Library of
Davidson College

# KENTUCKY PROFILES

Holman Hamilton

# KENTUCKY PROFILES
## Biographical Essays in Honor of Holman Hamilton

Edited by James C. Klotter
and Peter J. Sehlinger

The Kentucky Historical Society
Frankfort

ISBN: 0-916968-11-1
Library of Congress Catalog Card Number: 82-81154
Copyright © 1982 by The Kentucky Historical Society
All rights reserved.
Printed in the United States of America

# Contents

| | |
|---|---|
| Preface | vii |
| Introduction<br>*Thomas D. Clark* | 1 |
| Holman Hamilton: A Biographical Sketch<br>*James A. Ramage* | 11 |
| Henry "Light Horse Harry" Lee:<br>Kentucky's Last Virginia Governor<br>*Thomas E. Templin* | 31 |
| James Guthrie: Kentucky Politician and Entrepreneur<br>*Charles J. Bussey* | 57 |
| William Preston, Kentucky's Diplomat of Lost Causes<br>*Peter J. Sehlinger* | 73 |
| Civil War Romance: The Influence of Wartime Marriage on the Life and Career of John Hunt Morgan<br>*James A. Ramage* | 99 |
| Family Influences on a Progressive<br>The Early Years of Sophonisba P. Breckinridge<br>*James C. Klotter* | 121 |
| Augustus Owsley Stanley: Early Twentieth Century Democrat<br>*Thomas W. Ramage* | 155 |
| Holman Hamilton: A Bibliography<br>*Sherrill Redmon McConnell* | 181 |
| Contributors | 191 |
| Index | 193 |

# Preface

All too rarely a professor is so esteemed by his colleagues, friends, and students that they honor him with a collection of essays. But Holman Hamilton was a rare individual. He excelled — as scholar, teacher, mentor, leader, and gentleman — and brought excellence to all fields.

The idea came early for a book honoring Professor Hamilton. Work began in earnest after the Kentucky Historical Society gave final publication assurances in November 1979. The editors had already contacted the dozen and a half students whose dissertations had been directed by Dr. Hamilton and learned which ones could contribute an essay to this work. Many more wanted to remember their mentor through an article than could, because of other commitments. Virtually all — and many other students from other levels of graduate and undergraduate work — expressed their support for such a project.

In late February 1980, Holman Hamilton learned that he was dying of cancer. At that time, for the first time, he was told of the project. It was an emotional moment, and the pride he had felt for all his students was expressed. The knowledge that such a book was underway sustained him, he said, in the remaining months. He died in June 1980.

I

Such collections of essays — *Festschriften* — are frequently praised for the motives involved, but often damned for their uneven quality, themelessness, and disjointed nature. The editors, in an attempt to meet at least the last two criticisms, decided to follow the ideas presented by the person they sought to recognize. Professor Hamilton, in his presidential address to the Southern Historical Association, and in the classroom before that, stressed that people must have a place in the history we write. Individual actions could make a difference in history. While recognizing the value of other studies, he wanted faces and feelings in his history and those of his students. The editors thus asked contributors to use a biographical approach in their sketches.

A second Hamilton interest dictated another unifying theme: that the works deal with Kentucky. The Hoosier-born Hamilton loved his adopted state, but more than that, he saw the value of history at the state and local levels. Professor Hamilton, anticipating recent trends to case-studies focusing on smaller units, long advocated the value of historical work at all levels. He argued that only through combining such studies could full synthesis result.

And, finally, the editors asked contributors to remember another Hamilton dictum: Make your history readable. That may be the most difficult assignment he offered us as students. Yet, as scholar and teacher, he saw the vital need for interesting history. In his presidential address both the title — "Clio with Style" — and the words within showed the importance Dr. Hamilton placed on this matter: "There should be such style that history glows, that leaders and followers of bygone eras spring to life, that spent forces are recharged and move again with their old momentum." The articles, then, are aimed at not only the trained, professional historian but, perhaps even more important, the educated, discriminating reading public.

Of course, a desire for a unified theme and a desire to write readable history does not mean the authors have accomplished their aims. But the will to achieve and to excel *is* present. That desire was perhaps Holman Hamilton's most enduring legacy.

II

This collection of essays written by seven Hamilton students represents the efforts not of those few, but rather of many. The editors particularly wish to thank Dr. Thomas D. Clark, Dr. Otis Singletary, and Dr. Hambleton Tapp. It was Dr. Clark who professionally trained Holman Hamilton; it was he who worked with him for many fruitful years in the history department of the University of Kentucky. His introduction ably reflects on those relationships. University of Kentucky President Singletary supported the project from the earliest moments. His aid and the university's support recognize that professors such as Holman Hamilton are what makes a university great. Dr. Hambleton Tapp, now editor emeritus at the

Kentucky Historical Society, gave the editors a hearing, aided their cause, and helped bring the work to realization. The efforts of Drs. Tapp, Singletary, and Clark all are tributes to the man whose friendship they shared.

The authors enlisted the counsel of several people and wish to acknowledge that aid as well:

James A. Ramage wishes to thank Mrs. Holman Hamilton, Dr. Thomas H. Appleton, Jr., of the Kentucky Historical Society, Anne Coke of the University Press of Kentucky, Burton Milward of Lexington, and the editors, for assistance in the sketch of Dr. Hamilton. For his article on Morgan, he expresses appreciation to his wife Ann for her reaction to his interpretations and for typing the manuscript. He also thanks Richard Shrader, director of the Southern Collection at the University of North Carolina, and manuscript librarians at the University of Kentucky, Duke University, and the Filson Club. The author is grateful to Michael C.C. Adams of Northern Kentucky University for reading the manuscript.

Thomas E. Templin wishes to acknowledge the aid of Dr. Lance Banning of the University of Kentucky and Dr. Patrick J. Furlong of Indiana University at South Bend for reading the article, and that of the University of Kentucky and other libraries whose manuscript collections were used.

Charles J. Bussey thanks James R. Bentley of the Filson Club, the Western Kentucky University Faculty Research Committee, and former Western Kentucky graduate student Walter Hixson for the support given.

Peter J. Sehlinger wishes to express his appreciation to Charles C. Hay, Archivist at Eastern Kentucky University, James R. Bentley, Secretary of the Filson Club, and Wilbur E. Meneray, Head of Manuscripts and Rare Books at the Howard-Tilton Memorial Library, Tulane University, for making manuscript materials available. The author also is grateful to three historians at the Indiana University School of Liberal Arts: Sabine Jessner for her invaluable research assistance and Bernard Friedman and Ralph D. Gray for reading the manuscript and offering helpful suggestions.

James C. Klotter wishes to thank, from the Kentucky Historical Society, William R. Buster, Robert B. Kinnaird, Anne

McDonnell and the entire library staff, as well as the publications department's Dr. Thomas H. Appleton, Jr., Cheryl Conover, James Russell Harris, and Mary Lou Madigan, for support both in the editorial process and in his article. Dr. Helen L. Horowitz of Scripps College and Dr. Nancy Schrom Dye of the University of Kentucky kindly read the manuscript article and offered needed suggestions, as did several staff members at the Society. He is appreciative also of aid given by the Filson Club, the University of Kentucky Library, the University of Chicago Library, the Library of Congress, and the Edith Abbott Memorial Library.

Thomas W. Ramage thanks his wife and the many others whose time and patience have made his work possible. He acknowledges aid given by the University of Kentucky and the Library of Congress.

Sherrill Redmon McConnell expresses appreciation to Mrs. Holman Hamilton, to Frank Stanger of the University of Kentucky Library, and to Natalie Schick of that school's history department for their aid in compiling the bibliography.

# Introduction

*by Thomas D. Clark*

In the course of an extended teaching career a university professor has an army of students pass through his classroom. This was true in my case, especially during the turbulent post-World War II decades. There were the undergraduates who flocked in for two or three semesters of introductory courses in either western civilization or United States history, and then went away to talk the rest of their lives about their like or dislike of history. Then there were the juniors and seniors who continued on in upper-level courses, some of whom became majors and the seed stock for graduate work. The latter established their personalities and talents in professors' minds and affections. It was the graduate student, however, who gained lasting recognition.

By the time a young scholar underwent extensive undergraduate training and was determined to make the study of history a career, he began that transformation of becoming a fellow scholar with his professor, bent on the eternal search for the truth, and the gaining of maturity as a historian.

In the years prior to 1931, the Department of History in the University of Kentucky was strictly an undergraduate division serving the needs of undergraduates and supplementing the work in other departments and colleges. In the decade, 1931-1941, there occurred some decided changes in its program. The ending of the Great Depression and the approach of World War II brought somewhat improved financial conditions for the University of Kentucky. Under the leadership of President Frank L. McVey the institution expanded its programs in several fields and began offering the doctorate in selected areas. In limited fashion the Department of History was able both to expand and improve its program, even to the extent of offering the doctorate in certain areas of American history. After 1941 the Department of History was set on a course of hiring competent scholars on its staff, of expanding the library collection,

**Holman Hamilton delivering a talk at Morehead State University**
Courtesy of John Kleber

and of encouraging professors to involve themselves in research and writing. Progress was slow, and, at times, tedious, but the department did improve its program. At the end of the war, and after a gruelling three years of offering courses to the Army Specialized Training Corps, there came the great avalanche of returning veterans. Never before in the history of American higher education were universities so overrun by so many mature students demanding better instruction. State universities, and many of the better private schools as well, began offering work leading to the doctorate. There was begun a search far afield for promising candidates to fill the newly organized graduate lecture courses and seminars. Those wise prophets who clambered up the educational statistical mountain to catch a glimpse of the bright gleam of the future came down to spread the gospel that not enough doctoral candidates could be trained to fill the needs of an ever-increasing academic population.

This was the somewhat hurley-burley world of graduate education which Holman Hamilton entered in 1951. His background progress toward making a final career decision had included a helpful and maturing newspaper experience, both as a reporter and an editorial writer. As an adjunct to his reportorial and editorial work he became a self-disciplined biographer. His two-volume life of Zachary Taylor and its hospitable reception by critical scholars reflected the cardinal facts: he had learned quickly to do mature historical research by using several approaches which ranged from a perceptive hunt for original manuscript sources to applying his skill as a newspaperman in conducting oral interviews with scores of persons who in some way could contribute pertinent information to the development of the Taylor story. Equally as important, Holman demonstrated conclusively that he could write in a more finished style than a majority of the trained and established historians of the era.

Almost inherently, Holman Hamilton possessed that precious trait so valuable and vital to the historian: he had both a love and respect for the past. To him its galaxy of personalities lived on into the present to speak their pieces. Such people as Zachary Taylor, Robert Wickliffe, Abraham Lincoln, Jefferson Davis, Franklin D. Roosevelt, and hundreds of others, including that homespun, colonel-making character, Governor Ruby Laffoon of Kentucky — all of these were as real to him as his colleagues next door. As a newspaper reporter standing off to the side observing public affairs, he became adept at mimicking participants to the later amusement of his students.

I first met Holman Hamilton in the office of that colorful character of Kentucky history, Otto A. Rothert, secretary of the Filson Club. "Uncle" Otto lived only partially in the world of gross realities, but far more in the shadows of the fixed past. I had gone to see him about an article pending publication in the *Filson Club History Quarterly,* and found him chatting with a round-faced "GI" who was hot on the trail of Zachary Taylor and his background in Louisville. The manuscript collection of the Filson Club contained a large body of papers relating both directly and indirectly to the life of Taylor and his times. It was in these papers that Hamilton was digging away under Rothert's fatherly guidance.

In that casual meeting I found the young man from Fort Wayne a personable individual who demonstrated an easy and warm Hoosier friendliness. I doubt that Otto Rothert knew much more about him at the time. Not long after the meeting in the Filson Club, Holman came on to Lexington. In some way he had learned about J. Winston Coleman, Jr., and his interests, perhaps through Louis Warren of the Lincoln Foundation in Fort Wayne. Coleman's collection of Kentuckiana was growing rapidly, and he gathered in with his books and pamphlets an astonishing amount of information about Kentuckians and their past. On that occasion Holman came as Winston's guest to a Saturday luncheon and afternoon of reminiscing by the Book Thieves. I am reasonably certain that it was on that occasion that he first met William H. Townsend, Charles R. Staples, Dr. Claude Trapp, Dr. Frank L. McVey, Judge Samuel M. Wilson, and Dr. John Sharp Chambers. All of these men had good private libraries, and in the case of Wilson and Townsend, their collections were of such quality that they enjoyed national recognition.

The jovial Book Thieves gatherings were often attended by guests who had kindred interests, many of whom were authors of genuine distinction. There was always a lot of yarn spinning, good natured arguments, and much serious discussion of historical matters. Perhaps Holman Hamilton got a somewhat perverted notion of life in the Blue Grass from these meetings. I know that some other guests, including W. Clement Eaton, the distinguished historian of the Old South, did. Many a good story was passed around on those carefree afternoons; as William H. Townsend was fond of saying on occasions, "Mere fact should never be allowed to discolor a good story."

As indicated, so far as the Book Thieves had a sober side it was a serious mutual interest in book collecting and writing. Most of its members had constantly in progress either books or extended articles. Whatever its virtues, or lack of them, this was just the kind of rich human associations which Holman Hamilton relished. I am sure it had considerable bearing on his wishing to return to Lexington to do graduate work and to establish his residence. I know these associations influenced him in later years when he became so much a part of the social and cultural life of the Blue Grass.

In the spring of 1951, I went up to Fort Wayne, Indiana, to speak before the local historical society. Holman and Susie Hamilton invited me to be their house guest. In the course of that visit Holman discussed with me the possibility of entering the University of Kentucky Graduate School to work toward a doctorate in history. He had an undergraduate degree from Williams College, and a "gentleman's degree" at that. Ordinarily this would not have satisfied our standards, but his Taylor volumes clearly demonstrated his capacity to undertake successfully mature historical study and writing.

At the time I was in Fort Wayne, the Department of History at Kentucky was being sorely beset by a persistent correspondent who had written and published a thin local history booklet which she wished to submit in lieu of a master's thesis. Even if the booklet had been of substantial quality, to have agreed to this proposal would have been to invalidate our graduate-research program. I was indeed wary of prospective graduate students who rushed forth with dog-eared publications to their credit, and who could not distinguish between black ink and scholarship. If their essays or books were worthy of reputable publication, they perhaps did not need to do further work. In Holman's case his research and writing were of a high standard, even exceedingly mature. It had stood well the test in the national crucible of review. He no doubt wrote as well or better than any member of our staff, or in the University for that matter. He, however, needed the training and discipline which a broader approach to the study of history would give him. We made to him the single concession of allowing him to waive the writing of a master's thesis, which in his case had no earthly purpose. Too, more and more doctoral candidates were bypassing this requirement. As Holman's graduate director I advised him to select early a dissertation topic which would have some broad national significance. That was the point when we agreed upon the study of the Compromise of 1850. He already had a well developed interest in the middle period in American history.

Holman Hamilton quickly adapted himself to the academic regimen. He was studious without being pedantic. For him the University Library became a happy hunting ground, and for the first time in his life he gained a concept of the broad areas of historical literature. By the end of his first semester he was certain that he not only wanted to be a reputable publishing historian but likewise a good classroom teacher. In close association with his far less experienced fellow graduate students, Holman practically became a father figure. He listened to their tales of woe, soothed their frustrations, guided them through the wilderness of paper writing and the making of seminar reports, and took them along as field scouts in his diligent exploration of the field of historical bibliography.

There never was any doubt that Holman Hamilton would achieve his doctorate, and do it brilliantly and on time. He wrote a good strong dissertation, was never in any difficulty in his general examinations, and in the end defended his thesis in a skilled, professional manner. With the usual additional research and polishing, his dissertation was made publishable under the title *Prologue to Conflict* (1964), a book which received favorable reviews in the professional journals, and added cubits to Holman's growing reputation as a scholar.

Had we not been sorely pressed to enlarge our teaching

staff in 1954, we most likely would not have employed Holman Hamilton, solely on the grounds that we felt it unwise in a young graduate department to in-breed the staff. We knew beyond all doubt that Holman had the makings of a superb teacher and would continue to be a publishing historian, and that he would be a fine asset to the department. Under other circumstances Holman was the kind of graduate we wished to establish in another good department to help give high credibility to our own graduate program. We knew also that we would have no difficulty placing him in a desirable position. He fitted nobly, as time proved, our own staff needs.

Never at any time during the years I was head of the Department of History did Holman Hamilton fail to live up to his bright promise. From the outset he was an excellent classroom teacher who attracted students to his classroom in swarms, and who now remember him with marked respect. As a graduate student he developed a wholesome perspective of professor-student relationship which he cultivated to the end of his active teaching career. No student ever came to me to complain about Holman; quite to the contrary, they praised him for his intellectual and humane qualities. To him the American past with its galaxy of colorful actors was as much alive as if it were still at center stage of the current moment. He was able to transmit his love of the past with dramatic effects.

I am sure Holman Hamilton never refused to see a student in his office, or to give as much time as needed to solve problems. If he ever complained about students interfering with his research and writing I never heard of it. With all his kindness and consideration in dealing with his students, he was quick to single out the slackers and triflers. Among his attributes as teacher and scholar was his mature capacity to read widely and critically. This gave a broad dimension to his teaching which got across to his students. Holman built for himself a respectable professional library, and was a constant fixture in the University Library. On several occasions I had reasons to be personally impressed with his knowledge of obscure sources, and his ability and skill in locating equally fugitive information.

With the ease of an experienced journalist, Holman Hamilton met his professional colleagues on common grounds. His established reputation as a biographer gave him a long lead over most recent graduate historians. Too, he reflected a secure family and social background which gave him a full measure of assurance in meeting and dealing with people on a plane of equality.

It was heartening indeed to see Holman Hamilton advance as a publishing scholar. His *Prologue to Conflict* confirmed my belief that it would be equally, if not more, significant than his two-volume Taylor biography. In brief space he was masterful in summarizing the background of Taylor, Lincoln, and Davis in *The Three Kentucky Presidents,* one of the Kentucky Bicentennial Bookshelf volumes. This latter book was to bring him joy by its warm reception in the closing weeks of his life.

For a decade and a half Holman Hamilton worked at writing a biography of Claude G. Bowers. He had known Bowers intimately during his newspaper days in Fort Wayne and greatly admired him. I am reasonably certain that when Holman first conceived the idea of this biography he had in mind a treatment of the friendly and droll Hoosier Democrat who was an eloquent correspondent, a successful author, political analyst, and public activist. Once he began examining the Bowers' record, however, he found his subject to be more complex than he had at first realized. Claude G. Bowers functioned as a diplomat in extremely delicate and troubled situations, a fact which reached far beyond the party struggles of Indiana and Washington.

Holman was in Chile as a Fulbright lecturer in 1966 largely for the privilege of savoring the nature of that country's political actions, folkways, and internal struggles. He sought to view these as Bowers had described them in reports, diary, and other personal papers.

It is a disappointment that Holman was never able to make an extended visit to Spain to sense the nature of life in that once troubled country. He could have found the material from which to weave a revealing chapter of pre-World War II affairs. This era of Bowers' career represented a far more complex one than his experiences in Chile, and it demanded more astute search, understanding, and interpretation.

Holman was comfortably at home with Claude G. Bowers,

the Hoosier Democrat, and his counter-foil, Albert J. Beveridge, the Republican. On several occasions Holman read papers describing the comical jousting of these two, to the delight of his audiences. He had free access, granted him by Bowers before his death, to a voluminous collection of papers which shed that intimate personal light on political affairs which is missing from more formal sources. It is possible that most of this part of Holman's writings can be salvaged by bright young historians.

Hamilton entered graduate school late in terms of his age, and time-wise he had a lot of catching up before him. He may have been denied the thrills of growing up as a callow youth with time enough to grow into a long career. Once underway, however, he made remarkably constructive use of his time. He was capable of a high degree of concentration, and he read with twice the rapidity of most of his colleagues, gathering and retaining information almost in encyclopedic manner. He expended an impressive amount of energy preparing and delivering his class lectures, and in keeping the necessary records of hordes of students. At the same time, as this collection of essays indicates, he directed the studies of an ever-growing number of doctoral candidates. These wrote dissertations on a wide variety of subjects in American history. He appears never to have steered his charges into the narrower channels of his personal interests, or used them to do spade work for his own research and writing.

In the course of his career in the University of Kentucky, Holman gained the respect of his colleagues. He was elected to the Hallam Professorship in the Department of History, to the special professorship in the College of Arts and Sciences, and the Alumni Association awarded him both its good teaching and research recognitions. In the years before his retirement he served as University Orator in a manner which would have won the applause of both Claude G. Bowers and Albert J. Beveridge.

Every university professor worthy of his calling and institution must assume responsibilities for internal operations. Many of these tasks are onerous and time-consuming, some even prove fruitless; others, however, are highly rewarding from an intellectual and scholarly standpoint. Holman Hamilton, in all of these demands, was a loyal citizen in the University of Kentucky community. He was fortunate in being made chairman of the Executive Committee of the University Press of Kentucky in the years when that consortium was embarked upon an exciting publishing program. In this position he left his impress upon one of Kentucky's most successful cultural ventures. In scores of other ways he exemplified the University, the student body, and his colleagues to both the academic and general public.

Just as Holman Hamilton reveled in the ways of the Blue Grass and associations with his non-academic friends, he cherished even more his association with members of his profession who perhaps lived somewhat less ebullient lives, but who were far more stimulating intellectually. He cherished the friendships of his fellow historians, and gloried in their learning and wisdom. To him the members of his profession formed a warm fraternal kinship which ever sustained his faith in the calling of historian.

# Holman Hamilton: A Biographical Sketch

*by James A. Ramage*

At 8:30 on the clear and mild autumn evening of 15 November 1979, the members of the Southern Historical Association gathered in the Georgian Ballroom of the Atlanta Biltmore Hotel. In this setting, with its elaborate chandeliers and classical decor, Holman Hamilton rose from his seat on the dais beside his wife Susie, greeted several friends, and made his way to the speaker's platform. The moment was one of high honor for Hamilton, an appropriate culmination of a lifetime's dedication to the history profession. In his fourth year of retirement from teaching, he was president of the 4,500-member association, one of the three national professional history organizations in the United States.

Determined that his address be meaningful, Hamilton had devoted many hours to its preparation. The charm, grace, and wit, the uplifting spirit of Hamilton, filled the room. Those who had been his students were inspired anew, as they had been many times in his classroom. Hamilton's voice was strong, and the address well received. Several times he was interrupted with laughter, and, at the conclusion, hardened professors applauded enthusiastically. The president had delivered a significant paper, one which demonstrated his love for history, his concern for the future of the profession, and his sympathy for young scholars attempting to enter the overcrowded vocation.

Hamilton reemphasized that history is in crisis — a crisis of declining enrollments, unemployed Ph.D.'s, and the removal of history from the curriculum. He called for united action on several fronts. First, historians should take advantage of the widespread national interest in historical sites and shrines, in preservation and restoration, and in family, state, and local history. If Clio's disciples teach and write with style, elementary and secondary students will enjoy history, and college freshmen will take history as elective courses, which will create the demand for more professors. "There should be," he

Holman Hamilton, portrait in oil by Alfred J. Domene, commissioned by the Kentucky Civil War Round Table in 1978

declared, "such style that history glows, that leaders and followers of bygone eras spring to life, that spent forces are recharged and move again with their old momentum."

Further, Hamilton stressed that the profession should protect humanist interests in the midst of a technological revolution. Computerization in scholarly research must not substitute breadth for depth of understanding; and microfiche, microform, and computer programs cannot replace books. He also insisted that television productions with historical themes should consult historical experts to insure accuracy, and challenged his colleagues to select and train the 5 percent of history students who have the ability to write with style.

To many, the central theme in the address was concern for the young scholar. Hamilton, first and foremost a teacher, advocated the interests of today's students. Expressing this same attitude, Holman wanted to avoid "the traditional presidential squeeze," a party given by the president in his suite. Because the affair usually included only established scholars and the president's special friends, Hamilton despised this time-honored custom that excluded so many young historians. Therefore, after his speech, the University of Kentucky hosted a reception in honor of President and Mrs. Hamilton in the hotel's Empire Suite, to which everyone was invited. Hamilton hoped that, for the benefit of the younger members, a precedent would be established.

That President Hamilton introduced such an innovation in a social aspect of the history convention evidenced his sociable nature. At an early age Holman had discovered the pleasure of sharing knowledge and insight, and the attraction of books and history. He gave himself unselfishly to others and became a cheerful, gracious, and charming gentleman, an outstanding scholar and writer, an exceptional academic citizen, and a great teacher.

I

Holman was born 30 May 1910, in Fort Wayne, Indiana, the hometown of his father Allen Hamilton, a respected, prosperous physician; his mother, Helen Knight Hamilton, was a native of northern Indiana. In this bustling urban setting the Hamiltons lived in a new house at 337 West Wayne Street. Fort Wayne was a growing industrial city of about 65,000 people when Holman was born; a decade later, its population had increased to about 85,000 and in 1930, to 115,000.

As was the custom then for general practitioners, Doctor Hamilton made house calls. At ages five and six, Holman accompanied his father on those visits to patients, and the lad observed the streetcars, counted railroad cars, and smelled the smoke rising from factory smokestacks. In the countryside, Holman saw farmers tilling the fertile soil, growing corn, and raising hogs. Cherishing these moments, he sat enchanted as his father quoted the poetry of Rudyard Kipling and other nineteenth-century British authors. The young boy began himself to recite verses which he could still quote from memory decades later.

Holman's elementary education was entrusted to his father's sister Katherine, who tutored her nephew five days a week. Along with training in Latin and modern languages, she encouraged his historical and literary interests. Holman never really considered becoming a physician like his father. "I never had any interest or ability in the sciences, and to spend months and years in the laboratory would have been torture. To me history and English literature are just naturally fun and not really work. How wonderful to be paid for doing something so enjoyable." He preferred the world of books and even as a boy became a familiar figure at the Fort Wayne Public Library, just down the street from his home.

As had his father, Holman attended St. Paul's School in Concord, New Hampshire, and Williams College in the hills of Massachusetts. At St. Paul's, he played intramural football, hockey, and other sports, and enjoyed debating and writing for the school newspaper. He graduated in 1928 at age eighteen. At Williams, Holman lived his first three years in the dormitory and ate his meals at his fraternity house. His two roommates were members of other fraternities, so the dormitory arrangement widened rather than confined his friendships. In his senior year he was president of Chi Psi and lived in the fraternity house. "I enjoyed college life enormously," Holman said. "Of course, Williams was a very small college and by your sophomore year you knew almost everyone in the student body." He majored in English, was managing editor of both the college literary magazine and the student newspaper, was a member of the senior honor society, and in his senior year won the Dunbar Prize for his essay, "Fraternities at Williams."

Graduating from college at twenty-two, Hamilton went in 1932 to New York to seek employment, preferably in newspaper or magazine work. After numerous frustrations, the country being in the deepest part of the Great Depression, he finally made the acquaintance of a retired executive of a defunct New York daily paper. "This man proved extremely helpful," Hamilton remembered, "because he spread out before me the pros and cons of journalistic apprenticeships in large cities and smaller communities. The upshot was that he counseled my returning to Fort Wayne. I did so and soon was hired as a reporter on the *Journal-Gazette.*"

Newspaper work was very exciting but not entirely satisfying to Hamilton. "It gave you a wide variety of experience and you met many people and had a lot of fun and excitement. When different reporters went on vacation I would cover their beats for a week since I was the junior in the crowd." Still, he longed for something of a more sustained nature. "Early I could see that there was something not wholly satisfying about doing a day's work, doing it as well as you could, submitting copy, having it printed, and then starting all over again the next day." Hamilton's yearning for something more enduring led him back to one of his favorite pastimes — the world of books, the reading of history and biography. Holman's love for books and history, which began in childhood, had been strengthened by his friendship with historian Claude G. Bowers.

Hamilton knew Bowers as the man who lived next door to his Aunt Mary Hoffman in Fort Wayne. In his early teens Holman read Bowers' *The Party Battles of the Jackson Period* (1922), and when he was fifteen Aunt Mary gave him as a Christmas present an autographed copy of Bowers' *Jefferson and Hamilton: The Struggle for Democracy in America* (1925). It was thrilling to know a historian personally, especially one who could make the past so vivid and exciting.

During his first year as a reporter, Hamilton's interest in American history began to mature. He read Bowers' eighth and latest book, *Beveridge and the Progressive Era* (1932), and, stimulated by that, reread some of Albert J. Beveridge's biography of Lincoln. He was impressed by the author's neglect of Zachary Taylor on the Washington scene in 1850. Holman likewise found the standard biographies of Taylor, including Oliver O. Howard's *General Taylor* (1892), completely inadequate. He knew that Taylor had been involved in four wars — an unusual record for a president. The idea of writing a biography of Zachary Taylor began forming in Hamilton's mind.

In the spring of 1933 Hamilton read widely in U.S. history of the late 1840s and 1850s. The young reporter became a fixture at the Fort Wayne Public Library, where he noticed that many books had been checked out only once before — by Claude G. Bowers. Bowers had been a friend of the librarian, who had expanded the holdings on this period by purchasing books Bowers needed for his own research.

Another institution important to Hamilton at this time was the library of the Lincoln National Life Foundation, which had one of the largest collections on Lincoln in the nation, as well as a collateral collection relating to the 1840s and 1850s but not primarily on Lincoln. There Hamilton read biographies of Calhoun, Clay, Webster, and others, and talked often with the director, Louis A. Warren, and his assistant, R. Gerald McMurtry. These two Kentuckians told him about the historical collections of the Filson Club, which they speculated might contain material on Taylor not available elsewhere.

In June 1933, the National Recovery Act reduced Hamilton's working hours to forty and raised his pay from $10 to $14 per week; he welcomed the additional free time for reading. That summer also he spent a week's vacation in Louisville, doing research on Taylor at the Jefferson County courthouse and at the Filson Club, where he formed a friendship with Otto A. Rothert, its secretary. Up to his death in the 1950s Rothert took great interest in Hamilton's work and he introduced Hamilton to Hambleton Tapp and other Kentucky historians. When the Hoosier returned to Fort Wayne, he was more than ever enamored of history and especially the life of Taylor.

At this point Hamilton decided to contact Taylor's great-grandson, Trist Wood, and his granddaughter, Mrs. Betty Taylor Stauffer, both of New Orleans. A cartoonist for Huey Long's newspaper, the weekly *Louisiana Progress,* Wood was a rather eccentric bachelor who proved very helpful and knowledgeable about Zachary Taylor. To Hamilton's letter, the spirited Mrs. Stauffer had replied: "Yes, I shall be glad to help you, even though you are a damyankee." So, on his vacation in 1934, he had lunch in New Orleans with Mrs. Stauffer. It was his twenty-fourth birthday and she was in her eighties. Mrs. Stauffer always wore black because she had taken a vow that if a relative recovered from a serious illness she would wear black clothing and go to church every day. After serving crepes suzette in a chafing dish in the dining room, she ushered the polite young Yankee into the parlor, where, surrounded by Taylor busts and portraits, he began examining Taylor manuscripts. He thought she had left for the afternoon, when, out of the corner of his eye, he saw a little figure entering the room. It was Mrs. Stauffer and she was clutching something to her breast. Rising to greet her, he beheld a bottle of pre-World War I "Old Taylor" whiskey. Handing him the container, Mrs. Stauffer said, "Mr. Hamilton, down South the ladies hand the gentlemen the bottle and turn their backs. Monroe [a servant] will be in every fifteen minutes to see that you have plenty of ice." Holman soon learned, however, that these were not standard conditions for historical research.

The more he read and researched, the more Hamilton became caught up in the Taylor biography. Reporting became an unwelcome interruption to what he enjoyed most. He had saved some money and with his family's financial help resigned from the *Journal* in early September 1934 to devote full time to research. That autumn he took his first extensive research trip of three months: Louisville and Frankfort, Kentucky; Orange County, Virginia, where Taylor was born; and Washington, D.C. The trip included Hamilton's first visit to the Kentucky Historical Society and the Library of Congress. In Lexington, introductory letter from Otto Rothert in hand, Holman called on J. Winston Coleman, Jr. and soon attended a dinner given by University of Kentucky President Frank L.

McVey. At the dinner, the Hoosier was introduced to Dr. Thomas D. Clark of the University of Kentucky History Department and to Lexington attorney and historian William H. Townsend. Along with Dr. Hambleton Tapp, these gentlemen were to become close friends.

In the spring of 1935 Hamilton was offered the *Journal-Gazette* editorial writer position, held earlier by Claude G. Bowers. Since the job would allow time for the biography, he decided to accept. From then until March 1942, he spent half of each day on the paper and half on the biography, and wrote nearly all the editorials for seven days every week. Even though he took no regular vacations, he could, by composing thirty or forty editorials in advance, find time for concentrated research and writing.

In the midst of this research, in October 1939, Holman Hamilton married Miss Suzanne Bowerfind — known as Susie — daughter of Henry and Clara Paul Bowerfind of Fort Wayne. A graduate of Tudor Hall in Indianapolis and Smith College, she contributed excellent judgment concerning such matters as style, emphases, and ideas in her husband's writing.

Such writing bore fruit. In late February 1941, Hamilton's *Zachary Taylor: Soldier of the Republic,* covering Taylor's life through 1847, was published by Bobbs-Merrill Company of Indianapolis and New York. War had broken out in Europe and the United States was strengthening its defenses; it was an opportune time to publish a book on a soldier. The volume was received with enthusiasm. *Newsweek* commented: "It is a good job, restoring the portrait of 'Old Zack' in all its strong color and homespun texture." The *New Yorker* complimented the author on "an excellent job, easy to read and exhaustively annotated." The New York *Times* declared that Hamilton had "ably filled another gap in the biographical record of the Middle Period in American history. Mr. Hamilton has painted a clear picture of army life on the advancing frontier." Equally gratifying was the positive reception by professional historians, one of whom wrote that Hamilton had "set a standard which few historians could surpass." In general, historians welcomed the book as the first critical, scholarly study of the life of Taylor. Claude G. Bowers, in the introduction to the book, commended Hamilton's conscientious research, and his appealing, straightforward style; he predicted accurately that it and the second volume to follow would become the definitive biography of Taylor.

*Soldier of the Republic* analyzes Taylor as the hero of the Mexican War. Of course, Americans loved his four victories, but, the author wrote, "More than anything else they liked the homespun qualities of the General — his simplicity, humility and rare common sense." Old Rough and Ready was a plain, straightforward man, who was better at inspiring his men than at planning broad strategy. At Buena Vista on 23 February 1847, his last and greatest victory, the battle was not going well until mid-morning, when Taylor appeared on the field "astride Old Whitey high on the plateau within sight of all. The effect of his presence on the struggling American soldiers was almost magical. For here was Old Rough and Ready in fact as well as in name, sitting calm and collected in the heat of battle. Instantaneously the combat stiffened. . . ." There was another, even more important reason for the great popularity of Taylor and his victories. Communications were primitive and each of the four battles was first reported through the United States as a defeat; then, when word of victory was proclaimed, the joy was sustained, making Taylor an even more glorious hero. The volume ends when Taylor retired from the army and before he ran for president.

Hamilton's research for the second Taylor volume was interrupted by Pearl Harbor and his enlistment in the army. Following basic training with the 5th Armored Division at Camp Cooke, California, Hamilton qualified, in summer 1942, for Officer Candidate School at Fort Knox, Kentucky. In January 1943, he was commissioned second lieutenant; in early 1945 he was promoted to captain and assigned to overseas duty. From May 1945 to February 1946, he was a staff officer at General Douglas MacArthur's General Headquarters for the Pacific Theater. In the Philippines he was promoted to major. Returning to civilian life in Fort Wayne — and to Susie and their daughter Susan, who was born during the war — Hamilton resumed the biography of Taylor. Financial assistance came with the Guggenheim Fellowship in 1946; and, beginning in 1947, he resumed editorial writing for the *Journal-Gazette*.

The second and final Taylor volume appeared in October 1951. *Zachary Taylor: Soldier in the White House* received even more acclaim than the first volume. The *Saturday Review* proclaimed: "This biography is a fine specimen of thorough, systematic, and judicial scholarship" and is "well-documented, carefully organized, and decidedly readable." "The writing is of a very high quality," announced the *New Yorker*.

As with the first volume, current events made publication of Volume II timely: in October 1951, General Dwight D. Eisenhower was becoming increasingly prominent as a presidential candidate for 1952. Journalists across the nation drew the parallel between Eisenhower and Taylor. More important, the history profession hailed the second volume as the completion of the definitive life of Taylor. In the opinion of Allan Nevins, the book furnished "a scholarly, judicious and interesting history of three critical years in the history of the nation, and a vigorous and convincing portrait of Zachary Taylor as Presidential candidate and President." Arthur Schlesinger, Jr., and Marquis James both praised the book highly. Perhaps most gratifying was to be congratulated by Claude G. Bowers, who wrote: "The actors appear in artistic and realistic portraits as flesh and blood. His narrative marches rapidly and throbs with life. A real achievement." Other reviews praised the author's exhaustive research, wealth of detail, and vivid, fast-moving style. Historians recognized that Hamilton had provided a fresh view of the role of Zachary Taylor as president. Hamilton established that Taylor, with roots in pioneer Kentucky, and with a lifetime on the frontier, had always been a nationalist who developed his policies as president not as a Louisiana planter but as a patriotic soldier. Once in the White House, Hamilton maintained, Taylor gained confidence daily and was improving as a statesman when he died. Hamilton's biography shows that Taylor was ready to meet threats against the union with force. While he lived, compromise was impossible. Hamilton theorized that, had Taylor lived, there might have been bloodshed, but, if secessionists had met armed force in 1850, perhaps the Civil War would have been prevented. Named "The Indiana Book of the Year" and mentioned in *Time* as one of the best biographies of the year, Hamilton's second volume was evidence that he had matured as a writer and had further developed the ability, characteristic of his mentor Bowers, to bring to life people and events.

## II

For years Hamilton had been more and more inclined toward history as a full-time occupation, and in summer of 1951, having completed the writing of *Soldier in the White House,* he had made the move. At age forty-one, he resigned from the *Journal-Gazette* for the second and final time to undertake graduate work in history at the University of Kentucky. Why Kentucky? "I liked Kentucky and Kentuckians: they're a combination of Virginia gentility and frontier earthiness. And I thought Susie and Susan would like Kentucky just as I did."

Dr. Thomas D. Clark, as Hamilton's director, made it clear that he would be required to take the full course at Kentucky and that the biography of Taylor would not be accepted as a dissertation. Hamilton passed his qualifying examinations in spring 1953. During his last semester in graduate school, Hamilton won the Pelzer Prize of the Mississippi Valley Historical Association for the best article written by a graduate student in the United States in 1954. The article, "Democratic Senate Leadership and the Compromise of 1850" *(Mississippi Valley Historical Review,* December 1954), emphasized the role of Henry S. Foote and other Democratic senators in the adoption of the compromise.

With graduation at age forty-four, the new Ph.D. began looking for a teaching position and was pleasantly surprised when the University offered a post as assistant professor of history beginning in fall 1954. According to Dr. Clark, "Hamilton became immediately a very industrious, good member of the staff." As a professor, Hamilton continued writing and publishing. His articles appeared in prestigious professional journals and, in 1964, a revised version of his dissertation was published by the University of Kentucky Press as *Prologue to Conflict: The Crisis and Compromise of 1850.* Historians welcomed this as the first intensive study of the process of the enactment of the compromise and the complexity of forces behind it.

In *Soldier in the White House,* Hamilton had revised Taylor's role in the compromise; now, in addition to reinforcing that interpretation, he analyzed the mechanics and maneuvers involved in the enactment of the compromise after Taylor's death.

Hamilton viewed the compromise as a bad move. The Fugitive Slave Law intensified extremism in the North, broadened the antislavery base, and created an atmosphere in which readers would readily accept *Uncle Tom's Cabin.* The territorial settlements were generally accepted. In California slavery was legal for several years and during the 1850s California congressmen aided the South more than the North. The slave pen and depot in the District of Columbia were eliminated, but trading within the District continued. Ultimately, Hamilton argued, the compromise was a mistake because Fillmore and Congress let pass a good opportunity to "confront disunionists with the bluntest sort of nationalism in the Jackson-Taylor tradition," calling their bluff or enforcing federal authority. Reviewers praised both the scholarship and the style, one writing, "His presentation has all the suspense of a novel, even though the informed reader knows the plot at the start." Well received nationally, *Prologue to Conflict* was reprinted in paperback by W.W. Norton & Company of New York in 1966 and won the Alice Hallam Book Award as the year's best historical work published by a University of Kentucky faculty member.

Other books flowed from the Hamilton pen. In 1958 the University of Florida Press had published Hamilton's *White House Images and Realities,* three lectures on presidents and the impressions Americans have formed of them. He also joined Carl M. Degler, Arthur S. Link, David M. Potter, and others in writing a successful textbook on U.S. history, *The Democratic Experience,* first published in 1963. Hamilton, with Gayle Thornbrough, edited *Indianapolis in the "Gay Nineties": High School Diaries of Claude G. Bowers* (Indiana Historical Society, 1964); he penned an enthusiastic biographical introduction and edited selections for *Three American*

*Frontiers: Writings of Thomas D. Clark* (University Press of Kentucky, 1968); he wrote a section of *Major Crises in American History* (Harcourt, Brace & World, 1962) and a biographical introduction for William H. Townsend's *Hundred Proof* (University Press of Kentucky, 1964); he contributed articles and sketches to the *Dictionary of American History, The History of American Presidential Elections, Notable American Women, Encyclopedia of American Biography,* and *Encyclopedia Americana;* and he wrote numerous book reviews for history journals, as well as articles, chapters, and sketches for other publications.

Hamilton was professionally active outside the field of writing. Before becoming president in 1979, he served on the Executive Council of the Southern Historical Association and on the Board of Editors of the *Journal of Southern History*. He chaired the program committee of both the Southern Historical Association and the Organization of American Historians, as well as the nominating committee of the latter.

Considered by President Otis A. Singletary of the University of Kentucky to be "a first rate academic citizen," Hamilton served on many departmental, college, and university committees, including two terms in the University Senate, and as director of graduate study for the Department of History. He took extreme pride in his contribution to the University Press of Kentucky, which he considered "One of the really great cultural achievements in the history of education in the state." Serving on the University Press Committee for seven years, he was chairman for four years of the Editorial Board.

Hamilton was an "academic citizen" of other institutions as well. He delivered the History of American Civilization Lectures at the University of Florida and the J.P. Young Lectures at Memphis State University, as well as the Haynes Lectures at Marshall University; he lectured at Indiana University, the University of Notre Dame, Morehead State University, Northern Kentucky University, Murray State University, Western Kentucky University, Berea College, Georgetown College, Hobart College, the University of Missouri, Lincoln Memorial University, and other institutions. Hamilton served on the Board of Trustees of Lincoln Memorial

University in Tennessee and was awarded honorary degrees by that school, Franklin College, Indiana University, and the University of Kentucky.

As a Fulbright Professor at the University of Chile in 1966, Dr. Hamilton conducted the first graduate course in U.S. history ever given in South America and, in addition, he lectured in Spanish in an undergraduate course. He also lectured in English at the Catholic University of Chile at Santiago, the University of Valparaiso, and the University of Temuco.

Hamilton's unusual ability as a teacher was recognized by his colleagues and students alike. At the University of Kentucky he was elected Hallam professor of history in 1969 and distinguished professor of the College of Arts and Sciences in 1972. In January 1970, his chairman, Dr. Carl B. Cone, wrote of him: "Professor Hamilton's role is exceptional in the amount of attention he gives to undergraduates. He enjoys teaching freshmen, yet carried a heavy load of graduate work . . . . His abilities make him particularly well-suited for service activity outside the university, and here he does a *very* important service for the university." When Hamilton retired in 1975, the university honored him with a retirement dinner and elected him Professor Emeritus. In 1980, he was present when the Alumni Association inducted him into the Hall of Distinguished Alumni.

Only a great teacher could move a class to interrupt his lecture with applause; Holman Hamilton could do so with a class of four hundred freshmen gathered at 9:00 on a cold December morning. Dr. Hamilton felt privileged to awaken young scholars. "Except for the rapture of love, and rapport with cherished kinsmen and friends," Hamilton said, "there is no experience more exciting unless it is the sensation of an artist who creates a masterpiece, or of a surgeon who saves a life, or a clergyman a soul."

Although he avoided being "too lighthearted at the very beginning of a course," Hamilton gradually would begin to share his personality. He brought to the classroom his wealth of experience as a reporter, editorial writer, army veteran, and civic leader as well as author and scholar. "I try to put in colorful material . . . to keep them awake, make them feel some of the color, the drama, the fascination of history. Their eyes, manner tell you they're interested." When it was relevant to a lecture, Hamilton would do impressions of characters in history — John L. Lewis, Theodore Roosevelt, F.D.R., W.C. Fields — complete with facial expressions and voice inflections; his impersonations truly brought history alive.

From his varied experience, particularly as a newspaperman, Hamilton enriched his lectures with lively anecdotes. Especially fascinating was a story about Franklin D. Roosevelt. As Hamilton told it, he was covering the appearance of F.D.R at a convocation at the University of Notre Dame in the early fall of 1935. "I sat with the press and when it was over, being young and brash and perhaps a little foolish, instead of going out of the hall, I went in the other direction and found myself backstage in a room where I recognized everybody else in the room, but of course no one recognized me.

"I was twenty-five and here were the president of the United States, the governor of Indiana, the president of Notre Dame, the postmaster general, several other cabinet members and so on. I got chicken and turned around and went out. I found myself going out a side door and down a ramp which had evidently been set up for the president. So I got down to the foot of the new ramp and here was a touring car drawn up very close. I found myself inside a cordon of Indiana state policemen, between them and the car — so I thought it would cause too much of a ruckus if I tried to get outside the policemen — so I stayed where I was. Pretty soon this parade came down the ramp, all these dignitaries, and finally the president. I had seen him walk once before, actually, in Connecticut in 1932. Of course he could do better on a ramp, in many ways, than he could on the ground. He moved by leaning on a rail with one arm and a cane in the other hand, and he made his way slowly but effectively down the ramp and came to the car. He backed up to the car and of course he had very strong arm and shoulder muscles; but no strength whatsoever in his legs — no give in them. So the thing was to put the cane aside and lift himself up by his arms and shoulders into the jump seat and then pick up his poor withered legs and swing them around and then lift himself into the back seat.

"While he was in the midst of this operation I was about a foot and a half from him. Some man he apparently knew came up to him and held out his hand and wanted to shake hands with the president. Well, the president *couldn't* shake hands because his hands were busy. He said to this guy, with a great toss of the head, 'Well, how are ya, ol boy?' Then he got seated and shook hands. Several things struck me: one was the physical courage of a person who could come out of an illness like that and become president of the United States, and, secondly, the fact that he did not lose his cool when this man held out his hand. He greeted it as something normal and ultimately shook hands."

In recognition of his teaching excellence, Hamilton was selected by university students to receive the "Outstanding Teacher Award," in 1968. The same year at commencement, he was honored as a "Great Teacher" by the Alumni Association. For Hamilton history was never an escape to an ivory tower; rather, it was something to share with others, like the poems he memorized to share with his father. He made friends far and wide. Former students have only to mention to other scholars and professors that we went to Kentucky and they say, "Did you know my friend Holman Hamilton?"

In the summer of 1955, for example, Hamilton was at the University of Texas doing research for *Prologue to Conflict*. At the vending machine in the hallway of the library he met Charles P. Roland. "We would take a break every morning," Roland says, "and in the middle of the afternoon and we soon became close friends. I was immediately struck by his remarkable congeniality, his genuine liking for people. In all my life I have never known a man who likes people more than Professor Hamilton does." A former student of Hamilton's ate at the "Jacaranda" Restaurant in Santiago, Chile, on a research trip. He was surprised to find that the waiters would ask him about Dr. and Mrs. Hamilton. When Hamilton was there doing research in 1966 the waiters gave him Spanish lessons while he ate his meals. Barkley Moore, president of Oneida Baptist Institute, experienced Hamilton's friendship on campus: "As a mountain boy from an Eastern Kentucky village of about 250 souls, U.K. seemed very large, rather impersonal, and I felt lost and scared. Holman Hamilton helped change that perspective. Whenever and wherever I saw him, he smiled, called me by *name,* often stopped to talk. He seemed to do so with everyone!"

The outstanding characteristic of Hamilton as a director of graduate students was his ability to inspire students. Many worked harder for him than for any other teacher, not because of fear or awe, but because they desperately wanted to please him. This quality in his teaching is the reason that his influence on students continues throughout their lives. Don Flatt, professor at Morehead State University, commented: "Dr. Hamilton is one of the few people who have really been able to inspire me. I have never left a conference with Dr. Hamilton or ended a telephone conversation without being challenged and inspired to face up to the task and give it all that I have. Few professors, if any, excel Dr. Hamilton in his ability to correct the graduate student without at the same time discouraging him."

### III

When Hamilton retired in 1975 his writing, teaching, lecturing, public service, and professional involvement continued. He planned to write a biography of Zachary Taylor for the Kentucky Bicentennial Bookshelf Series published by the University Press of Kentucky. In autumn 1976, while Hamilton was recovering from cancer surgery, Bruce Denbo of the Press suggested that the book also include Abraham Lincoln and Jefferson Davis, an idea which greatly appealed to Holman. Published in 1978, *The Three Kentucky Presidents: Lincoln, Taylor, Davis* describes the influence of the "western-southern Kentucky experience" on the three men and discusses how their lives intertwined.

Reviewers praised the work. Robert W. Johannsen wrote in the *Journal of American History* that "no one will question the appropriate inclusion of this finely-written 'appreciation' in this series." In *The Register of the Kentucky Historical Society* Lowell H. Harrison observed that the book is "written with grace and wit" and that it presents "a number of fascinating insights into the events and personalities of the era with which he is so familiar. This is a book to read and enjoy — and to think about." In *The Alabama Review,* T. Harry Williams declared that the study was written with "great skill," and was "a delight to read and can be read with profit by academic specialists or by lay readers."

When he retired from the University, Hamilton had been working on a biography of Claude G. Bowers, who had successful careers as a newspaperman, historian, Democratic politician, orator, and diplomat to Spain and Chile. While Visiting Distinguished Professor of History at the University of Houston in spring 1979, Hamilton did considerable studying and writing about Bowers. At the same time, he and Gayle Thornbrough worked on a second volume of Bowers' diaries, covering the years 1923-1933, the same period which Hamilton was studying for the biography. The diary was far along when Hamilton died, and Thornbrough is completing it for publication by the Indiana Historical Society.

During the period 1975 to 1980, Dr. Hamilton also spoke widely and frequently throughout the South and in Ohio. He gave a commencement address at Tennessee Technological University, read a paper at the Kentucky Historical Society's observance of Boone Day in June 1977, and appeared on the NBC Today Show's bicentennial tribute to Kentucky. When *The Three Kentucky Presidents* appeared, Holman received several invitations to talk on Jefferson Davis. On 3 June 1978, he was featured speaker at a gathering of Davis' descendants at his home, Rosemont plantation near Woodville, Mississippi. On 3 June 1979, he addressed the Jefferson Davis birthday celebration in Todd County, Kentucky, Davis' birthplace. In Montgomery, Alabama, Hamilton spoke in the Senate Chamber where the Confederacy was organized. After the address a candlelight reception for Dr. and Mrs. Hamilton was held across the street in the first executive mansion of the Confederacy.

Always untiring in community and state activities, Hamilton served as first president of the Friends of the Lexington Public Library and as a member of the Kentucky Historic Preservation Committee. Such service continued during his "alleged retirement." As chairman of the publications committee for the Lexington-Fayette County Historic Commission, Hamilton was recognized for his five-year contribution of time and scholarship in overseeing publication of five books and presented one of the three annual awards given in 1980. Conferring the award, Lexington Mayor James G. Amato remarked that Hamilton, a prominent author himself, "takes time to encourage others to write. A distinguished scholar, he stimulates them to write well. He presides with tact, consideration and the ability to inspire others."

Holman's enjoyment of the personal side of history found expression also in his work with the Kentucky Civil War Round Table. In eulogizing William H. Townsend, the first president of the Kentucky Civil War Round Table, Holman articulated his own philosophy of friendship: "Let it be underscored here and now that Bill Townsend in this organization built a solid community of spirit, an esprit, a delightful appreciation of man for man, a brotherliness, a rare achievement of affection without the slightest sign of affectation. This, do we not agree, is the best in Kentucky? Is this not the best in American life? This is the natural, the true, the unfeigned, the permanent. This is friendship. This is substantial evidence of confidence renewed and faith redeemed . . . ."

Under Hamilton's leadership as president from 1964 to 1975, the Kentucky Civil War Round Table increased in membership to 550 in 1975, thus becoming the largest organization of its kind in the nation. "The Round Table," he said, "stresses historical facts, to be sure, but emphasizes friendship even more. Mutual respect and liking are pervasive."

## IV

Holman possessed the remarkable ability, even in his last illness, to enjoy his friends, to cheer them, to make them feel uplifted. His lively wit and buoyant spirit were there in his letters as well. At the University of Houston he resided in several different locations, including two weeks in a seventeenth floor "roost" of a women's dormitory. From there he wrote: "The only live creatures visible from this chair are pigeons — not human ones — on the ledge outside. They coo away to their hearts' content, and must think they have it all over the strange critter in the interior who pounds away on his outdated Smith Corona."

On 7 June 1980, Holman Hamilton died at his home on Barrow Road in Lexington. Four days later a service was held in Memorial Hall, where Holman had delivered his lectures to hundreds of freshmen; the chimes rang in tribute to the life of a remarkable man. He was remembered as respected reporter and editorial writer, exceptional military officer, eminent scholar, prominent university and community leader, and charming gentleman. Yet, his most outstanding achievement was his great teaching. By inspiring students to enjoy history, Holman Hamilton made a lasting contribution to the cultural and intellectual life of Kentucky and the nation.

# Henry "Light Horse Harry" Lee
# Kentucky's Last Virginia Governor

*by Thomas E. Templin*

Henry "Light Horse Harry" Lee, an intriguing persona of American history, is generally well known — for his colorful name and exploits in the Revolutionary War, for his personal and political friendship with George Washington, and as the father of Robert E. Lee. One of the more vivid and interesting members of that remarkable group of men who created the United States, Henry Lee participated in the southern campaign which contributed to the British surrender at Yorktown, in the struggle to ratify the United States Constitution, and in the Whiskey Rebellion, among other important events.

Lesser known is Lee's role as Kentucky's last Virginia governor. That is, he was serving as governor of Virginia when, in 1792, Kentucky separated from Virginia to become a state in its own right. Although he in fact contributed little to Kentucky statehood, Lee is linked, in this formal sense, to the Commonwealth's origins. Furthermore, during his tenure as governor of Virginia, as well as at other times, he was substantively involved politically with Kentucky or matters of special concern to Kentuckians. Lee, as seen from a Kentucky perspective, also strikingly personified certain Virginian and eighteenth-century characteristics that would be embraced — and repudiated — by the inhabitants of Kentucky, Virginia's daughter state beyond the mountains. He embodied a set of traits and ideas, some that would persist and others that would quickly be lost or discarded as the new nation expanded westward.

Lee, who was approaching maturity at the outbreak of the War of Independence (he was nineteen in 1775), was essentially a creation of that struggle. He was steeped in the eighteenth-century concepts and ideals of republicanism that then held sway in Virginia, and on which the United States was founded. This, combined with his service in the Revolutionary army, gave him a deep sense of national feeling. Yet he also

**Henry "Light Horse Harry" Lee**
Courtesy of Independence Agency, Philadelphia

proved capable of powerful state, and even sectional, loyalties. Outraged, for example, by Alexander Hamilton's fiscal policies, which he considered anti-Virginia and antisouthern, Lee expressed unwillingness to live under the rule of an "insolent northern majority" and spoke of disunion, "dreadful as it is," being "a lesser evil than union on the present conditions."[1]

A combat officer and war hero, Lee was also an effective public official and political leader. He was an orator of some distinction, noted for forceful and occasionally memorable language. Though fundamentally thoughtful and responsible, he possessed an emotional intensity sometimes displayed in a hot temper and strong sense of honor.

In all these respects — temperament, oratorical ability, the combination of military and political aptitude, the strong but not unshakable nationalism — Lee resembled many subsequent Kentucky notables. Moreover, he lived, for much of his life, in the high Virginia plantation style so widely emulated by affluent Kentuckians and aspired to by those less fortunate in the state's early decades. Seen in this way, Lee represents — as well as any Virginian of his day, and better than most — the cultural heritage that flowed from Virginia to early Kentucky.

Yet Lee also illustrated much that would never exist or survive in Kentucky or the American West as a whole. A Federalist and basically an elitist, he had roots in the world of late colonial Virginia, where stability had been assured by aristocratic leadership of a public that was rather broadly enfranchised (excepting, of course, blacks and women) but politically unassertive. He was far more concerned with good government than with popular opinion, and he candidly voiced fears that the infant American republic might be wrecked by too much democracy. For such a man, politics could never in any sense be "the great game" it would so often be in Kentucky and nineteenth-century America.

Possessed of quite human foibles, Lee could never be successfully portrayed as a plaster saint. Yet he was notable — even measured against his many impressive contemporaries — for his courage and forthrightness, his independence of action, his determination to do what he thought right regardless of consequences. His life reflects many of the best virtues of a heroic age — and, on occasion, the troubles and excesses to which those virtues could lead.

## I

Born in 1756, Lee grew up beside the Potomac River at Leesylvania, his family's plantation in Prince William County, Virginia. His father, also named Henry Lee, was a respected, locally prominent man of moderate wealth who served in the House of Burgesses. The Lees' neighbors included George Washington, Mount Vernon being less than fifteen miles upriver from Leesylvania.

Young Henry — usually called Harry — was the eldest son. Lively and intelligent, he received a good education. At Princeton, then known as the College of New Jersey, Lee's fellow students included several — James Madison, Philip Freneau, Aaron Burr, Hugh Henry Brackenridge — who would figure significantly in his later life. Harry exhibited considerable intellectual ability at Princeton, winning college prizes for translating English into Latin and for reading Latin and Greek.[2] After his graduation in 1773, Lee intended to study law in England at one of London's Inns of Court, but was thwarted by the worsening relations with the mother country that would soon erupt in armed conflict.[3]

The Lees, like many of their fellow Virginians, strongly supported the American Revolution. The branch of the family that was associated with Stratford — a more splendid plantation than Leesylvania, located farther down the Potomac in Westmoreland County — gave to the Revolutionary cause a conspicuous group of brothers. Richard Henry Lee, Francis Lightfoot Lee, William Lee, and Arthur Lee all served politically or diplomatically in the struggle for American independence. Their young cousin Harry Lee was drawn to the military side of that struggle and, in June 1776, was commissioned a captain of light dragoons.[4]

Lee's performance as a cavalry officer soon revealed his natural military talent. General Charles Lee — no relation — said that the young Lee seemed "to have come out of his mother's womb a soldier."[5] Others, including George Washington, also promptly recognized his ability.[6] During his first two years in uniform, Lee served on such battlefields as Brandywine and Germantown, and endured the harsh winter at Valley Forge. In August 1779, he proposed and led one of the war's most daring operations: a raid on the British post at Paulus Hook, New Jersey. A mixed force of cavalry and infantry carried out this difficult venture, in which, after a stealthy night approach march, the garrison was surprised and overwhelmed. Washington acclaimed the triumph as "brilliant," and the Continental Congress voted Lee a gold medal — one of only twelve such medals awarded during the entire war.[7]

This lauded victory, however, had an ugly aftermath that may well have inflicted permanent psychological scars on Lee. Some of the troops and officers involved in the raid had been temporarily assigned to serve under him only for the Paulus Hook operation. Jealous of Lee's success and unhappy that the command had gone to him, one officer was urged by similarly motivated superiors to file a series of charges against Lee, who was put under arrest. A court-martial totally vindicated him, but the episode was nonetheless painful and disillusioning.[8]

Lee's most significant Revolutionary War service came in the South, during the pivotal year 1781. By autumn 1780 British and loyalist forces had won a large measure of control over Georgia and South Carolina, and it was feared that the Revolutionary cause in the whole region below Virginia might collapse. In this dark hour, General Nathanael Greene was sent to take command of the battered Revolutionary army in the South. With him Greene brought a recently formed elite force of about three hundred men, part cavalry and part infantry. Led by Harry Lee, now a lieutenant colonel, this force was to be famous as "Lee's Legion."[9]

Greene planned to offset enemy strength by using a strategy particularly dependent on rapid movement and partisan tactics. The Revolutionary conflict in the South was a bitter, half-guerrilla war — one that some scholars have compared to the twentieth-century war in Vietnam.[10] In conducting this sort of warfare, Greene received much assistance from local partisan leaders, such as Francis Marion, the "Swamp Fox." But Greene relied even more on Lee, whom he described as his most valuable subordinate and "one of the first officers in the world."[11]

The tide of war soon began to turn in the South, and Lee was in the thick of events that made this possible. His Legion served as Greene's rear guard during a perilous retreat across North Carolina — a retreat in which, after being hotly pursued by the army of General Cornwallis, Greene's smaller, weaker army escaped. Shortly afterward, Lee inflicted a crushing defeat on a large band of armed loyalists, producing a chilling effect on loyalism in North Carolina.[12] And Lee was with Greene when, on 15 March 1781, his army, temporarily enlarged by militia reinforcements, fought Cornwallis to a virtual standoff in the bloody battle of Guilford Court House.

These events had an important bearing on the conclusion of the Revolutionary War. Frustrated by his inability to defeat Greene decisively, disappointed by weak loyalist support, Cornwallis chose to carry the war northward into Virginia, a basic error in strategy which resulted in his entrapment six months later at Yorktown. Though Cornwallis surrendered to a Franco-American army led by George Washington, Greene rightly claimed a share of the credit for his own troops. On learning that Cornwallis was besieged at Yorktown, Greene said, "We have been beating the bush and [Washington] has come to catch the bird."[13]

Meanwhile, Greene's army had itself won a string of victories over the British and loyalists in South Carolina and Georgia. In a superbly conducted campaign, one in which Lee's Legion played a key role, Greene restored Revolutionary control to most of the lower South. This sweeping success was confirmed in September 1781 by the battle of Eutaw Springs, a tactical draw but strategic victory for Greene.

At Eutaw Springs Lee performed creditably enough under difficult circumstances. But the battle's sequel was disturbingly reminiscent of what had happened after his triumph at Paulus Hook. Circulating stories and rumors suggested that his performance at Eutaw Springs had been incompetent, even cowardly. These insinuations, evidently put into circulation by personal rivals or enemies, stung Lee, and he was further displeased that Greene's official report of the battle did not more explicitly vindicate him.[14]

Upset with Greene, angry at his detractors, depressed and disillusioned, Lee was seized by an irrational feeling that his contributions during the southern campaign had not been properly recognized. He left the army, early in 1782, in a bleak, aggrieved state of mind.[15] It marked an unfortunate ending to his impressive career as a Revolutionary soldier. At age twenty-six, however, much lay ahead of him.

## II

Lee's Revolutionary War service was a powerful formative experience which influenced the pattern of his life. First, it made him a hero. Wherever he went, whatever he did, he would always be "Light Horse Harry," his military renown lending a certain weight and aura to his presence. Second, his wartime experience affected his personality. The hardship, the glory, the unfair detraction engendered traits of pride, sensitivity, and determination. The challenges he faced evoked a personal force and boldness that sometimes made him unpopular. Alexander Hamilton, his friend and fellow officer, once said of Lee that he would have liked him better had there been less "of the Julius Caesar or Cromwell in him."[16]

Finally, and perhaps most important, Lee's Revolutionary War experience fostered a "continental" or nationalist outlook, which was the foundation of his later Federalism. In six years of warfare that took him from New York to Georgia, he saw repeatedly how the weakness of the separate states and the lack of effective central government hindered the effort to win independence. What was needed, he said, was "wisdom and vigor" in a central authority "created by the whole, for purposes of the whole."[17] He continued to hold this view after the war — as the infant American republic struggled to survive its early years. Much of Lee's postwar life was to be consumed by the public and political concerns of that struggle.

The first important event of Lee's private life after he left the army was his marriage in Virginia, in April 1782, to his nineteen-year-old second cousin Matilda Lee. Although the union of the attractive, vivacious Matilda and her famous cousin was a love match, it had further significance as well: She was principal heiress to the splendid estate of Stratford, and her marriage to Harry Lee made him one of Virginia's hundred wealthiest men.[18]

Lee had said, in the emotional distress of his departure from the army, that what he wanted was the comfort of "an obscure retreat."[19] Life with Matilda at Stratford probably did offer a psychological haven, but Lee's inclination to seclude himself did not last. In 1785, he was elected to the Virginia legislature, which designated him one of Virginia's delegates to Congress. By this time, the inability of government under the Articles of Confederation to cope with postwar problems was vexingly evident, at least to national-minded men like Lee. After several weeks in Congress, he wrote his father that "unless matters soon alter, the United States must inevitably become more insignificant than words can express."[20]

One very difficult issue facing Lee and his congressional colleagues — illustrative of the new nation's weakness and of the danger of a sectional split — was the question of free navigation of the Mississippi River. Spain contolled the lower Mississippi and, to discourage westward expansion by the United States, had closed it to American trade. Foreign Secretary John Jay had then proposed that the United States suspend for some years its claim to free navigation, now a dead letter anyway, in return for Spanish trade concessions. But to many settlers in the West — including many in the Kentucky country — use of the Mississippi River was far too important to be dealt away in this fashion. Some of them were prepared to defy the government of the United States and make whatever terms they could with Spain.

Lee initially took a stand in favor of Jay's proposal to yield free navigation of the Mississippi. His motivation stemmed partly from personal economic interest. He was involved with efforts to improve the navigability of the Potomac River, in the hope that it might someday carry Western goods that could now be boated only down the Mississippi. As a large-scale planter, he also stood to benefit if Spain could be induced to give more favorable treatment to American agricultural exports. Beyond this, however, Lee feared very rapid economic growth in the West. Like George Washington, he thought that free navigation of the Mississippi might encourage a sense of self-sufficiency in the region, dangerously straining its political ties to the Atlantic states.[21] Furthermore, Lee had no doubt that Americans would ultimately control the Mississippi anyway. Mincing no words, he wrote Washington that "the moment our western country becomes populous and capable, [it] will seize by force what may have been yielded by treaty."[22] But Washington, fearing disorder in the West, warned Lee that Kentucky's "many ambitious and turbulent spirits" might become "riotous and ungovernable" if the United States did not hold to its claim to free use of the river.[23]

In Congress, Lee supported Jay and opposed the other members of the Virginia delegation on this issue. But when the matter came up for actual debate in August 1786, Jay's proposal was so fiercely opposed by the southern states, which supported the western point of view, and the resulting contention between representatives of North and South was so alarming, that Lee changed his position. In a strong speech, he declared that keeping the union intact must take precedence over Jay's proposal, which he voted against and which failed to pass. Despite his preference for concessions on the Mississippi navigation issue, Lee had found it impossible to continue pressing for this at a time when it was clear that such advocacy was increasing the danger of national disruption.[24]

The overall weakness of national government under the Articles of Confederation already had spawned a movement for a more effective charter of government. This movement was strengthened by reaction to the disorders in Massachusetts known as Shays' Rebellion, which Lee described as a possible "beginning of anarchy."[25] In his letters to and associations with influential Virginians, Lee helped build and sustain support for the nationalist effort that climaxed in 1787 with the drafting of the United States Constitution. He, along with such others as John Jay and James Madison, spurred George Washington's active support of that effort.[26]

Lee strongly favored the Constitution, and fought to ensure his state's adherence to it at the Virginia ratifying convention of 1788. This convention was integral to the creation of an invigorated national union. Although the nine states necessary to ratify the Constitution had approved it before the Virginia

Convention acted, approval by that body was nonetheless vital. Virginia was the largest and by far the most populous of the thirteen states, as well as the home of George Washington, the one man who was widely acceptable to fill the new office of president. Without Virginia and Washington, the success of the new constitutional union was doubtful.

The Federalists (as the Constitution's advocates called themselves) enjoyed a small advantage in delegate strength as the Virginia Convention opened. But the Antifederalists also were strong, led by Patrick Henry, whose influence and great oratorical skill, it was feared, might sway enough delegates to tip the balance.

Lee, though not one of the convention's most frequent speakers, played a significant role. Perhaps none of Virginia's other leading Federalists could match him in the combination of personal force and oratorical power needed to counter Henry's flaming words, particularly in the convention's early stages. Lee rebutted Henry's attacks on the Constitution with a vigor and bluntness that few others could, or would have dared, equal.[27] Yet Lee also exhibited an ability to speak soothingly and — a rarity for him — somewhat deceptively when necessary. The delegates from Virginia's Kentucky counties feared that a stronger national government could more easily surrender free navigation of the Mississippi. Lee tried to reassure them by emphasizing the failure of Jay's proposal in Congress, but he obscured the fact that he had favored it until almost the last moment.[28] Partly through Lee's efforts, the Federalists did carry the convention by a final vote of 89 to 79 — actually a close margin, since a shift of only six votes, out of the 168 cast, would have reversed the outcome.

Returning to Congress for its last session under the Articles of Confederation, Lee pressed his colleagues to get the new government into operation as quickly as possible.[29] When in the spring of 1789, after years of struggle, the United States at last had a central government with effective powers, he had abundant cause for satisfaction. Moreover, Virginia's two foremost proponents of the Constitution, men politically and personally close to Lee, were in leading positions: Washington as president, and Madison rapidly emerging as the most influential member of Congress. The new government began its work in a flush of optimism, with widespread hope that the worst storms of nation-building were over and that the coming years would bring increasing harmony and stability.

But this did not happen. Within a year, Lee himself was profoundly angry with the new government, even to the point of saying that disunion would be "a lesser evil than union on the present conditions."[30] Stimulus for Lee's turnabout was the set of fiscal measures, commonly known as funding and assumption, proposed by Treasury Secretary Hamilton in January 1790.

Hamilton wanted the federal government to take over the Revolutionary War debts of the states, consolidate those debts with the national debt, and elevate the whole to par value. This plan, which rested on a liberal interpretation of the Constitution, would strengthen both the national economy and the federal government. But it would do so at apparent cost to most of the southern states, including Virginia, which had already paid off a large part of their war debts.[31] The immediate benefits would go mainly to northern men of commerce and speculators who owned depreciated government securities. Favorable to the North over the South, and to monied and commercial interests over the agricultural interest, Hamilton's proposals — which Congress enacted in the summer of 1790 — also stirred fears of a potentially corrupt concentration of economic power closely tied to the federal government.

Lee's social and philosophical outlook was basically agrarian. Though a nationalist, he was keenly sensitive to the dangers of an excessive concentration of economic and political power. His personal interpretation of the Constitution was somewhat strict. And he was disturbed by the prospect of injury to Virginia. So, despite his devotion to President Washington, who had accepted the Hamiltonian program, Lee joined Madison and other leading Virginians in attacking it. To Madison he wrote: "This government which we both admired so much will I fear prove ruinous in its operation to our native state." Hamilton's "treasury schemes" were, he declared, comparable to the "wicked measures adopted through necessity in corrupt monarchies."[32]

Lee was prominently involved in the protest which the Virginia legislature expressed against the Hamiltonian program.[33] He also had a major role, along with Madison and Jefferson, in the establishment of the noted anti-Hamiltonian newspaper, the *National Gazette*. Located at Philadelphia but circulated nationally, it was edited by Philip Freneau, who had been a fellow student with Lee and Madison at Princeton. Lee helped persuade Freneau to come to Philadelphia, promoted the paper's circulation in Virginia, and may even have contributed to its financing.[34]

Lee was now among the leaders of the Virginia legislature, which late in 1791 elected him governor of the state — the first of three one-year terms he would serve in that office. Lee's election was likely due in part to his military knowledge and experience, for there was particular danger in Virginia's western areas, including Kentucky. Humiliating defeats of American forces by the northwestern Indians, in 1790 and again in 1791 had exposed the thinly settled region south and east of the Ohio River to an alarming upsurge of raids. Under legislation already passed, Kentucky would become a state 1 June 1792 and was already largely responsible for its own defense. Therefore, Lee directed his attention to the other threatened frontier areas. The initial crisis existed on the near northwestern frontier, comprising a large part of present-day West Virginia, but another group of Indians, the Creeks and Cherokees, posed a serious threat in southwestern Virginia.

Under Lee's general direction, steps were taken to strengthen the state's defenses, including the recruitment of more militia, increased use of scouts and patrols, and the establishment or reinforcement of a number of small fortified outposts. Lee himself made a long personal inspection trip through the western part of the state in summer 1792. Despite such efforts, the Indian depredations continued; only the westward advance of the frontier permanently ended them. But, for Virginia, the problem would never again be as troublesome as it was during these years.[35]

The period of Lee's governorship, late 1791 to late 1794, was one of the most eventful of his life. He had been desolated by the death of Matilda Lee in 1790, but by 1793 was ready to marry again. His bride — destined to be the mother of Robert E. Lee — was Ann Hill Carter, a gentle girl of beauty and firm character, and a daughter of one of Virginia's leading families. They were wed in June 1793, at her father's plantation, Shirley, on the James River not far from Richmond. She was twenty years old, Lee thirty-seven.[36]

For Lee the year 1793 was also a time of political transition, with changing conditions pushing his political outlook from that of Madison and Jefferson toward that of Washington and Hamilton. The basic cause of this shift was the French Revolution. Initially sympathetic in his view of that Revolution, Lee was increasingly dismayed by the violence and disorder it was spreading across Europe.[37] Moreover, when war broke out in 1793 between Britain and Revolutionary France, Lee feared, as did Washington and Hamilton, that radical pro-French elements in the United States might plunge this country into a ruinous war with Britain. He was particularly disturbed by the rise of the Democratic-Republican Societies, a network of pro-French political clubs which quickly became centers of harsh criticism of government policy. Lee shared the opinion of Washington and Hamilton that these clubs were a form of democratic excess, whose fervor not only could lead to war but also might imperil existing domestic political institutions.[38]

By 1793, the division of views in the United States was beginning to crystallize into political parties — administration opponents as the Republican party, supporters as the Federalist party. Though Lee was by no means reconciled to the Hamiltonian fiscal program, his overriding concern about the twin specters raised by the French Revolution — the danger of war, the threat of democratic excess — aligned him with the Federalist party.

In fall 1794, in the last months of his governorship, Lee helped quell the Whiskey Rebellion, which Federalists particularly considered a critical challenge to national authority. Since its enactment in 1791, the federal tax, on whiskey had been exceedingly unpopular in the West, from the Georgia back country up through Kentucky to the mountains of Pennsylvania. Opposition to the tax, aggravated by other discontents, finally exploded into defiant disorder in western Pennsylvania in 1794. The federal government responded by calling thirteen thousand militiamen from four states, including Virginia, to be sent into western Pennsylvania to restore order. President Washington appointed Governor Lee to command this army.

While Lee favored using all necessary force to put down the whiskey rebels, he was, unlike many who took part in this expedition, restrained and basically conciliatory in his attitude and conduct. The militia army contained numerous officers and men who looked upon the people of the West with vindictiveness, even hatred. Alexander Hamilton, traveling with the expedition, presided aggressively over a series of inquisitorial tribunals that were often conducted in an unfair or abusive fashion. By contrast, Lee's actions were moderate and, on the whole, fair-minded.[39]

There were several major instances of Lee's moderation, one conspicuous example being his treatment of Hugh Henry Brackenridge, a lawyer and writer who was Pittsburgh's leading citizen. While trying to pacify local extremists, Brackenridge had spoken and acted in a way that had caused many to believe him a dangerous foe of federal authority. Hamilton was intensely suspicious of him, and threats against his life had been voiced within the army. Lee — who had known Brackenridge two decades earlier when they had both been students at Princeton — stood against this wave of suspicion and hostility. He stated his opinion that Brackenridge was a virtuous man, insisted on his innocence until guilt could be proven, and openly treated him with courtesy and friendship. Soon Brackenridge was, in fact, cleared of any wrongdoing.[40]

Abusive acts, including physical mistreatment of local inhabitants, were committed by the militia troops under Lee's command. This behavior was contrary to his orders and largely the inevitable result of poor discipline in the unwieldy militia army. Lee tried to deal justly with the western Pennsylvanians, and, though some of his actions were not popular with them, the basic propriety of his conduct was recognized.[41] In a situation where a considerable number of those who held posts of authority behaved in a vindictive or harshly punitive spirit, Lee, by his performance, showed the depth and solidity of his sense of public responsibility.

Although politically less active during the next few years, Lee did return to the Virginia General Assembly. His legislative positions on important national issues demonstrated continuing Federalism. He supported Jay's Treaty, which assured the preservation of peace with Britain. He opposed the Virginia Resolutions of 1798, which argued that the states could rightfully judge the constitutionality of federal legislations.[42]

Lee was now a confirmed, staunch Federalist — but not an extreme one. Like most southern Federalists, he was generally associated with the party's moderate wing, not with the increasingly authoritarian, militaristic wing led by Alexander Hamilton. This is evident from his record in the United States Congress, from 1799 to 1801, when he represented a five-county district of northern Virginia.

In the first significant action of his term, Congressman Lee was chosen as the principal orator at services held at the national capital to commemorate the death of George Washington, who died in December 1799. In his eulogy, Lee praised his longtime friend as "first in war, first in peace, and first in the hearts of his countrymen" — thereby coining a noble, memorable phrase that would pass into American lore as a lasting expression of Washington's historical stature.[43]

The major questions before Congress during Lee's tenure arose essentially from two difficult, closely related problems. One was the undeclared naval war that had broken out in 1798 between the United States and France. The other concerned the proper use and legitimate scope of the federal government's powers in a time of foreign danger and bitter domestic political division. Lee favored vigorous measures to defend the nation and uphold its government against any threat, foreign or domestic. He voted to renew the Sedition Act and expand the federal judiciary, and he wanted to maintain an enlarged army until the troubles with France were settled. He also supported President John Adams' successful effort, which the extreme Federalists angrily opposed, to make peace with France.[44] In Lee's mind, the attainment and preservation of peace had become almost a sine qua non of national well-being. In truth, Adams' move to end hostilities with France was a key step in dampening the severe political strife that had developed during the 1790s, thus easing the danger that such internal conflict might permanently damage the nation's still-fragile political fabric.

Lee was, however, extremely reluctant to see the Federalists, defeated in the elections of 1800, lose control of the national government. When the electoral vote tie between Thomas Jefferson and Aaron Burr, the Republican presidential and vice-presidential candidates, threw the presidential election into the House of Representatives, Lee supported Burr, whom he believed more susceptible to Federalist influence. Most other Federalists in the House did the same, but few with more determination and persistence than Lee. Finally, when it became obvious that Burr could not win (but before it was certain that Jefferson himself could get enough states' votes to be elected), Lee evidently participated in a vain, short-lived effort to have Congress "make a President by Law" — that is, bypass both Jefferson and Burr and install someone else as president.[45]

Lee's unwillingness to have Jefferson become president no doubt stemmed partly from political partisanship, and was almost surely reinforced by personal antipathy, for Lee and Jefferson seem never to have much liked or trusted each other. Lee was further motivated by a deep-seated fear that the Jeffersonian philosophy of limited government might gravely weaken the nation. Having expended so much effort to strengthen the national government, he was willing to go to extreme lengths to thwart the election of one who, he feared, would move dangerously far in the opposite direction.

While Lee did not again hold state or national office after his congressional term ended in 1801, his life continued eventful. Of particular significance was the birth at Stratford, on 19 January 1807, of his son Robert Edward Lee, who would become the most famous of all the notable men produced by the Lee family. Yet for Henry Lee the years after 1800 were shadowed by deepening financial trouble. Partly because of the gradual economic decline of tidewater Virginia, but mainly because of years of unwise, impetuous, or unlucky investments and land speculations, Lee had fallen heavily into debt. As a result of his debts, he was arrested and imprisoned in 1809.[46]

This disagreeable circumstance, however, did not divert Lee from a literary project in which he soon became absorbed — and from which, in fact, he hoped money could be made. During his imprisonment Lee did much of the work on a book he set out to write on the Revolutionary War in the South. Finally published in 1812, his *Memoirs of the War in the Southern Department of the United States* was the best account yet written of the war by an American officer. It did not benefit Lee financially, but despite occasional error and bias was an excellent military history that graced many libraries of that day. In the decades since, it has come to be recognized as a substantial, even classic, contribution to the literature of the Revolutionary War.[47]

With settlement of the financial problems that had led to his imprisonment, Lee was set free in 1810. He and his family soon moved from Stratford to the Potomac River town of Alexandria, where they lived in modest comfort mainly on Ann Carter Lee's inheritance from her father.[48] During the months following their move to Alexandria, it became increasingly clear that the United States was headed toward war with Britain. The resentment and frustration generated by years of British impressment of American seamen and interference with American commerce had stirred a rising war sentiment, which was concentrated in the majority Republican party.

Lee, like most Federalists, opposed the drift toward hostilities. Having long feared the effect of war on the young American nation, he vehemently urged, in correspondence with his old friend President James Madison, that every effort be made to settle the points at issue between the two countries without war.[49] But war did come. Lee's disapproval of it, plus his staunch Federalism, led to his involvement in one of the most dramatic and brutal political disorders in American history, the Baltimore riots of 1812.

Baltimore was an intensely Republican city, and very rapid growth during the preceding twenty years had given it a rough, boom town atmosphere. In June 1812, the Baltimore *Federal Republican,* one of the nation's most extremely partisan Federalist newspapers, published a vitriolic editorial condemning the Republican-controlled government's decision to go to war. Reacting to this, a mob destroyed the paper's offices and razed the building in which they were located. But the editors refused to be silenced and, a month later, sought to restore the paper to circulation. Lee, probably in Baltimore for the express purpose of backing the *Federal Republican*'s editors, joined a number of Federalists at the house where the paper was being distributed.

That night, an angry mob besieged and assaulted the house. Under Lee's direction, the men inside withstood the mob, killing one man and wounding several. Toward morning, after hours of tumult, rock-throwing, and some gunfire, the city authorities finally intervened. Lee and the other Federalists, were escorted to the local jail where they could be protected. But the security actually provided was very meager, and the next night a vicious mob successfully stormed the jail. One of the Federalists, the Revolutionary veteran General James Lingen, was stomped to death. Many others were brutally beaten, slashed with knives, and burned with hot candle grease. Lee suffered deep, disfiguring cuts of his nose, cheek, and lip, and was badly beaten about the eyes; he never again regained his health.[50]

The Baltimore riots produced shock and revulsion, and were politcally damaging to the Republicans. To many, these events offered at least partial confirmation of the oft-repeated Federalist warning that the intolerant brutality of the French Revolution could be transferred to America. Republicans argued, with some justice, that the editors of the *Federal Republican* had acted provocatively, but this could not justify the barbarism of the mob or the failure of Baltimore's city authorities to protect persons in their custody.[51] For Lee, these events provided a cruel substantiation of his long-held fear of the excess to which popular passions could lead, especially when not checked by responsible, competent governmental authority.

Despite his dislike of the war, Lee intended to serve the nation. He sent advice to President Madison on the security of American forces wintering near the Canadian border and told the president he was willing to serve in any military capacity as soon as he could recover his health.[52] But recovery did not come, and, in the spring of 1813, hoping that a sojourn in a balmier climate might have a restorative effect, Lee left Virginia and sailed for the Caribbean. His family, whom he was never to see again, remained behind. There were two grown children from his first marriage to Matilda Lee, as well as his wife Ann and their five surviving children, including young Robert, age six.

Although Robert was raised primarily by his mother, Harry Lee's influence on his son's life was far from negligible. The example of his father seems to have helped turn Robert toward the military, and to have spurred his determination to become a highly capable officer. Also, Robert's remarkable self-discipline and self-control were in part reactions against the impetuous, combative aspect of his father's personality. Despite this and other obvious differences between them, father and son had deep similarities of outlook and belief. Imperatives of duty and public service were of extreme import to both. The two, though devoted to Virginia, were essentially nationalists, lovers of the union — Robert E. Lee's role in the Civil War notwithstanding. Each, though a slaveholder, disliked slavery. And both revered George Washington who was, for Henry and Robert, the foremost human ideal and exemplar.[53]

In the Caribbean, Lee landed on the British West Indian island of Barbados about the end of June 1813. There he began a series of communications with the island's governor, Sir George Beckwith, to promote a negotiated settlement of the conflict between Britain and the United States. Although some evidence does suggest that Lee may have been acting as an unofficial agent of the American government, most indications are that he was acting mainly or entirely on his own, trying to help extricate the United States from a war that, in his view, could only damage the nation.[54] In any event, nothing came of his peacemaking efforts and he was gone from Barbados by early 1814.

Lee spent the next four years voyaging the Caribbean, visiting one island, then another in a futile search for restored health. Apparently no serious obstacle to his returning home existed after early 1815, when the cessation of hostilities between the United States and Britain ended the Royal Navy's blockade of the American coast. But Lee chose to stay in the Caribbean. Possibly this was solely for reasons of health, but the greater likelihood is that his disfigurement, his financial situation, and the desire not to burden his family also influenced him. Certainly his thoughts were often with his wife and children during these years, as shown in a number of poignant letters of love and concern he wrote to them.[55]

When finally Lee did try to return home, he failed to survive the trip. Stricken seriously ill on the northward voyage, he was put ashore at Cumberland Island, Georgia. On the island was a plantation which once belonged to his Revolutionary commander, Nathanael Greene, and was now the home of Greene's daughter and her husband. They took Lee in and saw that he was well cared for. He died there, in March 1818, at the age of sixty-two.[56] Thus ended a stormy, vivid life — and one heavily devoted to the military and political tasks of founding the new American nation. While epochal achievement is often equated with the greatest names associated with it, surely it could not have been done without such less acclaimed, but nonetheless able and dedicated, men as Lee. They too made a difference, or helped to do so, as Lee himself did in the southern campaign of 1781, at the Virginia Convention of 1788, and on other occasions.

The prime political objective Lee wished to see realized was creation of a strong, harmonious, socially conservative republic. His outlook was not monolithic, however, as he showed in the early 1790s when his fear of excessive concentration of power and his concern for Virginia superseded, for a time, his belief in energetic central government. Lee was quite capable of acting unwisely, of being carried to excess — as in his stubborn resistance to Jefferson's becoming president. Yet the total record of his public life displays a basic unity, which lies not only in his support for establishing the United States on firmly national principles but also in the responsible, useful service he gave toward that end. Lee was deeply imbued with eighteenth-century ideals of civic virtue and, whatever his mistakes or failings, driven by an impressive desire to serve the public good as he perceived it.

While his strong emotions were sometimes exhibited in petulance, irascibility, or outrage, Lee was by and large a man of political moderation. The positions he took and his public and private comments on a number of issues reveal this. Yet he was also a courageous, outspoken, intensely determined man who pursued his aims with uncommon directness and vigor. One statement he made at the Virginia Convention — "I shall brave all storms and political dangers" — aptly describes his approach to public life.[57]

In an important sense, the specific conception of the American Revolution to which Lee was dedicated did not succeed. The harmonious, cohesive, socially conservative republic he wanted could not rise and flourish in a new nation whose society was already being reshaped by the centrifugal forces of democracy, individualism, and the frontier. Kentucky, the first state in the West, was an early stage on which that process appeared full-blown — a fact that lends a certain appropriateness to Lee's having been the last of Kentucky's Virginia governors.

The generation to which Lee belonged left an enduring legacy, one that survives in many of the institutions and ideals of late twentieth-century America. Lee himself actively served three important causes that were at the very foundation of that legacy: the winning of independence, the creation of a federal union under a strong constitution, and the placing of national government on a firm footing of authority. He was a justly renowned Revolutionary soldier, George Washington's good friend, and Robert E. Lee's father. But it is for his overall efforts in behalf of the new American nation, both military and political, that he most properly deserves to be remembered.

## Footnotes

[1]Henry Lee to James Madison, 3 April 1790, Madison Papers (Library of Congress).

[2]John Maclean, *History of the College of New Jersey* (2 vols., Philadelphia, 1877), I, 312n.

[3]Robert E. Lee, "Life of General Henry Lee," in Henry Lee, *Memoirs of the War in the Southern Department of the United States* (New York, 1869), 16. Henry Lee is sometimes referred to (as in this citation) as General Lee. His highest rank in the Revolutionary army was lieutenant colonel, but he held the rank of major general in the U.S. Army from 1798 to 1800 and was also a major general in the Virginia militia.

[4] Francis B. Heitman, *Historical Register and Dictionary of the United States Army* (2 vols., Washington, 1903), I, 624.

[5] Charles Lee, "Proposals for the Formation of a Body of Light Troops Ready to be Detach'd on Emergent Occasions," *Collections of the New York Historical Society* (31 vols., New York, 1868-99), VI, 287.

[6] George Washington to Henry Lee, 20 January 1778, in John C. Fitzpatrick, ed., *The Writings of George Washington* (39 vols., Washington, 1931-44), X, 322.

[7] George Washington to Henry Lee, 10 August 1779; Washington to the President of Congress, 23 August 1779, in Fitzpatrick, ed., *Writings of Washington*, XVI, 72-73, 155; Lynn Montross, *Rag, Tag and Bobtail: The Story of the Continental Army, 1775-1783* (New York, 1952), 465.

[8] Alexander Hamilton to John Laurens, 11 September 1779, in Harold C. Syrett, ed., *The Papers of Alexander Hamilton* (26 vols. to date, New York, 1961-  ), II, 168 and 165n; Henry Lee to Joseph Reed, 27 August 1779, in William B. Reed, *Life and Correspondence of Joseph Reed* (2 vols., Philadelphia, 1847), II, 126-27.

[9] In the military parlance of the time, a legion was a force of mixed arms — in Lee's case, cavalry and infantry. Besides being called "Light Horse Harry," a reference to his ability as a leader of light cavalry, Lee was also sometimes called "Legion Harry."

[10] See, for example, Russell F. Weigley, "American Strategy: A Call for a Critical Strategic History," and Richard Buel, Jr., "Time: Friend or Foe or the Revolution?" in Don Higginbotham, ed., *Reconsiderations on the Revolutionary War: Selected Essays* (Westport, Conn., 1978), 39-40, 124-25.

[11] Nathanael Greene to the President of Congress, 18 February 1782, quoted in R.E. Lee, "Life of Lee," in Henry Lee, *Memoirs of the War*, 41; Greene to Anthony Wayne, 7 October 1781, quoted in Douglas Southall Freeman, *George Washington: A Biography*, completed by John Alexander Carroll and Mary Wells Ashworth (7 vols., New York, 1948-57), V, 355n.

[12] Theodore Thayer, *Nathanael Greene: Strategist of the American Revolution* (New York, 1960), 323.

[13] Nathanael Greene to Henry Knox, 29 September 1781, in F.S. Drake, *Life and Correspondence of Henry Knox* (Boston, 1873), 68.

[14] William Johnson, *Sketches of the Life and Correspondence of Nathanael Greene* (2 vols., Charleston, 1822), II, 220-35.

[15] Nathanael Greene to Henry Lee, 27 January and 18 February 1782, in Henry Lee [1787-1837], *The Campaign of 1781 in the Carolinas* (Philadelphia, 1824), Appendix, xvi-xx; Lee to Greene, [19] February 1782, HM 22708 (Henry E. Huntington Library, San Marino, California).

[16] Alexander Hamilton to John Laurens, 11 September 1779, in Syrett, ed., *Papers of Hamilton*, II, 168.

[17] Henry Lee to Thomas Sim Lee, 18 September 1780, Thomas Addis Emmet Collection (New York Public Library).

[18] Ethel Armes, *Stratford Hall: The Great House of the Lees* (Richmond, 1936), 225-26, 240-41; Jackson T. Main, "The One Hundred," *William and Mary Quarterly*, 3d Ser., 11 (1954), 377.

[19]Henry Lee to Nathanael Greene, 26 January 1782, in Johnson, *Greene*, II, 321.

[20]Henry Lee to [his father] Henry Lee, 19 April 1786, Edmund Jennings Lee Papers (Virginia Historical Society).

[21]George Washington to Benjamin Harrison, 10 October 1784; Washington to Henry Lee, 18 June 1786, in Fitzpatrick, ed., *Writings of Washington*, XXVII, 471-80; XXVIII, 459-61.

[22]Henry Lee to George Washington, 7 August 1786, in Edmund C. Burnett, ed., *Letters of Members of the Continental Congress* (8 vols., Washington, 1921-36), VIII, 417.

[23]George Washington to Henry Lee, 26 July 1786, in Fitzpatrick, ed., *Writings of Washington*, XXVIII, 484-85.

[24]Worthington Chauncey Ford et al., eds., *Journals of the Continental Congress 1774-1789* (34 vols., Washington, 1904-37), XXXI, 594-96, 600-07, 610-13; Minutes of Proceedings, 18 August 1786; Burnett, ed., *Letters of Congress*, VIII, 439. In voting against Jay's proposal, Lee was also obeying instructions from the Virginia legislature, but private letters and the content of his speech show that his earlier view had changed as a result of his concern for the union.

[25]Henry Lee to George Washington, 17 October 1786, in Burnett, ed., *Letters of Congress*, VIII, 486.

[26]Marcus Cunliffe, *George Washington: Man and Monument* (Boston, 1958), 140-41.

[27]Jonathan Elliot, ed., *The Debates in the Several State Conventions on the Adoption of the Federal Constitution* (5 vols., Philadelphia, 1891), III, 41-43, 176-87; David John Mays, *Edmund Pendleton, 1721-1803; A Biography* (2 vols., Cambridge, Mass., 1952), II, 237, 244.

[28]Elliot, ed., *Debates*, III, 333-34.

[29]Ford et al., eds., *Journals of Congress*, XXXIV, 367-68, 396, 515-16.

[30]Henry Lee to James Madison, 3 April 1790, Madison Papers.

[31]Actually, in the final crediting and settlement of accounts, the Hamiltonian measures treated Virginia and most other low-debt southern states equitably, if not more than equitably. But it was not at all clear initially that this would be so.

[32]Henry Lee to James Madison, 13 March 1790, 8 January 1792, Madison Papers. In the 1792 letter, Lee expressed hostility not only to Hamilton's "funding schemes" but also to the full Hamiltonian program as of that date, including the Bank of the United States and the Report on Manufactures.

[33]Virginia *House Journal* (1790), 3-5, 35-36, 44, 80-81, 140-41.

[34]Memorandum by Nicholas P. Trist, quoting James Madison, 25 May 1827, in Henry S. Randall, *The Life of Thomas Jefferson* (3 vols., New York, 1858), II, 74-75; James Madison to Henry Lee, 18 December 1791, in Gaillard Hunt, ed., *The Writings of James Madison* (9 vols., New York, 1900-10), VI, 69; Samuel E. Forman, *The Political Activities of Philip Freneau* (Baltimore, 1902), 31-32.

[35]G.W. Jackson and others to Henry Lee, 12 December 1791, A. Lewis and J. Preston to Lee, 7 February 1792, in William P. Palmer, et al., eds., *Calendar of Virginia*

*State Papers and Other Manuscripts* (11 vols., Richmond, 1875-93), V, 405, 437-38, and V, VI, VII, *passim;* Lee to the County Lieutenants of western counties, 12 December 1791, Lee to Henry Knox, 7 September 1792, 29 April 1793, Executive Letter Books (Virginia State Library).

[36] Armes, *Stratford Hall,* 271-78.

[37] Henry Lee to John Graves Simcoe, 15 March 1793, de Coppet Collection (Princeton University Library).

[38] Henry Lee to George Washington, 14 June and 17 September 1793, Washington Papers (Library of Congress); Lee to Alexander Hamilton, 15 June 1793, in Syrett, ed., *Papers of Hamilton,* XIV, 549-50.

[39] Leland D. Baldwin, *Whiskey Rebels: The Story of a Frontier Uprising* (Pittsburgh, 1939), 69-75, 105, 225, 234, 240-50; Orders of Major General Lee, 21 November 1794, Lee to Captain d'Hebecourt, 22 November 1794, *Pennsylvania Archives, Second Series* (19 vols., Harrisburg, 1887-96), IV, 392-93, 395-96.

[40] Hugh Henry Brackenridge, *Incidents of the Insurrection in the Western Parts of Pennsylvania in the Year 1794* (3 vols. in 1, Philadephia, 1795), II, 50-61, 73-82; Claude Milton Newlin, *The Life and Writings of Hugh Henry Brackenridge* (Princeton, 1932), 145-75.

[41] Henry Lee to the Commandants of Divisions, Brigades, Regiments, and Corps, [21?] October 1794; Lee to Gov. Thomas Mifflin, 25 October 1794, Lee to Gen. William Irvine, 9 November 1794, *Pennsylvania Archives, Second Series,* IV, 353-54, 376-77; William Findley, *History of the Insurrection in the Four Western Counties of Pennsylvania* (Philadelphia, 1796), 218; Brackenridge, *Incidents,* II, 65, 80-82.

[42] Virginia *House Journal* (1795), 91-92; *Alien and Sedition Laws: Debates in the House of Delegates of Virginia* (Washington, 1912), 82-87.

[43] *Annals of Congress,* 6th Cong, 1st Sess. (26 December 1799), X, 210, 1310.

[44] *Ibid.,* 273-77, 360-66, 369, 403-04, 713-14; 2d Sess., 903, 915, 960-63, 975-76, 1014-15, 1019; Stephen G. Kurtz, *The Presidency of John Adams: The Collapse of Federalism, 1795-1800* (Philadelphia, 1957), 375, 384; [Henry Lee], *Plain Truth: Addressed to the People of Virginia* ([Richmond?], 1799), 4-5, 9-10, 36-39.

[45] Alexander Hamilton to James McHenry, 4 January 1801, in Bernard C. Steiner, *The Life and Correspondence of James McHenry* (Cleveland, 1907), 484; Henry Lee to Hamilton, 6 February 1801, Hamilton Papers (Library of Congress); Washington *National Intelligencer,* 13, 16, 18 February 1801; Albert Gallatin to Henry A. Muhlenberg, 8 May 1848, in Henry Adams, ed., *The Writings of Albert Gallatin* (3 vols., Philadelphia, 1879), II, 664; Randall, *Jefferson,* II, 608.

[46] Thomas Boyd, *Light-horse Harry Lee* (New York, 1931), 179-85, 245-48, 280-97.

[47] Charles G. Sellers, Jr., "The American Revolution: Southern Founders of a National Tradition," in Arthur S. Link and Rembert W. Patrick, eds., *Writing Southern History: Essays in Historiography in Honor of Fletcher M. Green* (Baton Rouge, 1965), 44-45.

[48] Boyd, *Lee,* 301, 303; Armes, *Stratford Hall,* 322-31.

[49] Henry Lee to James Madison, 19 August 1811, 21 June 1812, Madison Papers.

[50] David Hackett Fischer, *The Revolution of American Conservatism: The Federal-*

*ist Party in the Era of Jeffersonian Democracy* (New York, 1965), 141, 173, 217; J. Thomas Scharf, *The Chronicles of Baltimore* (Baltimore, 1874), 309-39.

[51] Henry Adams, *History of the United States of America During the Administrations of Jefferson and Madison* (9 vols., New York, 1889-91), VI, 408-09; Richard Buel, Jr., *Securing the Revolution: Ideology in American Politics, 1789-1815* (Ithaca, N.Y., 1972), 286-88.

[52] Henry Lee to James Madison, 15 January 1813, Madison Papers; Boyd, *Lee*, 330-31.

[53] Douglas Southall Freeman, *R.E. Lee: A Biography* (4 vols., New York, 1934-35), I, 22-23, 37-38, 65-67, 371-73, 420-25, 453; IV, 400-01; Henry Lee to Robert Goode, 16 May 1792, quoted in Boyd, *Lee*, 207; Henry Lee, *Memoirs of the War*, 215, 215n.

[54] "Major-General Henry Lee and Lieutenant-General Sir George Beckwith on Peace in 1813," *American Historical Review*, 32 (1927), 284-92. Lee's departure for the West Indies was specially arranged. It came soon after Albert Gallatin and James A. Bayard sailed for Russia on an official peace mission, and before he left Lee discussed the diplomatic situation with Madison and Secretary of State Monroe. But other evidence indicates pretty clearly that Lee was not acting as an unofficial diplomatic agent. See, for example, Henry Lee to Rufus King, 19 November 1813, in Charles R. King, ed., *The Life and Correspondence of Rufus King* (6 vols., New York, 1894-1900), V, 354.

[55] R.E. Lee, "Life of Lee," in Henry Lee, *Memoirs of the War*, 57-78; Armes, *Stratford Hall*, 346-54.

[56] Lee was buried in the Greene family cemetery on Cumberland Island, but in 1913 his remains were moved to Lexington, Virginia, where they now rest beneath the Lee Chapel at Washington and Lee University.

[57] Elliot, ed., *Debates*, III, 187.

# Bibliographical Essay

The most important sources for a study of Henry Lee are his surviving letters and papers. These are scattered among a number of repositories, including the Library of Congress, the Virginia Historical Society, the Virginia State Library, the University of Virginia Library, the Robert E. Lee Memorial Association at Stratford Hall, Virginia, the Henry E. Huntington Library at San Marino, California, and the William L. Clements Library at Ann Arbor, Michigan. A sizable portion of Lee's letters is accessible in the various editions of the published papers of such contemporaries as George Washington, Alexander Hamilton, and James Madison; but many of

Lee's letters remain unpublished.

A basic source for Lee in the Revolutionary War is his *Memoirs of the War in the Southern Department of the United States* (New York, 1869), originally published in 1812. (The 1869 edition is of particular significance in that it contains a biographical essay on his father by Robert E. Lee, in which are extended quotations from a number of the elder Lee's letters, especially family letters.) Henry Lee also wrote a few political pamphlets, which shed light on his view of some specific issues and on his general thinking and attitudes.

Certain public documents are important for Lee's political activities. Indispensable among these are Worthington Chauncey Ford et al., eds., *Journals of the Continental Congress, 1774-1789* (34 vols., Washington, 1904-37); Jonathan Elliot, ed., *The Debates in the Several State Conventions on the Adoption of the Federal Constitution* (5 vols., Philadelphia, 1891), Volume III; William P. Palmer et al., eds., *Calendar of Virginia State Papers and Other Manuscripts* (11 vols., Richmond, 1875-93); and the *Annals of Congress,* 6th Congress.

The most comprehensive biography of Lee is the author's doctoral dissertation, "Henry 'Light Horse Harry' Lee: A Biography" (University of Kentucky, 1975). An older biography, Thomas Boyd, *Light-horse Harry Lee* (New York, 1931), is essentially sound and remains useful. A notable recent book is Charles Royster's interesting and impressive thematic study, *Light-Horse Harry Lee and the Legacy of the American Revolution* (New York, 1981).

# James Guthrie: Kentucky Politician and Entrepreneur

*by Charles J. Bussey*

In 1792, the same year that Kentucky entered the Union as the fifteenth state, James Guthrie was born on 5 December in Nelson County near Bardstown. The youth and the state grew up together during the early years of American history, with Guthrie destined to play a major role in Kentucky's development during the tumultuous years of Jacksonian Democracy. At a time when Whig Henry Clay overshadowed his fellow Kentucky politicians on the national level, Guthrie patiently made his reputation in the state legislature as a Democrat. Competent and fair to all factions, Guthrie was president of the Kentucky Constitutional Convention in 1849. He became nationally prominent as President Franklin Pierce's secretary of the treasury from 1853 to 1857. In February 1861, the former secretary played the key role at the Washington Peace Conference which aimed at reversing the headlong rush toward the Civil War. When that tragic conflict developed despite his efforts, Guthrie gained respect as a staunch Unionist. In 1865, by then in his seventies, he was elected to the United States Senate. This study will thus focus on the public service of James Guthrie — his impact on both his state and nation, his role in state politics, his crucial reforms as secretary of the treasury, and his efforts to avert the Civil War.

I

Adam Guthrie, James' father, came in 1776 from Ireland to Pennsylvania and, from there, to Virginia. Adam's adventuresome spirit eventually led him to settle in Nelson County, Kentucky, where he became a prominent citizen and represented his district in the state legislature for several years. Young James Guthrie had a fairly typical frontier childhood; he studied in a log schoolroom, and, having shown aptitude, spent

**James Guthrie**
Courtesy of Louisville & Nashville Railroad

several years at McAlister Academy in Bardstown. During the War of 1812, Guthrie interrupted his education and engaged in the flatboat trade to New Orleans. He would purchase produce from his neighbors, float it down river to sell, and return home on foot.[1] Dissatisfied with that life, Guthrie abandoned commerce to read law under the direction of Judge John Rowan, one of Kentucky's foremost nineteenth century lawyers. Guthrie passed his bar examination in 1817, set up practice in Bardstown, and, when Governor John Adair appointed him a commonwealth attorney in 1820, moved to Louisville, which was to be his life's home. The following year Guthrie made a fortunate marriage to Elizabeth Prather, daughter of a prosperous Louisvillian; their union produced three daughters.[2]

Once settled in Louisville, Guthrie established himself as a lawyer and talented businessman, and during the 1820s he became active in party politics. The great political rivalry between Tennessee's Andrew Jackson and Kentucky's Henry Clay was maturing in the mid-1820s, and Guthrie aligned himself with the Jackson Democrats against Clay's Whigs. "From 1825 on he was an active, influential and efficient Jacksonian Democrat," in a city which was predominantly Whig.[3] Despite his party's minority status, Guthrie served in the state house of representatives from 1827 to 1830 and in the state senate from 1831 to 1840. In 1835, he also was the unsuccessful Democratic candidate for the United States Senate.[4]

As a highly respected member of the state legislature, Guthrie enhanced his reputation as a man with a flair for finance. He was instrumental, for example, in chartering the Bank of Kentucky in 1834. Following the "Great Bank War" in which President Andrew Jackson succeeded in destroying Henry Clay's National Bank, Guthrie's Bank of Kentucky enabled his state to withstand a period when many states floundered in financial chaos. Guthrie, "a veritable picture of strength and endurance," maintained his law practice, his banking interests, and his political activities throughout the 1830s.[5] One estimate is "that one-third of the laws made in Kentucky in the decade 1830-1840 either originated with Mr. Guthrie or were passed by his influence."[6] In addition, Guthrie was quite civic-minded, helping to found a school for the blind in Louisville and beginning a thirty-two-year tenure on the

University of Louisville's Board of Trustees. Also in the 1830s, Guthrie began his interest in railroads — he helped develop the Louisville, Maysville, and Lexington Railroad, which he served as president until 1853.[7]

Beginning in the early 1840s, there was considerable discussion and effort among public-minded Kentuckians to effect change in the state constitution. By 1849, with the focus on the relation of the state to slavery, the election or appointment of state officials, the use of state credit for internal improvements, and a common school system, enough people had been convinced to vote to convene a constitutional convention in October 1849. That convention met in Frankfort, where Guthrie was elected president by a vote of 57 to 43 over Archibald Dixon, a Whig from Henderson.[8]

Much of that convention's time, perhaps stimulated by antislavery meetings in Maysville and Lexington in February and a state emancipation convention in Frankfort in April, was given over to the question of slavery. President Guthrie led the convention in its proslavery sentiment, using the problems of the poor in industrial-urban Massachusetts to bolster his argument that slavery was tolerable. Arguing that a free, biracial society could not exist in Kentucky, Guthrie contended that emancipation would injure all concerned, including blacks, but especially society at large. Ultimately, the Kentucky Constitution of 1850 supported slavery and prohibited the migration of free Negroes into the state.[9]

On other issues, however, Guthrie proved much more democratic. He made clear his judgment that the appointive power should be limited and that "the people should select all officers, including the judges, for a term of years." Again, the new constitution reflected Guthrie's opinion, as it did on the questions of slavery and immigration. Several thousand foreigners had come to Kentucky, especially to the Louisville area, and, as the nation moved into a nativist, Know-Nothing Party period, there was discussion of making them second-class citizens. Guthrie argued: "I am not willing that any man shall be a citizen of this commonwealth and not be entitled to all the privileges of citizenship. I do not want to see a class here who shall be less than citizens."[10]

Guthrie emerged from the constitutional convention with his state reputation and stature at its highest level. In 1852, he refused Governor Lazarus Powell's offer to appoint him to the United States Senate seat left vacant by the death of Henry Clay. That vacancy was filled instead, for a period of fifty-six days, by David Meriwether, one of Guthrie's political friends. In September, however, the state legislature sent Guthrie's old Whig rival Archibald Dixon to Washington to replace Meriwether. Had Guthrie accepted the original offer, the course of history might have been altered: Dixon might never have gone to the Senate and thus could not have played a key role in forcing Illinois Senator Stephen A. Douglas to raise the slavery issue in such blatant form in his explosive Kansas-Nebraska bill in 1854.[11]

In 1850, the year after the Kentucky Constitutional Convention, America's national unity was in grave danger as the nation appeared to be on the verge of dividing. Explosive issues polarized Americans as never before: a new Fugitive Slave Law, the status of slavery and the slave trade in the District of Columbia, California's demand for statehood, the Texas boundary and debt question, and territorial governments for Utah and New Mexico. The Thirty-first Congress met in Washington, D.C., and after a long and complex process, reached a tenuous agreement. A "final" solution to the problem of slavery was purported to have been achieved, and the nation generally agreed with that analysis. The calm, moderate mood of the people was probably superficial, but it prevailed from September 1850 to the quadrennial presidential election in 1852.[12]

Both major party presidential candidates in 1852, New Hampshire's Franklin Pierce for the Democrats and General Winfield Scott for the Whigs, were second-choice candidates, the selections of deadlocked conventions. The ensuing campaign was essentially devoid of substantive discussion of fundamental issues. Pierce and Scott simply represented themselves as national candidates who viewed compromise as a legitimate method of solving national disputes; both supported the Compromise of 1850, including the new Fugitive Slave Law, "as a [final] settlement in principle and substance" of the nation's problems. The only discordant note was sounded by the Free Soil ticket of John P. Hale and George W. Julian. Hale, a former senator from New Hampshire, and Julian, a one-term representative from Indiana, ran on a platform denying that compromise could be a viable policy on such a public issue as slavery.

Thus, the American voter had a chance to express his considered opinion on the Compromise settlement in the 1852 presidential election. Considering the nation's pro-Compromise mood between mid-1851 and November 1852, the result was not surprising. Pierce was the only presidential candidate to receive a popular majority after 1840 and prior to 1864; and though his popular majority of 58,227 was small, his victory in the electoral college was immense — 254 to 42. Hale and Julian attracted few popular votes, far fewer than the Free Soil ticket had received in 1848, and no electoral votes. Clearly the people had spoken and issued a mandate. They were tired of hearing about slavery and having turmoil thrust upon them; it was time to get on with the business of developing America and its vast resources.[13]

Pierce approached his first political task, the selection of a cabinet, on the principle that no one would be proscribed because of previously held political convictions. In seeking to appoint a cabinet balanced among the three major Democratic factions (Unionist, Free Soil, and Southern Rights), Pierce was logical and probably correct — up to a point. But he was indecisive, and the selection process dragged on through November and December 1852 and into January and February 1853. The cabinet finally was composed of New York's William Marcy as secretary of state, Jefferson Davis of Mississippi as secretary of war, Michigan's Robert McClelland heading the Interior Department, North Carolinian James Dobbin as secretary of the navy, Massachusetts' Caleb Cushing as attorney general, and Kentucky's James Guthrie in the treasury slot. The cabinet clearly leaned toward the southern wing of the party in ideological terms. And Marcy, though on friendly terms with northern Free Soilers and a strong national figure, had attracted his share of critics over his long political career. In many respects, it was a good cabinet, one which inspired confidence and strengthened Pierce's administration, which "was as strong in administrative integrity as it was weak in political strength and skill."[14]

Named to head the Treasury Department, Guthrie came to his post as a southern unionist without national recognition.[15] A self-made man, this Kentucky native and Louisville resident was a successful railroad entrepreneur and lawyer with a reputation for work at once "clear, brief, logical and precise." Although "very strong,"[16] he was "not polished" and had "none of the courtly graces." Nevertheless, on the state level, Guthrie had proved himself an important and effective Jacksonian Democrat.[17] While Guthrie may have brought to the Pierce administration no major political assets, neither did he reflect liabilities associated with men like Davis and Cushing. The New York *Times* gave a fair assessment of the tall, sturdy Kentuckian when it described him as "a clear-headed, practical business man, of known and steady integrity . . . not a mere politician. . . . He is a lawyer of mature experience and profound judgment."[18] A Whig journal in Louisville expressed a similar view: "Mr. Guthrie will make a good and efficient Secretary of Treasury. . . . He undoubtedly possesses strong sense, great industry, an unconquerable will and a moral courage that nothing can daunt."[19] That was high praise from the opposition.

Invoking his abundant energy and determination, Guthrie assumed supervision of his very complicated department, which "included customs service, revenue-cutter service, a light-house system, bureau of weights and measures, and a bureau of construction, as well as the accounting system established by [Alexander] Hamilton."[20]

The new secretary faced four principal problems: (1) the Whig members employed in his staff of four to five hundred; (2) an awkward surplus which was accumulating in the treasury; (3) a number of fraud charges against the department; and (4) non-enforcement of the Independent Treasury Act, which resulted in a considerable amount of federal money being reposited outside the treasury. Guthrie acted with dispatch and effectiveness, and with some ruthlessness according to his enemies, in cleaning up his department. He earned the nickname "prairie plow."[21]

Immediately, Guthrie laid plans to use the treasury surplus

to pay off a part of the national debt, due in July 1853. He also began to buy up United States stock certificates at market prices, thus further reducing the national debt and the unwieldy surplus. Critical of the previous administration's questionable policy of having the treasury contract with financiers such as New York's Simon Draper to keep public funds, Guthrie began to cancel such contracts.[22]

In many respects, Guthrie's most heroic feat as secretary was to break the hold which the Corcoran and Riggs banking firm held over the treasury. W.W. Corcoran throughout the 1840s and into the early 1850s had been perhaps the most powerful man in the United States; his extraordinary influence on government policy reached into the very inner circles. His relationship, for example, to Daniel Webster, one of the nineteenth century's greatest heroes, was nothing short of scandalous, with Webster essentially a bought man who did what Corcoran wanted in exchange for funds. Upon taking office Guthrie withdrew Corcoran and Riggs' "government deposits of $493,000." Corcoran strongly protested and enlisted the support of ex-Secretary Robert Walker who "urged . . . others to join in support" against the determined Guthrie.[23] By discontinuing the practice of having private firms act as repositories, Guthrie returned over two million dollars to government vaults and, "after years of controversy and partial reform, the Independent Treasury was at last to be fully instituted."[24]

When in December 1853 Guthrie made his first report to Congress, as mandated by the United States Constitution, he had several accomplishments to report. The national debt had been reduced by $12,703,329, many accounts (some over five years behind) had been settled, the independent treasury was in fact working, and the privileged position of W.W. Corcoran had been ended. Although there remained the troublesome problem of the surplus, Guthrie was at work on a plan to revise the tariff by increasing the free list of imports and thereby reduce revenue to a manageable sum.[25]

Throughout his tenure, the theme of Guthrie's reports would be consistent. He continued to urge tariff reduction and provided Congress with a remarkably detailed and comprehensive analysis of America's economic life. Additionally, Guthrie in his four years expressed grave concern over the 1,300 state banks whose "practically unlimited issue of paper money was a constant menace to the financial system." Guthrie proposed taxing them out of existence, a plan that was finally put into effect during Abraham Lincoln's tenure. In his final Treasury report to Congress in 1856, Guthrie reported that during his four years the national debt had been reduced from $60,129,937 to $30,963,909. He left the Treasury in stable condition, with no hint of scandal and with staff morale at a high point.[26]

II

Leaving office in 1857, Guthrie returned to Louisville, where he assumed the vice-presidency of the Louisville and Nashville Rail Company whose construction was then stalled because of financial difficulty. Guthrie reorganized the company, put it on sound fiscal footing, and "on October 31, [1859], the first train ran from Louisville to Nashville — thus connecting Louisville directly to the South by rail." In 1860, he was named president of the company, a position he held until 1868.[27]

When sectional voting resulted in Lincoln's election to the presidency in 1860, South Carolina led southern states in a movement to break up the Union. The crisis worsened daily, intensified by lame-duck President James Buchanan's refusal to take action, and hope waned for a secure and peaceful future. In an effort to dramatize the crisis and to search for a meaningful solution, Virginia's state legislature called for a National Peace Conference to meet in February 1861 in Washington, D.C.[28] Twenty-one states responded by sending 132 delegates, including former President John Tyler, six former cabinet members, nineteen former governors, fourteen ex-United States senators, and fifty former United States congressmen. Included in the Kentucky delegation was James Guthrie, now nearly seventy years old. The setting would be one of his finest hours and because of Guthrie's efforts the Peace Conference held together and succeeded, although Congress subsequently failed to implement its proposals.

No southern "Fire Eaters" attended the conference —

they refused — but present were such outspoken antislavery men as Salmon P. Chase of Ohio and George Boutwell of Massachusetts, who made the task of compromise difficult for the Unionists. Antislavery outbursts threatened to throw the conference into chaos until Guthrie proposed a stablizing procedure. He moved the establishment of a Committee of 21 (one member from each state) to hear all proposals and resolutions and then report those which seemed "right, necessary, and proper to restore harmony and preserve the Union." Guthrie chaired the committee, which met from 6 February to 15 February, and played the key role at the conference.[29]

The Guthrie Committee formulated seven articles which it hoped the whole conference would endorse and send on to the United States Congress as a proposed Thirteenth Amendment. Similar to Kentucky Senator John J. Crittenden's compromise proposal then pending in the Senate, the seven articles of the Guthrie Committee included: (1) the protection of involuntary servitude in territories south of the Missouri Compromise line and the prohibition of involuntary servitude north of that line; (2) no additional territory would be acquired without ratification by four-fifths of the Senate; (3) Congress would not interfere with slavery in Washington, D.C., without Maryland's consent and could not regulate or abolish slavery in states where it already existed; (4) the Fugitive Slave Law would be strictly enforced; (5) the importation of slaves was forbidden forever; (6) nothing in the United States Constitution relating to slavery could be changed without the consent of all the states; and (7) slaveholders were to be compensated for slaves lost through violence or intimidation.[30]

In delivering his committee's report, Guthrie made his pro-Union position clear: "I hate that word secession, because it is a cheat! Call things by their right names! The Southern States have . . . originated a revolution."[31] The debate over the committee's proposals was long and often heated, and Guthrie himself spoke sixty-one times in favor of its agenda. At one point a radical element issued a resolution calling the Guthrie Report "useless," whereupon Guthrie, dejected and furious, walked out briefly. That resolution lost. In the end, the committee's proposals were accepted, and Guthrie wrote a preamble, which was approved without a recorded vote and sent on to Congress.[32] In the Senate, Crittenden withdrew his proposal for compromise in favor of the Peace Conference's agenda; but it was defeated in the Senate, as were all Unionist efforts late on 3 March 1861. Guthrie felt strongly that Lincoln could have made the difference and "have prevented all the states but South Carolina from going out [of the Union] by advising his friends in the Senate" to support the peace proposals.[33] Guthrie returned to Kentucky to watch the Union come apart despite his efforts to preserve it.

As the war came, Guthrie prepared to do all that he could to support the Union. That he gave his allegiance to the North is not surprising, even though he had strongly opposed Lincoln's election and though "his sympathies were with the South" in the sense of culture and taste. Guthrie, basically a realist and a businessman, was also a Unionist, so the South's move to secession offended his sense of order. "I was born," he said, "under the Constitution and I desire to die in the Union."[34] As president of the Louisville and Nashville, the only such railroad from the North into the South, Guthrie stood in good position to provide aid, even to the extent of supporting General William T. Sherman's takeover of the railroad in 1864. Sherman, in his *Memoirs,* wrote: "I have always felt greatful [sic] to Mr. Guthrie who had sense enough to subordinate the interest of his railroad company to the cause of his country."[35]

In the midst of the war, as a delegate to the 1864 Democratic Convention in Chicago, Guthrie supported the nomination of General George B. McClellan. Active in the contest in Kentucky, which McClellan won over Lincoln 61,478 to 26,592 votes, Guthrie was himself elected to the United States Senate and served from March 1865 to February 1868. Though clearly past his prime, Guthrie served admirably as a moderate and gave support and counsel to beleaguered President Andrew Johnson, who had succeeded the martyred Lincoln. The Kentuckian resigned his seat early in 1868 because of ill health and returned home to Louisville, where he died 13 March 1869, at age seventy-six.[36]

An individual's ability to affect the course of history depends upon the era in which he lives and his position within the power structure, as well as his natural talents. James Guthrie's effectiveness was limited by the former rather than the latter. In those areas in which he had authority, his presence made a difference. In the 1830s, primarily through Guthrie's efforts, Kentucky remained financially stable. And, as secretary of the treasury, Guthrie was able to clean up a dismal situation and to break the hold which certain financiers had on the nation's treasury. Later, at the 1861 Washington Peace Conference Guthrie persuaded disparate factions to support a peace proposal and secured success of the conference; it was the United States Congress which failed. Finally, during the Civil War, Guthrie's actions contributed to the preservation of the Union.

Guthrie was often aligned with the minority — a Democrat in a Whig town, a moderate in a period of radicalism — but his personal ability and integrity served his state and his nation well.[37]

## Footnotes

[1]Louisville *Courier Journal,* 14 March 1869; Frankfort *Tri-Weekly Journal,* 5 November 1859; J.S. Johnston, *Memorial History of Louisville* (2 vols., New York, 1896), I, 371-75; Gabrielle Robertson, "James Guthrie" (Master's thesis, University of Chicago, 1920), 4-10.

[2]Robertson, "James Guthrie," 5-6; John Livingston, "James Guthrie, Secretary of Treasury," pamphlet in the Kentucky Library (Western Kentucky University).

[3]Johnston, *Memorial History,* I, 371-75; Robertson, "James Guthrie," 14.

[4]R.S. Cotterill, "James Guthrie, Kentuckian," *Register of the Kentucky State Historical Society,* 20 (1922), 290.

[5]Robertson, "James Guthrie," 20-30. At one point in 1839 when Guthrie was poised to leave the state legislature, three hundred members of the opposing Whig Party petitioned him to remain in Frankfort. Johnston, *Memorial History,* I, 373.

[6]Cotterill, "James Guthrie," 290-92.

[7]*Ibid.,* 291.

[8]*Debates and Proceedings of the Kentucky Constitutional Convention* (Frankfort, 1849), 15.

[9]*Ibid.,* 38-39, 41ff, 93ff.

[10]*Ibid.,* 47-48, 256, 269.

[11]Robertson, "James Guthrie," 54.

[12] The primary and secondary source material supporting this position is overwhelming. See Holman Hamilton, *Prologue to Conflict* (New York, 1966), 166-90, and Charles J. Bussey, "The Lost Opportunity of 1853" (Ph.D. dissertation, University of Kentucky, 1975).

[13] Arthur M. Schlesinger, Jr. et al., eds., *History of American Presidential Elections* (4 vols., New York, 1971), II, 930-35; Roy F. Nichols, *The Democratic Machine, 1850-1854* (New York, 1923), 129-47.

[14] Franklin Pierce to Jefferson Davis, 7 December 1852, 12 January 1853, Pierce Papers (Library of Congress); Pierce to William L. Marcy, 7 November 1852, Marcy Papers (Library of Congress); Lewis Cass to Howell Cobb, 18 December 1852, in U.B. Phillips, ed., *The Correspondence of Robert Toombs, Alexander H. Stephens, and Howell Cobb* (2 vols., Washington, 1913), II, 322; New York *Times*, 8 March 1853; Jacksonville *Floridian*, 12 March 1853; Allan Nevins, *Ordeal of the Union* (2 vols., New York, 1947), II, 47, 321; Henry Cohen, *Business and Politics in America from the Age of Jackson to the Civil War: The Career Biography of W.W. Corcoran* (Westport, Conn., 1971).

[15] A number of prominent persons recommended Guthrie for his position, including F.P. Blair, Kentucky Governor Lazarus Powell, and Tennessee's A.O.P. Nicholson. Powell to John C. Breckinridge, 10 February 1853, Breckinridge Family Papers (Library of Congress); Pierce to Guthrie, 5 February 1853, Guthrie Papers (The Filson Club, Louisville); Francis J. Grund to Caleb Cushing, 1, 24 January 1853, Cushing Papers (Library of Congress).

[16] New York *Herald*, 28 December 1852; Robertson "James Guthrie," 1-5.

[17] Robertson, "James Guthrie," 8.

[18] New York *Times*, 7 March 1853.

[19] Louisville *Daily Journal*, 9 March 1853; George A. Caldwell to Guthrie, 15 February 1853, Guthrie Papers.

[20] Roy F. Nichols, *Franklin Pierce* (Philadelphia, 1931), 270; Nevins, *Ordeal*, II, 160.

[21] Baltimore *Sun*, 16 March, 13, 14, 18 April, 17 May 1853.

[22] New York *Herald*, 18, 20 April 1853; New York *Times*, 6, 7 May 1853; Baltimore *Sun*, 18 April 1853.

[23] Cohen, *Business and Politics*, 93-96.

[24] *Ibid.*

[25] *Cong. Globe*, 33d Cong., 1st Sess., *Appendix*, 2-5; United States Congress, 33d Cong., 1st Sess., *Treasury Report, House Executive Document 3*, 5-7, 13-14, 31-41.

[26] United States Congress, 34th Cong., 2d Sess., *House Executive Documents 1, 2*, 840-46, 893-94.

[27] Maury Klein, *History of the Louisville and Nashville Railroad* (New York, 1972), 30; Thomas D. Clark, *The Beginning of the L & N* (Louisville, 1933), 48.

[28] Robert G. Gunderson, *Old Gentlemen's Convention: The Washington Peace Conference of 1861* (Madison, 1961), 5-36.

[29] *Report of the Kentucky Commissioners to the late Peace Conference Held at Washington City, Made to the Legislature of Kentucky* (Frankfort, 1861), 3-78; E. Crittenden, *A Report on the Debates and Proceedings of the Washington Peace Conference* (New York, 1864), 120-35.

[30] *Report of Kentucky Commissioners*, 3-78; Crittenden, *Report on Debates*, 120-35.

[31] New York *Times*, 18-21 February 1861; Crittenden, *Report on Debates*, 136-87.

[32] New York *Times*, 26 February 1861; Gunderson, *Old Gentlemen's Convention*, 91.

[33] Guthrie to Paul G. Washington, 13 March 1861, Guthrie Papers.

[34] Louisville *Daily Journal*, 18 March 1861.

[35] William T. Sherman, *Personal Memoirs of General W.T. Sherman* (2 vols., New York, 1891), II, 12; Nevins, *Ordeal*, II, 130; Klein, *History*, 29-36.

[36] Nichols, *Franklin Pierce*, 526; Nevins, *Ordeal*, II, 98.

[37] One of Guthrie's most admirable traits, except with respect to slavery, was his consistently democratic approach to public questions. A statement from an 1853 speech he made sums up that attitude: "I for thirty years raised my voice . . . in favor of democratic principles [in Kentucky]." Louisville *Daily Democrat*, 11 July 1853.

# Bibliographical Essay

The secondary literature on James Guthrie's life is sparse. Historians from R.S. Cotterill in 1922 to Allan Nevins in 1947 to Charles Bussey in 1975 have called attention to the shameful neglect which Guthrie has suffered. After all, Guthrie was active in Kentucky politics and business for over thirty years and was a national figure from 1853 to 1869. Still there is no Guthrie biography and very few articles. In 1920, Gabrielle Robertson, later a professor at Western Kentucky University for many years, completed a master's thesis on Guthrie at the University of Chicago. While deficient in some respects, Ms. Robertson's thesis provides an unusual source. It was based to a large extent on interviews which the author conducted with Kentuckians who had known Guthrie. In 1922, R.S. Cotterill published a short essay on Guthrie in the *Register of the Kentucky Historical Society*. Aside from scattered references to Guthrie in major works like Roy F. Nichols' *Franklin Pierce* (Philadelphia, 1931) and Nevins' *Ordeal of the Union* (2 vols., New

York, 1947), and mention of Guthrie in such volumes as J.S. Johnston's *Memorial History of Louisville* (2 vols., New York, 1896), little else exists.

One can find information about Guthrie's life and career in a variety of primary sources. These would include legislative and congressional records, Kentucky and national newspapers, and various manuscript collections. The largest collection of Guthrie material is in the Filson Club in Louisville, Kentucky. The moment one begins to research in Guthrie manuscripts the reason for the absence of a Guthrie biography is clear: it is virtually impossible to read his writing. Even his contemporaries found his script practically indecipherable. A friend of Guthrie's, Jacob Smyser, recalled that only one person in Guthrie's law firm (a clerk named Quarier) could translate his scribbling. One day Quarier sat in the office deep in thought; someone spoke to him and Quarier responded, "Don't disturb me. I am trying to think what Mr. Guthrie was thinking about when he wrote this." I hope someday a full-length biography of Guthrie will appear. Unless a modern Quarier appears, however, I remain doubtful.

**William Preston**
Kentucky Historical Society Collection

# William Preston, Kentucky's Diplomat of Lost Causes

*by Peter J. Sehlinger*

Better known as a politician and soldier, William Preston of Kentucky also served both the United States and the Confederacy as a diplomat. For three years, from 1858 until the outbreak of the Civil War, the Jefferson County native represented his country at the Spanish court. Preston's diplomatic goals in Madrid were the purchase of Cuba by the United States and the resolution of long-standing economic disputes between the two governments. Although Spanish hostility and the growing sectional conflict at home frustrated these initiatives, a study of Preston's Madrid years illuminates a serious attempt to divert the Union from its divisive course and offers insights into American foreign relations in the prewar period. Mexico, to which Preston was appointed Confederate envoy in 1864, relented to international pressure and refused to recognize the Confederacy; the Kentuckian never reached his second diplomatic post.

## I

William Preston's early social and economic background explains the politically conservative, proslavery views he would espouse later as a politician and a diplomat. The only son of a prominent Virginia family, he was born in autumn 1816 on his father's plantation just outside of Louisville. After the death of his father William Preston, the four-year-old lad was reared, with his five sisters, by his mother Caroline. Although always short of cash, the family had inherited a large estate upriver from the falls of the Ohio, property granted by Governor Thomas Jefferson to William's grandfather, a colonel in the American Revolution. This landed wealth provided young William with a confident sense of "entitlement" and gave him automatic social standing. After elementary schooling in

Louisville and a secondary education in Bracken County and in Bardstown, Kentucky, William ventured north to New Haven, Connecticut, first to study the humanities at Yale University, then to receive an LL.B. degree in jurisprudence from Harvard University in 1837.

Returning to Louisville the next year, William Preston practiced law and managed his family's extensive properties in Jefferson County. Dissatisfied with the routine life of an attorney, he soon asked his brother-in-law Albert Sidney Johnston, then secretary of war for the independent Republic of Texas, to obtain a diplomatic appointment for him in Europe as that Republic's representative. Unsuccessful in this request, Preston remained in Kentucky, where he courted his second cousin, Margaret Howard Wickliffe of Lexington. Her father Robert Wickliffe, probably the largest slaveholder in Kentucky, was certainly one of the wealthiest men in the Commonwealth. Wed in 1840, William and Margaret took residence in one of the first stone-front mansions in Louisville. They enjoyed a pleasant married life and were the parents of five daughters and a son. Except for one year of military service as a lieutenant-colonel during the Mexican War, Preston was occupied principally as an attorney in Louisville until 1852.

During these years William Preston displayed both the physical and intellectual traits which would characterize him for the remainder of his life. Friends often remarked that he was imposing in appearance, his sharp features endowing him with a strikingly handsome countenance. Although of average height, he possessed an erect carriage and projected a vigorous and commanding air. In fact, his decisive bearing connoted a measure of hauteur which indicated his aristocratic station. Like many contemporaries, Preston had a carefully trimmed mustache which complemented his often serious mien. While his correct appearance betrayed his concern for detail and precision, it belied the definite sense of humor he often displayed among friends. When in his later years Preston became increasingly bald, he parted his hair carefully to obscure this. His high forhead was marred by furrows while he read and imparted a certain impression of a dignified intellectual.

Preston's social beliefs and political attitudes were fully

developed by the mid-1840s. His genteel background and economic interests combined to reinforce his conservatism. With a definite belief in the correctness of slavery, he was an outspoken defender of the institution. Like many whites, South and North, he was convinced that the Negro was inferior and must be held "in bondage because we are unwilling to amalgamate with them, and desire to keep our Teutonic blood pure and uncorrupted by any baser admixture, because we prefer that their untutored labor should be directed by the superior intelligence of our race to useful industry . . . ."[1] Despite his racist views, Preston's confident sense of superiority was tempered by his upper-class sense of paternalism which made him a benevolent master. The owner of eighteen slaves in his own right, in addition to the two hundred he received from his father-in-law's estate, Preston observed during the Civil War that he never bought a slave, except to free him, and that he never sold a servant, "except for crime, but I did not consider it wrong to inherit them, & thought it was right for me to hold, govern, protect & direct them according to the best of my ability . . . ."[2]

Although Preston believed in the racial superiority of whites, his aristocratic upbringing also inculcated in him a conviction that members of the upper-class should bear the burden of noblesse oblige and provide direction for their socially and economically inferior brethren. A staunch supporter of universal male suffrage for those of his own race, Preston nevertheless knew that political leadership should rest with the better educated and socially prominent sectors. He assumed that such elite direction was natural and preferable, given the political success of his aristocratic friends and of his own relatives. The list is formidable. His maternal grandfather, George Hancock, had served as a congressman from Virginia, and William's father-in-law was an influential Whig legislator in Frankfort. Preston's brother-in-law Albert Sidney Johnston, as mentioned, was secretary of war in Texas and later commanded the Confederate forces in the West; Albert's brother, Josiah Stoddard Johnston, was United States senator from Louisiana. William's uncle James Patton Preston was governor of Virginia, while another uncle, Francis Preston, served as a congressman from that state. Cousin William Campbell Preston represented South Carolina in the Senate; and another cousin, John C. Breckinridge, a prominent Kentucky Democrat, was vice-president from 1857 to 1861. Cousin James McDowell was governor of Virginia, and the illustrious Senator Thomas Hart Benton of Missouri was married to cousin Eliza McDowell. Preston's maternal aunt was the wife of Governor William Clark of Missouri, a younger brother of George Rogers Clark. Among Preston's many socially prominent friends were Basil W. Duke and Simon Bolivar Buckner, who also shared political leadership in Kentucky with others from their ranks.

At a time when United States political and economic life was becoming more broadly based and business oriented outside of the South, Preston's assumed views on the nature of governmental and social leadership were at variance with a changing reality. Like many Kentucky gentry, he believed that a definite virtue of southern society was its upper-class domination. During the Civil War, Preston came close to stating this assumption when he wrote, "I entered the service of the Confederacy to which I was allied by my birth, my education, and my convictions of justice."[3] In his generally successful political campaigns, the Kentuckian received the electoral support of many hard-working immigrants and middle-class merchants in Louisville, but his circle of friends was confined to members of the socially prominent and rather pecunious upper classes.

William Preston was elected a member of the 1849 convention called to rewrite Kentucky's constitution, and he served from 1853 until 1855 in the House of Representatives. In both Frankfort and Washington the conservative representative was a consistent defender of slavery and a strong advocate of states' rights. Preston actively supported the successful efforts to incorporate an article into the new Kentucky charter which declared, "The right of the owner of a slave to such a slave . . . is . . . as inviolable as the right of the owner to any property whatever."[4] He also argued that the new document should define a voter narrowly as a "qualified elector of this Commonwealth" rather than in broader national terms as a "citizen of the United States."[5] As a congressman, the Kentuckian was a conscientious member of the Foreign Relations Committee, but he is better remembered for the role he played as a partisan southerner in urging passage of the Kansas-Nebraska Bill, the most important piece of legislation considered in 1854. Preston originally was a very partisan Whig, but the growth of abolitionist strength in the North during the 1850s had divided both the Whig and Democratic parties into pro and antislavery factions, making the traditional political groupings meaningless. Democratic Senator Stephen Douglas of Illinois sought to gain southern allies by sponsoring the Kansas-Nebraska Bill, which allowed the settlers in the new territories of Kansas and Nebraska to determine the fate of slavery in their districts at a later date. Despite truculent abolitionist opposition, Douglas' proposal became law after three months of acrimonious debate. Preston was so involved in working for the Kansas-Nebraska Bill that he once complained the measure "kept me up without interruption two days & all one night."[6]

In his 1855 bid for reelection, Preston was challenged by his congressional predecessor, Humphrey Marshall. The major issue of the campaign was immigration. Large numbers of Germans and Irishmen had settled along the Ohio River in cities like Louisville and Cincinnati during the 1840s and 1850s, causing many of the native-born to fear the aliens' competition for jobs. Unlike the vast majority of original settlers of the Commonwealth, many of the recently arrived foreigners were Roman Catholics whose customs, such as drinking on Sundays, were viewed with suspicion. A former Whig, Marshall was the nominee of the American or Know-Nothing party and served as the spokesman for the populace most strongly opposed to continuing immigration. Preston ran as an independent supported by the Democratic Party, and he was forthright in praising the beneficial contributions of the naturalized citizens to the economic and social development of the state. After a bitter and emotional campaign, Marshall defeated his opponent on 6 August 1855, an election day so characterized by violence that it is known in the annals of Louisville history as "Bloody Monday." On that day so-called "executive committees" of the American party took over the voting precincts, often admitting only their own partisans and depriving naturalized citizens of their franchise. By the evening of 6 August, Know-Nothing mobs had set fire to dozens of houses of German and Irish Americans, destroyed a German-owned brewery, and killed a Roman Catholic priest and several immigrants.

Folowing his defeat in 1855 and the demise of the Whig party, Preston became a Democrat. In June 1856, he represented the Commonwealth as an at-large delegate to the Democratic national convention in Cincinnati. There he nominated his fellow Kentuckian and cousin John C. Breckinridge for the vice-presidency and was a strong backer of James Buchanan as the party's presidential nominee. In September Preston met with Buchanan at his Pennsylvania home and promised to address electoral rallies in the Keystone State, a pledge he enthusiastically redeemed. The Kentuckian himself noted: "I exerted my voice so much that I am hoarse."[7] He also campaigned for the Democratic ticket in New York, Illinois, and throughout his native state. Preston confidently wrote Breckinridge before the election: "I am assured we are to have a peaceful solution to the great sectional question at issue, and that the happiness and grandeur of the Republic are to be established for many a year, by this triumph of the Democracy."[8] Preston's predictions concerning the outcome of the contest were correct, but, unfortunately, his optimism that a Democratic victory would bridge the widening North-South breach would prove ill founded.

From 1858 to 1861 William Preston added a new dimension to his record of public service when he became United States Envoy Extraordinary and Minister Plenipotentiary to the Spanish court in Madrid. Four candidates for the post were suggested to President Buchanan; he finally selected the Kentuckian only after refusing to consider one nominee and after the other two had declined the assignment. August Belmont, a prominent New York Democrat and financier, was promoted for the diplomatic opening by his uncle, Senator John Slidell of Louisiana. Buchanan sought to persuade Slidell to serve as minister to Paris and feared charges of favoritism if he also appointed Belmont. Having passed over the New Yorker, the president asked Slidell's second choice, Senator Judah P. Benjamin of New Orleans, to represent the United States in Madrid, but Benjamin preferred to remain a legislator. Senator

Stephen Mallory of Florida also refused Buchanan's offer. William Preston was next in line and, when asked in October 1858 to accept this responsibility, he enthusiastically agreed. The Senate unanimously approved his appointment without submitting his nomination for the customary committee action.

Both Preston and Buchanan were quite satisfied with this appointment. As a political ally of the president, the Kentuckian had urged the Democrats at their Cincinnati convention in 1856 to nominate the already victorious Buchanan by acclamation and had campaigned for him in four states. Despite their political association, Preston and Buchanan never enjoyed a close personal friendship.[9] In 1858, the Kentuckian was actively seeking a position in the Buchanan administration. Having declined offers to run again for Congress, Preston likewise had decided not to try for the Democratic gubernatorial nomination, an honor he probably would have received and which would have made him the favorite for election. However, his close friend Vice-President Breckinridge had previously committed his support to Beriah Magoffin as the Democratic candidate, and Preston's father-in-law Robert Wickliffe counseled him not to run.[10] The Louisvillian's political ambitions possibly included the presidency, and his wife Mag, his nephew William Preston Johnston, and some influential southern Democrats had urged him to aspire to this position.[11] In autumn 1858, Preston definitely viewed the Madrid offer as a most promising step to future advancement, and his wife and father-in-law concurred. Preston's appointment allowed President Buchanan the pleasant opportunity to select a political ally and at the same time strengthen his support among southern lawmakers.

Although the Buchanan administration is generally remembered by historians for its domestic problems and failures, the president pursued a vigorous foreign policy. He sought to reduce growing sectional differences over internal issues such as slavery by building public support for his expansionist goals abroad. The key to this diplomatic offensive was United States acquisition of Cuba, the most valuable colony in Spain's remaining empire. Strong trade ties between northern ports and Havana and the South's search for additional slave territory had made the annexation of the Caribbean isle a popular subject in both regions for decades. Thomas Jefferson, John Quincy Adams, James Monroe, John C. Calhoun, and Henry Clay were among earlier statesmen who believed Cuba should become a part of their country. As secretary of state for President James K. Polk, Buchanan himself had offered Spain one hundred million dollars for Cuba in 1848, but the money was refused.

By the 1850s the issue of Cuba, like so many others, developed into a heated matter of regional controversy. Abolitionists charged that southerners were interested only in gaining the island to guarantee the political power of the slave states, and these northerners created a political block adamantly opposed to Cuban annexation. In 1850 and 1851, hundreds of this country's southerners served with Narciso Lopez, a Venezuelan filibusterer who unsuccessfully invaded Cuba and tried to wrest it from Spanish control. President Franklin Pierce asked Congress in August 1854 to appropriate ten million dollars for purchase of the "Pearl of the Antilles," but the legislators decided to postpone action on this controversial request until December. Disturbed by the delay, three United States ministers, James Buchanan in London, John Mason in Paris, and Pierre Soulé in Madrid, met in Ostend, Belgium, and issued a highly publicized declaration in October. In this Ostend Manifesto these three proslavery Democrats stated that Cuba should be incorporated into the North American union and threatened war if Spain would not agree to sell the island. The Pierce administration was quick to repudiate this act, but it furnished yet another point for debate between North and South.

President Buchanan was particularly confident that his administration would be successful in purchasing Cuba. In his second annual address to Congress on 6 December 1858, he argued that Cuba could and should be acquired by "honorable negotiation." Several signs seemed to indicate that Spain at long last might be willing to sell her most important colonial possession. The president had met secretly in 1857 with Christopher Fallón, a Spaniard by birth who lived in Philadelphia and was well connected with both the European financial community and the Spanish royal family. Also closely associated with the Rothschild banking interests through their agent August Belmont, Fallón was involved in Spanish railroad bonds through his ties with the Baring Brothers in England and as a representative of Leon Lillo et Compagnie of France. As the United States agent of the French firm, Fallón had invested monies of the Spanish queen mother in land purchases in Pennsylvania. The Spanish-American financier managed to convince an optimistic Buchanan that business pressures could succeed where diplomacy had failed in regard to Cuba. With the Madrid government deeply in debt to international capitalists, both major parties in Spain might "reluctantly" agree to sell Cuba, provided a generous share of the purchase price would find its way into the pockets of the politicians in Madrid. Furthermore, the queen mother had a just reputation in Spain for seeking money in exchange for political favors, so her influence in any Cuban scheme might be purchased by the United States.

With a letter from Buchanan in hand, Fallón sailed for Europe in December 1857, to convince European investors and Spanish leaders of the monetary advantages which would accrue to them from North America's purchase of the Caribbean isle. In the Old World he met with the impecunious queen mother, as well as worried Spanish bondholders and politicos, but he claimed that outspoken opponents in the United States were frustrating his best efforts to guarantee the purchase of Cuba.[12] Nevertheless, Fallón reported to Buchanan in February 1858: "I feel *now* convinced that with judicious management the purchase can be made on fair terms, honorable & beneficial to both countries."[13] He urged Buchanan to appoint a United States envoy to Madrid and correctly remarked that public hostility to the sale of Cuba was so great in Spain that the president should carefully refrain from mentioning this object in his instructions to the new minister.[14] Buchanan definitely believed that the right appointee and a large enough supply of money would enable the United States to persuade the traditionally corrupt Spanish politicians to barter away their Caribbean prize.

Preston sailed from New York on 9 January 1859, confident of his chances for success in acquiring Cuba. He sincerely believed on the eve of his departure that "a big pile of *cash* (not *credit*) at Madrid" would permit him "to seize any golden opportunity that Fortune might cast upon the current [so that] I might make a stroke that would not alone signalize me, but benefit my country."[15] In this assertion, the Kentuckian was repeating the opinion of Fallón who had written to him on 6 January, after scheduling problems had prevented their meeting in Philadelphia. The financier had informed Preston that Cuba was the United States' for the taking, if only the Madrid officials could be given "assurances of success and confidence that the terms of contract if any will be fulfilled."[16] Buchanan's secretary of state, Lewis Cass, told the new minister that the purchase of Cuba was so obvious a goal that he should seek specific instructions in this regard from the president and that he must enjoy full powers to negotiate such a deal.[17] Of his White House meeting, the Kentucky diplomat optimistically reported: "The President is polite and lets me have everything my own way. After a long and full interview, he acceded fully to my views. . . ."[18] As Fallón had suggested, Preston's official instructions contained no mention of Cuba. The Kentuckian also visited Spain's minister to Washington, Gabriel García y Tassara, and sought to assure them that the United States would not go to war over the Caribbean colony. The Spaniard found Preston personally appealing, but nonetheless warned the foreign office in Madrid that the new envoy was an outspoken proponent of Cuban annexation.[19]

The day following Preston's departure for Europe, Senator John Slidell of Louisiana introduced a resolution which requested an appropriation of thirty million dollars "to facilitate the acquisition of the island of Cuba."[20] As soon as the Foreign Relations Committee approved the measure, it was turned immediately into a sectional issue, with most southerners urging its passage and northern Republicans denouncing the purchase of Cuba as a proslavery plot. The Louisville *Daily Courier,* the Washington *Union,* and the *Constitution* in the capital favored the bill, while the New York *Times* opposed such a "financial conquest" of the island and observed pointedly "that this money is wanted for purposes of *bribery* — that if voted it will be spent in purchasing support for the Cuban scheme in the Spanish court."[21] Preston ignored such statements and campaigned actively for support of the Caribbean initiative and wrote his friends "to press home upon the country the necessity of consolidated public opinion & full endorsement of the Cuban policy."[22]

As Slidell's proposal became an increasingly prominent issue in the feud between the pro and antislavery forces, northern Democrats exercised an expedient silence regarding their president's attempt to purchase Cuba. Realizing the Senate would not take a favorable stand on his resolution, the Louisiana solon withdrew it from it from consideration on 26 February, promising to reintroduce the measure in the next session. The congressional elections in October and November, however, cost the Democrats their majority in the lower house and doomed future passage of Slidell's bill. Buchanan's attempt to use Cuba to unify his party and bring North and South together in a common enterprise had failed; the problem of slavery had proved stronger than the desire for expansion on the eve of the War between the States. The Cuban failure correctly augured the importance that slavery would play as an issue in Abraham Lincoln's successful campaign the following year.

After "a rough but not stormy passage," William Preston and his family spent a week in London and then proceeded to Paris, where he was presented to the Emperor Napoleon III at the Tuileries.[23] In the French capital, their home for the next few weeks, the Prestons placed their daughters in a convent school, Sacré Coeur. Despite the establishment's waiver of its rule not to accept Protestants, the parents six months later transferred their children to a second convent in the suburb of Auteuil to avoid "the bigotry the order evinced."[24] In Paris Margaret "Mag" Preston pursued private lessons in French, while her husband William complained that he was "heartily tired" of too many formal dinners and balls.[25] To see them through their Madrid stay, the couple also purchased and shipped to Spain several carriages, five loads of furniture, six boxes of carpets, iron skillets and tea, linens and four containers of porcelain, two boxes of silver plate, and a large shipment of wines, liquors, beer, and truffles.[26] They left by train from Paris for Marseilles, where they boarded a ship for Alicante, a Spanish Mediterranean port. Traveling from the coast up to the Castilian plateau, the Prestons reached Madrid on 4 March 1859.

Preston's optimism over the possible cession of Cuba quickly proved to be at variance with every circumstance he observed in Spain. Even before he received the news of the failure of Slidell's resolution, the Kentucky envoy realized that no Spanish government of any political persuasion would remain in power if it agreed to sell the nation's prize colony. Reacting to President Buchanan's appeal in his December message to purchase the island, the members of Spain's parliament, the Cortes, voted unanimously in January against the sale of Cuba. When Preston had his first interview on 9 March with the minister of foreign relations, Saturino Calderón Collantes, the Spaniard warned the Kentuckian that "any proposition to purchase Cuba would result in the immediate cessation of all intercourse between the two nations . . . ."[27] Four days later the new envoy presented his credentials to Her Catholic Majesty, Queen Isabel II, carefully refraining from mentioning Cuba during the audience. Unfortunately for Preston, his earlier expectation of using the weakness of Spanish partisan politics to his own advantage proved impossible. In the late 1850s the nation was governed by the rather efficient Liberal Union coalition, headed by General Leopoldo O'Donnell, formerly a captain-general in Havana. Instead of encountering ministerial instability which was so characteristic of nineteenth-century Spain, Preston in 1859 confronted a united government determined to retain its colonial empire. By late April, the Kentuckian was so disgusted with United States congressional opposition and Spanish refusal to discuss Cuba that he wrote Secretary of State Cass, "I have no longer a desire to remain at this Court . . . ."[28]

With his grand plan for Cuba ruined, Preston turned his attention to another cause: resolving the outstanding controversy between the two nations over the *Amistad* claims. This complex affair had plagued Spanish-United States relations since 1839, when some fifty Cuban slaves being transported from Havana mutinied and tried to force two Spanish subjects aboard the schooner *Amistad* to sail them back to Africa. Instead, the white pilots deceived the slaves and finally guided the vessel into Long Island Sound in August 1839. There a North American brig took the Cubans to New London, Connecticut, where they were charged with murdering their ship's captain and a cook. Under the treaty of 1795 between the United States and Spain, both nations were committed to care for and return to the true owner all vessels and merchandise of any kind which were rescued from pirates and brought into a port of the other country, "as soon as due and sufficient proof shall be made concerning the property . . . ."[29]

The Cuban and Spanish owners of the *Amistad's* goods and human cargo of course filed suit for restoration of their property, but northern abolitionists organized a legal offensive to win freedom for the slaves. President Martin Van Buren and Attorney General Henry D. Gilpin favored the return of the ship and its entire cargo to their owners as the treaty of 1795 stipulated, but the abolitionists carried their arguments to the courts. Decisions of district and circuit tribunals and even the Supreme Court affirmed in 1840-41 that the blacks were not the legal property of their supposed owners because of the circumstances surrounding the Negroes' capture and their recent importation from Africa into Cuba. The *Amistad* and its merchandise were sold in October 1840 to repay the claims of the vessel's salvors, an act which further enraged the original owners and the Spanish government. Van Buren's successors — Presidents Tyler, Polk, Fillmore, Pierce, and Buchanan — recognized Spain's constant claims regarding its citizens' financial losses in the *Amistad* affair as legitimate. Consequently, bills were introduced into Congress in 1844, 1847, 1848, 1852, 1858, and 1859 to appropriate either $50,000 or $70,000 to satisfy the *Amistad* claims. Opponents successfully blocked passage of these resolutions, arguing either that the United States should never reimburse illegal slave owners or that the decisions of the courts should not be violated.

A second Spanish-North American dispute soon exacerbated the difficulties between these governments over the *Amistad* claims. In 1844, following a devastating hurricane, Spanish authorities in Havana issued a decree permitting the importation of certain foodstuffs and building materials into the island free of duties for half a year. The administration in Madrid countermanded the decision of its colonial officials after shipments of goods had left the United States for Cuba. More than one hundred North American investors and firms unexpectedly were forced to pay Spanish levies on their exports, thereby trimming their profit margins and even causing unanticipated losses. Spain agreed in 1858 to reimburse North Americans for the amounts they had paid in export levies because of the recision of the 1844 Havana decree; these damages were determined to be $128,635.54.[30]

In November 1859, Preston and Secretary of State Calderón reached a tentative understanding on how to resolve the impasse concerning both the *Amistad* and the 1844 claims. Spain agreed to pay the sum of $128,635.54 in full, but without interest, a proposal acceptable to Secretary of State Cass.[31] Calderón told Preston that public pressure would not permit Spain to pay the full amount until the United States would agree to satisfy the *Amistad* claims. Although the Kentuckian formally protested this declaration, it was obvious that both the United States and Spain would have to resolve their long outstanding differences simultaneously. Both men decided that an agreement should be made to create a commission to arbitrate all unresolved claims against each government. In December 1859, President Buchanan formally recognized the justice of Spain's *Amistad* claims, and the Spanish minister in Washington subsequently reported, "The arrangement of the claims appears to be proceeding very satisfactorily."[32]

On 5 March 1860, Preston and Calderón signed a "Convention for the settlement of claims between the United States of America and Her Catholic Majesty."[33] This document stated that Spain would accept responsibility for paying $128,635.54 to satisfy the Cuban claims and would turn over to Washington $100,000 of this sum immediately. A three-man board of commissioners, one appointed by each government and a third chosen by the first two, would be created to hear the *Amistad* and all other claims, determining by at least a vote of 2-1 the amounts due each litigant. In a complex clause, the agreement stated that the remaining $28,635.54 due the United States for the Cuban claims would eventually be paid Washington if the

American government would directly reimburse the Spanish claimants in the amount agreed upon by the commissioners. If the United States did not do so, Spain itself would pay the litigants their determined awards and not surrender this amount to Washington. Preston returned to the United States in April to present the treaty to the administration and to handle financial affairs related to the estate of his father-in-law Robert Wickliffe, who had died in Lexington the previous year.

President Buchanan was quite pleased with the convention which apparently would end two decades of diplomatic discord between Spain and the United States. He submitted the treaty on 3 May 1860 to the Senate, where a two-thirds majority was required for ratification. Leading the attack on this agreement, Republican solons argued that the United States could not morally pledge itself to reimburse illegal slave owners in the *Amistad* case in defiance of the previous decision of the judiciary. On 27 June, by a vote of 26 yeas and 17 nays, an antislavery faction of twelve Republicans and five allies was responsible for the narrow rejection of this attempt to submit outstanding Spanish-North American disputes to bipartisan arbitration. Unresolved, the *Amistad* claims remained a problem for the Lincoln administration.

Preston's other diplomatic duties in Madrid were generally unexciting and often routine. Attending state functions; overseeing the actions of subordinate United States consuls in such cities as Gibraltar, Havana, Barcelona, Manila, Cádiz, San Juan, Valencia, and Tenerife; informing Washington of Madrid's ratification of international accords; and notifying the respective United States agencies of changes in Spanish tariff laws and navigational regulations proved to be time-consuming tasks. Looking after rather minor problems of North American citizens trading with or traveling in Spain, Cuba, Puerto Rico, or the Philippines required a great deal of the envoy's patience and effort. Arrests of United States sailors and tourists, complaints from irate Spanish merchants over legal difficulties, and burial arrangements for North Americans in the Church of England cemetery in Madrid were but a few of the myriad difficulties the Kentuckian encountered in his foreign post.[34] To assist in his ambassadorial duties, Preston chose his brother-in-law Robert Woolley Wickliffe as secretary of the legation; one employee, John De Havilland, handled the translation of correspondence from Spanish to English.

The election of Lincoln in 1860 and the dissolution of the American Union in 1861 signaled the end of Preston's service in Madrid and permitted a confident Spain to expand her Caribbean empire. On 5 March 1861, the Kentuckian tendered his resignation, but he was unable to leave the capital until 25 May, the day after he was granted his final audience with the queen. Very aware of Preston's prosouthern politics, Lincoln's new secretary of state, William H. Seward, pointedly wrote the envoy that the president expected him to report promptly any information about Confederate efforts to gain Spanish support.[35] Reporting that no Confederate agents had come to Madrid, the Kentuckian loyally informed Seward that he believed Spain's attitude toward the American conflict would depend on the policy of Napoleon III in France. Preston presented the Spanish court with a copy of Lincoln's inaugural address and even followed his instruction to notify the Spanish government that the United States was closing rebellious southern ports to commerce.

When Spanish forces at the request of some islanders took possession of the Dominican Republic in spring 1861, Preston energetically protested this action as a violation of the Monroe Doctrine and sent full reports about this recolonization effort to the Republican administration in Washington. So faithful was Preston to the government he was serving that Seward wrote him in May 1861, "It gives me great pleasure to add that your official conduct during your residence at Madrid has been entirely acceptable to the President."[36] Lincoln also complimented his fellow Kentuckian in Madrid for "the zeal with which he has fulfilled his former instructions."[37] Nevertheless, Preston's proslavery attitudes did rankle the new secretary of the legation, Horatio J. Perry, who was chosen by Seward to replace Robert Woolley Wickliffe. Perry denounced Preston to Washington for using his official position, money, and time to spread propaganda hostile to the United States.[38] These assertions, however, appear to have stemmed more from Perry's expressed personal contempt for the Kentuckian's southern allegiance than from any of his official actions.

Preston's preparation and abilities as a diplomat were no doubt superior to most North American representatives before the Civil War. In the 1850s high government positions were determined by political factors and were awarded to men who enjoyed a definite social standing. Professional diplomatic training was unheard of and specialization was not considered necessary for preferment in public service. Preston's knowledge of the Spanish language and customs was of course inferior to that of Washington Irving, who had lived in Spain and written several volumes on Iberian history before serving as United States minister to Madrid in the 1840s. But very few envoys were as well prepared as Irving, and Preston had previously demonstrated in his speeches and writings a familiarity with the lives of such noteworthy Spaniards as Hernán Cortés, the conquistador of Mexico, and Father Bartolomé de las Casas, the Renaissance humanist who defended the Indians during the settlement of the New World.[39]

Evidence indicates that Preston had but a rudimentary knowledge of Spanish, which placed him ahead of most American emissaries before the Civil War who rarely spoke the language of the country to which they were accredited. Surprisingly, the Kentuckian did read and understand enough French to serve him at social functions and to handle some official chores. Since French was the second language of educated Spaniards and very much the lingua franca of international relations in the nineteenth century, Preston was able to communicate with Spanish officials and members of the diplomatic corps not conversant in English. When negotiating official business with Spanish counterparts, the envoy did not trust his command of French and had to request an interpreter to avoid misunderstandings.[40] William's wife Mag was most straightforward about her husband's language problems when she remarked, "Just imagine that he is obliged to say all he has to say in Spanish and French. I die with laughter to see what an exertion it costs him."[41]

Preston's impressions of Spain were similar to those of other North American contemporaries who were confronted with the very foreign and extremely medieval version of Roman Catholic culture which still dominated the Iberian peninsula. The pre-Lenten carnival days in Spain appeared to the

Protestant Preston "a scene which seems to delight the people very much but is to me a melancholy sort of foolery."[42] Even less did the Louisvillian appreciate the Puritanical rigors of Holy Week which required that all members of the upper class and the diplomatic corps go on foot to their destinations, rather than ride in their carriages as usual. The envoy described Spain as "priest ridden." He reported with disbelief that the only Protestant worship service allowed in the capital, which his family attended in the home of a British diplomat, was attacked by a Madrileño newspaper as a gathering of heretics. For the rationalist Preston, this proved "to show how far Spain is behind the rest of Europe in religious liberty. . . ."[43]

William and Margaret Preston were determined to establish themselves as social leaders in Castile. On their arrival the husband wrote his sister Susan that "Madrid is old fashioned, proud and more expensive than Paris or New York," and he spoke eloquently of the capital's many fountains and the "miles of carriages on the Prado," the main downtown boulevard.[44] Preston bragged that his "house is now very handsome & by far the most comfortable in Madrid"; certainly its imported French furnishings made it the envy of many less fortunate colleagues.[45] He made full use of his diplomatic immunity from customs taxes by importing literally thousands of Havana cigars and bottles of French wines with which to regale his guests; and Margaret sent her Negro cook Fanny Green to Parisian chefs to learn how to cater to the gourmet appetites of their associates.[46]

Such lavish entertaining won Preston many friends in the diplomatic circle. But, as the legation's Republican and jealous charge d'affaires Horatio Perry observed: "He spends his money freely and flatters certain classes here . . . ," referring to the Kentuckian's particular friendship with aristocratic courtiers and military officers.[47] Preston proudly reported that "the Queen thanked me on behalf of the society here for the addition we had made to the social engagements of her capital," and in her final audience with the envoy she assured him "of the universal esteem that you have acquired and the special regard that my Husband and I always shall have for you."[48] Such an ostentatious life-style cost far more than the annual salary of twelve thousand dollars that Preston received, but he wrote his sister Susan: "I am greatly pressed here for money to make a creditable appearance, and if the question is between my patrimony & a decent show for the country, the acres must go."[49] His nephew William Preston Johnston in Louisville oversaw Preston's assets, selling certain properties as directed and renting the houses the family owned in Louisville and St. Louis.

Unfortunately, the Prestons disliked life in Madrid almost from the moment of their arrival, and their correspondence is filled with hopes that soon they might be returning home. After only one month at his post, Preston wrote: "I wish sometimes that I was back in Kentucky," and before long he was describing Spain as "this land of discomforts."[50] Margaret particularly detested Madrid, asserting after only four months there: "We all suffer dreadfully with homesickness. William often declares that he will stand it no longer, that life here is infernal. . . . I always encourage him in his discontent, and tell him that the children are ready and more than willing and that I am more anxious than they are."[51] Mrs. Preston's opinions were always given great consideration by her husband, and her distaste for Spain certainly colored his impression of the country. Even the queen's minister to Washington, Gabriel García y Tassara, realized after meeting the Prestons on several social occasions that Mrs. Preston "without entering into either political or diplomatic questions, has a great influence on her husband . . . ."[52] The heat of Madrid and the trouble and expense of moving temporarily to a rented house outside of the capital at La Granja where the court spent the summers also made life more disagreeable for the Prestons. On several occasions William and Margaret complimented themselves on sending their daughters to school in Paris rather than keeping them in Madrid. Both parents, however, were happy with the progress of their son and daughters' experiences in Europe. Peg and Carrie greatly improved their French; son Wick stayed in Madrid where he learned to speak Spanish "passably."[53]

In March 1860, when Preston left for the United States to bring the proposed arbitration treaty to Washington and to attend to his father-in-law's estate, the envoy was determined to resign his post. Diplomatic disappointments and personal circumstances dictated this course. Against his wishes the Kentuckian was convinced by Buchanan to serve in Madrid for the months remaining in his administration. Preston returned in September to Paris, where he had left Margaret living in a rented house on the fashionable Champs Elysées. Returning to Spain, they boarded a ship in Marseilles, but the vessel was shipwrecked not far from port. Fortunately, the passengers and crew members were saved, but not before all the travelers had experienced many anxious moments. The Prestons then proceeded by land via Barcelona to Madrid, where they remained until May 1861.

Preston's record of diplomatic disappointments in Madrid obviously can be credited to the growing sectional strife in the United States which doomed attempts to purchase Cuba and to settle the *Amistad* claims. The envoy's advocacy of these causes was consistent with his prosouthern stance. Unfortunately for him, the growing strength of the Republican party in the 1850s was depriving the southerners of their northern allies and frustrating their political goals. Preston commented bitterly on the deleterious results this North-South animosity was having on United States foreign policy. Dejected over the Senate's refusal to approve either Slidell's resolution or the treaty with Spain, the Kentuckian attacked the "eternal vaporing of Congress" and ruefully observed: "I firmly believe that I could do things deemed impossibilities, but for the unhappy party dissension at home, the rancour of the Republicans & the combination of perfidious Democrats against the President."[54] Preston concluded that Buchanan was unequal to the challenge facing him and remarked: "As to old Buck, I have surrendered all hope, long since, that he could help us — I pity him."[55]

The Kentuckian's disappointment with Congress blinded him to other reasons which also made his goals unattainable. He continued to believe that only a lack of sufficient funds was frustrating the acquisition of Cuba. Long after the rejection of Slidell's resolution, Preston reassured Washington in October 1859 that the Spanish-Moroccan War which had just erupted would have permitted him to purchase the Caribbean colony if only he had thirty million dollars on hand.[56] Obviously, the Kentuckian was mistaken in this judgment. Historical studies and any acquaintance with Spanish politics of this period convincingly demonstrate that Cuba could have been wrested from the mother country in the 1850s only at the price of war.

Following his diplomatic mission to Spain, William Preston served the Confederacy as a colonel and brigadier general through most of the war years, until he was appointed minister to Mexico City in January 1864. After a series of evasive answers and delays, it became apparent that Maximilian, the new emperor of Mexico, did not intend to receive the southern envoy, so Preston never reached the Aztec capital. At the end of the conflict he spent several months in England and Canada before returning to Lexington in late December 1865. Preston's political activities in the postwar period were limited to serving a single term in the state legislature and to attending the Democratic convention in 1880 as a delegate. Most of his energies were devoted to overseeing the large estate inherited from Robert Wickliffe in Lexington. Politician, diplomat, and soldier, William Preston died in 1887, a heroic figure to a generation of Kentuckians for whom the Old South and the Civil War were becoming more and more the substance of legend.

## Footnotes

[1]William Preston (hereinafter WP), *Remarks* (Washington, n.d.), 3. This is a reprint of Preston's speech in the House of Representatives, 20 December 1853.

[2]WP to son [Robert Wickliffe Preston], 10 February 1865, Preston Family Papers, Davie Collection (hereinafter Davie) (The Filson Club, Louisville).

[3]WP to General Almonte, 6 June 1864, Davie.

[4]Kentucky *Constitution* (1849), Article XIII, Section 3.

[5]R. Sutton, ed., *Report of the Debates and Proceedings of the Convention for the Revision of the Constitution of the State of Kentucky* (Frankfort, 1849), 302.

[6]WP to Susan [Mrs. Howard Christy], 4 March 1854, Davie.

[7]WP to [John C.] Breckinridge, 19 September 1856, Breckinridge Family Papers (Manuscript Division, Library of Congress).

[8]WP to Breckinridge, 20 October 1856, *ibid*.

[9] Gabriel García y Tassara to the Primer Ministro de Estado [Saturino Calderón Collantes], 4 January 1859, Correspondencia, Estados Unidos (Archivo del Ministerio de Asuntos Exteriores, Madrid, Spain).

[10] WP to Susan, 8 October 1858, Davie.

[11] William Preston Johnston to Aunt Susan [Mrs. Howard Christy], 4 February 1856, Preston Family Papers, Joyes Collection (hereinafter Joyes) (The Filson Club).

[12] Christopher Fallón to James Buchanan, 12 February 1858, Christopher Fallón Papers (Historical Society of Pennsylvania, Philadelphia).

[13] *Ibid.*

[14] Fallón to James Buchanan, 14 January 1858, *ibid.*

[15] WP to William [Preston Johnston], 17 December 1858, and WP to R[euben] T. Durrett, 14 December 1858, Albert Sidney Johnston Papers, Mason Barret Collection (hereinafter Mason Barret) (Special Collections, Howard Tilton Memorial Library, Tulane University).

[16] Christopher Fallón to WP, 6 January 1859, Fallón Papers.

[17] Lewis Cass, Diplomatic Instructions of the Department of State (hereinafter Diplomatic Instructions), 3 January 1859 (National Archives).

[18] WP to William [Preston] Johnston, 17 December 1858, Mason Barret Collection.

[19] G. García y Tassara to the Primer Ministro de Estado, 21 December 1858, Correspondencia, Estados Unidos.

[20] Craig L. Kautz, "Beneficial Politics: John Slidell and the Cuban Bill of 1859," *Louisiana Studies,* 13 (1974), 124.

[21] Louisville *Daily Courier,* 11 January, 19 February 1859; Washington *Union,* 30 December 1858; Washington *Constitution,* 18 June 1859; New York *Times,* 1 March, and 21 January 1859.

[22] WP to R[euben] T. Durrett, 14 December 1858, Mason Barret Collection.

[23] WP to Susan, 24 February 1859, Davie.

[24] WP to Susan, 27 September 1859, *ibid.*

[25] WP to Susan, 24 February 1859, *ibid.*

[26] Expendientes relativos a Preston, W. (hereinafter Expedientes), 24 November 1859, through 30 March 1861, Archivo del Ministerio de Asuntos Exteriores (Madrid, Spain).

[27] WP to Lewis Cass, 9 March 1859, Despatches of U.S. Ministers to Spain (hereinafter Despatches) (National Archives).

[28] WP to Lewis Cass, 25 April 1859, *ibid.*

[29] Treaty of 1795, Article IX, in W.M. Mallory, comp., *Treaties, Conventions, International Acts, Protocols and Agreements* (4 vols., Washington, 1910-38), II, 1644.

[30] A[ugust Caesar] Dodge to Lewis Cass, 20 October 1858, Despatches.

[31] WP to Lewis Cass, 14 October, 27 November 1859; Cass to WP, 18 January 1860, *ibid.*

[32]G. García y Tassara, to the Primer Ministro de Estado, 6 February 1860, Correspondencia, Estados Unidos.

[33]Convention included with letter of WP to Cass, 6 March 1860, Despatches.

[34]See Despatches, *passim,* 1859-61.

[35]William H. Seward to WP, 9 March 1861, Diplomatic Instructions.

[36]*Ibid.,* 1 May 1861.

[37]Abraham Lincoln to Queen Isabel II, 25 March 1861, Expedientes.

[38]Horatio J. Perry to Seward, 20 April, 27 May 1861, Despatches.

[39]WP, "Journal in Mexico, 1847-48" (handwritten copy by William Preston Johnston), Mason Barret; WP, *Remarks,* 3.

[40]WP to Cass, 9 March 1859, Despatches.

[41]Mrs. William Preston to Susan, 14 July 1859, Davie.

[42]WP to Susan, 8 March 1859, *ibid..*

[43]WP to Cass, 25 April 1859, Despatches.

[44]WP to Susan, 8 March 1859, Davie.

[45]*Ibid.,* 20 January 1860.

[46]Expedientes, 24 November 1859 through 30 March 1861; Louisville *Times,* 20 March 1940.

[47]H. Perry to Seward, 20 April 1861, Despatches.

[48]WP to Susan, 17 February 1861; *ibid., Grazeta de Madrid,* 26 May 1861.

[49]WP to Susan, 9 April 1859, Mason Barret.

[50]*Ibid.,* and 20 January 1860.

[51]Mrs. William Preston to Susan, 14 July 1859, *ibid.*

[52]G. García y Tassara to the Primer Ministro de Estado, 4 January 1859, Correspondencia, Estados Unidos.

[53]WP to Susan, 20 January 1860, Davie.

[54]WP to Susan, 16 February 1860, Mason Barret; WP to Susan, 20 January 1860, Davie.

[55]WP to William [Preston Johnston], 16 February 1860, Mason Barret.

[56]WP to Cass, 23 October 1859, Despatches.

# Bibliographical Essay

Although many primary sources exist on William Preston, there is very little literature about him. The only article devoted entirely to this Kentuckian is J. Frederick Dorman's very brief sketch, "General William Preston," in *The Filson Club History Quarterly*, 43 (1969), 301-08. Dorman also offers some biographical material on Preston in a newly published manuscript, *The Prestons of Smithfield and Greenfield in Virginia* (Louisville, 1982). Other family histories with some information about William Preston include John M. Brown's *Memoranda of the Preston Family* (Frankfort, 1870) and William Preston Johnston's *The Johnstons of Salisbury* (New Orleans, 1897). Additional information about Preston's life is found in the autobiographical *Reminiscences of General Basil W. Duke* (New York, 1911), the work of a friend and fellow Kentucky Confederate. Charles Roland's *Albert Sidney Johnston: Soldier of Three Republics* (Austin, 1964), William Johnston's *Life of General Albert Sidney Johnston* (New York, 1879), and Arthur M. Shaw's *William Preston Johnston: A Transitional Figure of the Confederacy* (Baton Rouge, 1943) include material about William Preston.

Most of the primary sources on William Preston are found at the Filson Club, the University of Kentucky in Lexington, and Tulane University in New Orleans. The Filson Club's splendid Davie and Joyes Collections of Preston family papers include hundreds of letters to and from Preston. James R. Bentley's "Calendar of the Preston Family Papers — Joyes Collection" (Master's thesis, The College of William and Mary, 1972) is a helpful aid to the use of this set of documents. Other valuable correspondence and reports on Preston at the Filson Club are found in the Johnston Family Papers. The Special Collections division of the Margaret I. King Library of the University of Kentucky houses the Preston-Johnston Papers which include thousands of pieces of correspondence to and from William, Margaret, and Wickliffe Preston, as well as newspaper clippings, awards, and memorabilia. The University of Kentucky also has a diary and account book, a letterbook, and an annotated Greek-Latin lexicon of Preston's. The Johnston and the Mason Barret Collections are found in the Special Collections section of the Howard Tilton Library at Tulane University and contain large compilations of papers which include hundreds of Preston letters. In addition, Tulane owns the only handwritten copy of Preston's account of his Mexican War experiences, "Journal, 1847-1848."

Historical literature on United States efforts to annex Cuba and to resolve the *Amistad* affair is plentiful. Robert E. May's *The Southern Dream of Empire* (Baton Rouge, 1973) and Charles H. Brown's *Agents of Manifest Destiny: The Lives and Times of the Filibusters* (Chapel Hill, 1980) note the importance of Caribbean expansion in southern politics and actions in the decades before the Civil War. Craig L. Kautz's article, "Beneficial Politics: John Slidell and the Cuban Bill of 1859," *Louisiana Studies,* 13 (1974), 119-29, is a thorough study of the Louisiana senator's unsuccessful attempt to have funds appropriated to purchase Cuba. Irving Katz's *August Belmont: A Political Biography* (New York, 1968) offers interesting material on this Democratic financier-diplomat's ideas on how to acquire Cuba. "The *Amistad* Claims: Inconsistencies of Policy," R. Earl McClendon's piece in the *Political Science Quarterly,* 48 (1933), 386-412, traces the complex history of this international issue from 1839 until 1861. Samuel Flagg Bemis devotes a chapter to "The Africans of the *Amistad"* in his important biography, *John Quincy Adams and the Union* (New York, 1956). For a Spanish account of United States efforts to purchase Cuba, see Jeronimo Becker, *Historia de las relaciones exteriores de España durante el siglo XIX,* 2 (Madrid, 1924), 313-96.

Several studies of United States history focus on the prewar years and the Buchanan administration. Roy F. Nichols' *The Disruption of American Democracy* (New York, 1948) and David M. Potter's *The Impending Crisis, 1848-1861* (New York, 1976) are two such well respected works. *President James Buchanan: A Biography* (University Park, Pa., 1962) by Philip S. Klein and *The Presidency of James Buchanan* (Lawrence, Kan., 1975) by Elbert B. Smith are standard studies.

Important primary sources relating to United States-Spanish relations from 1858 to 1861 are found in three institutions. The National Archives in Washington, D.C. has four valuable collections dealing with this topic: Diplomatic Instructions of the Department of State, 1801-1906, Spain; Notes to the Spanish Government, 1858-1863; Notes from the Spanish Government, 1858-1861; and Despatches of Ministers to Spain, 1792-1906. The Madrid Archivo del Ministerio de Asuntos Exteriores contains three sets of documents relevant to United States relations during this period: Correspondencia, Estados Unidos, 1856-1861; Expedientes relativos a Preston, W.; and Política, Estados Unidos, 1855-1860. The James Buchanan and the Christopher Fallón Papers at the Historical Society of Pennsylvania in Philadelphia include many letters concerning United States efforts to purchase Cuba. The twelve-volume *Works of James Buchanan* (Philadelphia, 1908-11), edited by John B. Moore, contain a great deal of correspondence about the administration's policies toward Spain.

# Civil War Romance
# The Influence of Wartime
# Marriage on the Life
# and Career of John Hunt Morgan

*by James A. Ramage*

On the northern bank of the Cumberland River, Colonel John Hunt Morgan reined his horse to a halt and settled back in the saddle. The exhilaration of victory glowed in his grayish-blue eyes; the thrill of the moment had to be shared with the young lady who in seven days would be his bride. Slinging his right leg over the saddle, he removed his gloves, and, using the top of his cavalry boot as a rest, began writing: "Hartsville battlefield, Dec. 7, 1862, Dear Mattie . . . ." As he wrote, the air was filled with sounds of the aftermath of battle: the crackling of flames as they consumed Union tents and supplies which could not be carted away, the splashing of water as Morgan's men escorted 1,800 federal prisoners across the icy Cumberland, and the barking of commands by Confederate officers who had accomplished what historian Kenneth P. Williams regarded as "one of the boldest and most successfully executed minor operations in the war."[1]

Morgan had won probably the most significant test of his ability to lead men in battle. During the previous twenty-four hours, he had marched four regiments of cavalry and two regiments of infantry thirty miles through middle Tennessee. Many of the Confederate infantrymen had only old rags on their feet to protect them from the wet snow and freezing cold; several were armed only with shotguns. Before the attack, at daybreak, Morgan's adjutant and brother-in-law, Basil Duke, rode up and exclaimed: "You have more work cut out for you, than you bargained for." About half of the cavalry had been delayed crossing the river and, as the 104th Illinois Cavalry hastily formed long blue lines at the edge of a wooded area beyond a snow-covered meadow, it was obvious that Morgan was out-

**John Hunt Morgan and his wife Martha Ready**
Kentucky Historical Society Collection

numbered almost two to one, and a few miles away a large force of enemy troops was camped at Castalian Springs. Three months later, at a dinner party, Morgan said: "I dared not fail than. In a few days I was to be married, you know. And besides I had to take them or they would take me."[2]

Morgan's bride, Martha (Mattie) Ready, profoundly influenced his life and career. After the war Basil Duke stated that Mattie "certainly deserved to exercise over him the great influence she was thought to have possessed." There were hints that Martha slowed Morgan down, took away his strength and courage, and sent his career on a downward spiral. The wedding came at the peak of his career, one day after his promotion to brigadier general. But instead of encouraging him to settle down to regular cavalry service, the relationship with Martha seems to have added to the psychological pressure to continue independent raids, even to the point of recklessness and insubordination.[3]

Martha Ready was a daughter of Charles Ready, one of middle Tennessee's most prominent lawyers and gentlemen farmers. The spacious two-story Ready home near the square in Murfreesboro frequently entertained suitors calling on the three Ready sisters — Mary, Martha, and Alice. And when Ready was a United States congressman from Tennessee from 1853 to 1860, the young ladies were favorites in Washington, D.C. Martha was medium in height, with a trim figure, and she had dark brown hair, thin lips, a prominent nose, and sparkling gray eyes which hinted that beneath her beautiful appearance and aristocratic manner there lingered a smouldering intensity, a spirited loyalty. Her favorite beau in Washington had been Illinois Representative Samuel Scott Marshall. Their courtship failed to survive the Civil War — Marshall remained loyal to the Union, while the Ready family, including Martha's brother Horace, became ardent Confederates. Martha told Alice that she was glad the romance had ended: "It is a good thing for it would have been more than I could stand — with him on one side and brother Horace on the other."[4]

Both Martha and her younger sister, Alice, kept diaries, and even though Martha's was destroyed in a fire, Alice's extant journal expresses the passionate dedication of her family and most of the people of middle Tennessee to the southern cause. Alice noted that when a Tennessee regiment passed through on the way to Virginia, Mattie presented the men a banner on which she had inscribed the words: "Victory or Death." After Fort Henry fell, Mattie and Alice wept, and their mother began packing for a swift retreat. When Albert Sidney Johnston abandoned the Kentucky defensive line and withdrew south of Nashville to a line running through Murfreesboro, the family experienced war firsthand. Colonel Ready opened the home to southern officers and it became a favorite gathering place for General William J. Hardee and others. One day when the colonel was strolling through the army camp, he met John Hunt Morgan and invited him to dinner. He sent a slave home with word that "the famous Captain Morgan" was coming. "Tell Mattie that Captain Morgan is a widower and a little sad. I want her to sing for him."[5]

When Morgan was twenty-three he had married eighteen-year-old Rebecca Gratz Bruce of Lexington. Five years later Becky bore a son who died shortly after birth. Becky remained an invalid for nearly eight years, and there were rumors that John pursued worldly pleasures while his wife suffered. Frances Peter, a young lady in Lexington who sympathized with the Union and hated Morgan, wrote in her war diary that "his character here was always that of a gambler and libertine." Basil Duke answered John's accusers: "General Morgan was certainly no 'saint' — his friends may claim that he had no right to that title and not the slightest pretension to it. . . . Like the great majority of the men of his class — the gentlemen of the South — he lived freely, and the amusements he permitted himself would, doubtless, have shocked a New Englander almost as much as the money he spent in obtaining them." Becky died in July 1861, and two months later John joined the Confederate army.[6]

By April 1862, Morgan's fame was widespread. He had attracted the attention of the press by conducting scouting expeditions behind enemy lines in southwestern Kentucky before Johnston's army retreated from the state. The southern people, in need of heroes, embraced Morgan as an officer who won battles while the commanding generals were ordering retreat.

In early April, the Atlanta *Confederacy* asserted that Morgan was "a perfect terror to the Yankees, and has inspired them with greater fear than all the army of General Johnston." Northern papers were already calling him a skulking freebooter, spy, guerrilla, land pirate, and "one of the greatest scoundrels that ever went unhung." He received credit for many accomplishments which did not involve him at all and, according to claims, had been killed several times and captured by innumerable soldiers. Before the end of April, his fame reached Europe. The Edinburgh *Scotsman* printed a New York *Times* article which stated: "The name of this mysterious marauder . . . is on the lips of every one, for his coolness and disregard of fear has become a byword even among our own [Union] army." Historian E. Merton Coulter wrote that eventually Morgan became as great a hero to the southern people as General James E.B. (Jeb) Stuart.[7]

In her diary on 3 March 1862, Alice referred to "the already celebrated Capt. John H. Morgan." She told how Morgan came to the Ready house direct from a raid. A large crowd gathered outside to catch a glimpse of the man they cheered as "bold, daring and fearless," and "the best scout in the service, the Marion of the War." For a few people the attraction of fame overcame propriety and they edged into the house and stood in the hall at the parlor door, gazing at the cavalry officer.[8]

Morgan was very comfortable in the role of hero for the Confederate cause. The eldest son in the wealthy family established by his grandfather, John Wesley Hunt, in Lexington, Kentucky, John was a southern aristocrat in manners and conversation. When someone met him for the first time in the drawing room, he seemed modest, shy, and personable, and nothing about him suggested daring or recklessness. But Morgan seems to have recognized the importance of appearance to effective leadership. In his cavalry uniform, from his boots and spurs to his beard and mustache and sparkling eyes, he looked the part of a southern hero. A lady from Louisville dined with Morgan when he was in Kentucky during General Braxton Bragg's invasion in 1862. "She, like all the ladies who see him, fell perfectly in love, was perfectly fascinated with his elegant and fine personal appearance," reported her friend.[9]

John felt at home with the Ready family and found excuses to return — to bring captured newspapers or to pick up their mail for delivery to a nearby town. After several visits, one night after dinner, as the servants poured refreshments from the colonel's fine wine cellar, John overcame his shyness and began recounting his exploits — how he had burned bridges, captured stragglers, intimidated telegraph operators, and taunted the Yankees on his scouting expeditions. "He would become excited, his eyes flash, and cheeks flush," Alice noted.[10]

Romance blossomed — fairytale romance between the famous cavalry officer and the charming southern belle. And the gallant horseman set his heart upon winning new laurels for the princess. On Friday, 7 March 1862, John halted a command of twenty-six men before the Ready house, dismounted, and asked for Mattie and Alice. He informed them that in their honor he was on his way to Nashville to capture a Union general to exchange for General Simon Bolivar Buckner. After promising to deliver the prisoner to their door upon his return, Morgan mounted and rode away at the head of his men.[11]

By Saturday night Morgan had not returned and the Readys grew worried. On Sunday morning Alice and Mattie were in church when they received a note from Morgan saying that he was on his way with prisoners. Unable to sit through the sermon, the girls left and began spreading the word that Morgan was coming. A large crowd had gathered in front of the Ready home when the heroes rode into town. "The first signal of their approach was a number of Texan Rangers galloping by here on horseback to the first street crossing the one below. In a much shorter time than I can write it, the grand Cavalcade appeared from that street. There was I suppose 60 or 70 horsemen including prisoners and with Morgan and Wood at the head. As soon as they came in sight it seemed impossible for any one to sustain their enthusiasm. There were heartfelt cheers and waving of handkerciefs," Alice recorded. Morgan's small band had not located a general, but they had thirty-eight captured Union soldiers — more than their own number.[12]

Halting the center of the column at the Ready door,

Morgan raised his hat and said to the sisters: "Ladies, I present you with your prisoners, what disposal shall be made of them?" Mattie replied: "You have performed your part so well, we are willing to entrust it all to you." With their prisoners, the heroes remained fifteen or twenty minutes, savoring the moment of glory.[13]

Leaving on an expedition to Gallatin a few days later, Morgan told Colonel Ready, who had accompanied them to the outskirts of town: "Tell the young ladies I will bring them a trophy on my return." While Morgan was gone a Union cavalry regiment conducted a reconnaissance in Murfreesboro and withdrew to the major encampment eight miles northwest of the town. Desiring to pass through Murfreesboro on his way south to link up with the withdrawing Confederate army, Morgan sent Mattie a note asking whether the town was clear of Federals. She hurriedly penned a reply: "They are eight miles from here. Come in haste," and handed it to a courier who returned to Morgan, ten miles to the north. A few hours later, in the early morning, Morgan appeared with five prisoners. He and Mattie talked until daylight and family tradition holds that they became engaged on that March nineteenth. At dawn John bade good-bye to Mattie by forming the soldiers on the square and leading in the singing of "Cheer, Boys, Cheer" in the "sweetest tones." Tom Morgan, one of John's five younger brothers, sang the solo part and "all seemed to mellow and soften their voices to suit the time and occasion."[14]

Later that day Union troops occupied Murfreesboro, bringing difficult times to the Ready family. Mrs. Ready locked the doors and pulled down the shades. The colonel refused to take the oath of allegiance and was forced to spend a few weeks in the penitentiary in Nashville. When the Union army withdrew to defend Kentucky against General Braxton Bragg's invasion, the colonel lost ten of his best slaves when they ran away with the Union army. After the battle of Perryville in October 1862, Bragg retreated to Murfreesboro, and once again the Ready house became a gathering place for southern officers, including Morgan, who had been promoted to colonel in command of the Second Kentucky Cavalry.[15]

The courtship resumed in earnest and in December, in the

atmosphere of jubilation over the Hartsville raid, word spread through the camp that Miss Ready and Morgan were to be married on Sunday, 14 December. On Friday, the Ready servants were decorating the parlor with holly, cedar, and mistletoe and stocking u on turkey, ham, and other delicacies, when Jefferson Davis arrived in town. On Saturday, Davis reviewed the troops and signed promotions, including Morgan's to brigadier general.[16]

The wedding on Sunday night in the Ready home was one of the most romantic social occasions in the Civil War. Beautiful Mattie, twenty-one years old, wore an elegant lace gown. John, thirty-seven, stood proud in his general's uniform. He was attended by Mattie's brother Horace, an officer in General William J. Hardee's staff, and by English soldier of fortune George St. Leger Grenfell. General Leonidas Polk, an Episcopal bishop, performed the ceremony and Generals Bragg, Hardee, Benjamin Cheatham, John C. Breckinridge, and many other officers attended. After an elaborate dinner, at least two regimental bands played outside and one came in to play for dancing. On the street, hundreds of Morgan's men gathered to build bonfires and cheer. One of Mattie's friends congratulated her: "It is certainly the match of the Times — 'The Belle of Tennessee' & the dashing leader whose name rings throughout the civilized world."[17]

The courtship and wedding occurred in an intoxicating atmosphere of military success, fame, and glory. The cheering of crowds and playing of bands, winning of laurels in Mattie's name, proposing when enemy troops might appear any moment, winning promotion from the president in person, and marrying in the presence of high commanders — all provided an unusually stimulating background for romance. Then on 21 December, one week after the wedding, Mattie and John stood in the reviewing stand together as he conducted his first complete regimental review. "Company after company moved forward into line with horses prancing, firearms glistening, bugles blowing, and flags waving," wrote one of the men. "It was a grand and imposing scene."[18]

Even though Colonel Grenfell participated in the wedding, he said later that he had tried to prevent it, warning that it would cause Morgan to become cautious and less enterprising as a partisan raider. Mattie's relatives admonished: "You must remember your promises, not to restrain the General in his career of glory, but encourage him to go forward." Morgan had an opportunity to react to the warnings when Bragg ordered him and Nathan Bedford Forrest on separate raids. Morgan's raid into Kentucky at Christmas, during the second and third weeks of his honeymoon, was successful in itself, but it caused Morgan to be absent from the significant battle of Stones River at Murfreesboro. Had he been at Stones River, he would have had an excellent opportunity, in command of four thousand men and at the pinnacle of his career, to demonstrate to himself, his wife, and others that he could carry out significant cavalry operations in support of infantry in a major battle. It would have been a good time to change his military métier from partisan raiding to regular support. The participation of Morgan's men in the battle might not have changed the outcome, but they would have been more useful there than in Kentucky.[19]

Instead of providing a settling influence on Morgan's career as a daring raider, the marriage seems to have intensified pressures on him to continue flashy, independent raids. From the beginning John was Mattie's hero, and to preserve his self-esteem there was a ceaseless need for honor and glory, for confirmation of his status. Mattie also felt the pressure. In January 1863, during the retreat from Stones River, she observed that there was a general clamor for Morgan to come to the rescue. "There was one continual inquiry at the front door, 'When will Genl. Morgan be here?' " She had promised not to hinder him, and, in a few months, when he had not made news lately, and his status seemed to be declining, she felt partially responsible. The Nashville *Daily Union,* a Union paper, had the wartime gall to bring the issue into the open. "Morgan seems to have been losing his character for enterprise and daring; many of his rivals, ladies particularly, are unkind enough to attribute his present inefficiency to the fact that he is married. The fair Delilah, they assume, has shown him of his locks. Maybe so."[20]

The deep, intense love which Mattie and John had for each

other only exacerbated the pressure. In his recent *At Odds: Women and the Family in America from the Revolution to the Present,* Carl Degler sets forth that modern American marriage, based in part on mutual affection or romantic love, began around the beginning of the nineteenth century. At midcentury, in the marriage of Mattie and John, romance was fully bloomed. On the Christmas raid, nine days after the wedding, he declared: "How anxiously I am looking forward to the moment when I shall again clasp you to a heart that beats for you alone." Three months later he proclaimed: "I am the happiest fellow upon Earth. Darling I love you more than life. My whole existence is perfectly wrapt up in you & I am perfectly miserable. When absent, days are so long, they seem innumerable & when with my pretty Mattie they pass so rapidly."[21]

On 20 March 1863, several of Morgan's enlisted men and four officers were killed in skirmishing at Milford, Tennessee. The next evening he declared: "All day yesterday my darling while in the hottest of the engagement was I thinking of my *dear* beautiful 'Mattie' & precious one. I am satisfied your prayers must have saved me. My coat sleve [sic] was nearly torn off by a ball, but my arm escaped unhurt. It even tore through the lining of *'your'* green jacket. When I again get back to you 'pretty one,' shall give it up & let you keep it. Darling, I am so anxious to see your sweet dear face & to have you tell me, that you Love me, so much & in knowing that I am perfectly happy, indeed I am the happiest Soldier, in the Confederacy, or in the World. Who has such a wife? You are the best & sweetest one of all."[22]

After the Battle of Stones River, Mattie became a refugee, retreating from Murfreesboro ahead of the Confederate army. From Winchester, southeast of Murfreesboro, she wrote to John on 6 January 1863: "Come to me my own Darling quickly. I was wretched but now I am *almost* happy and will be quite, when my precious Husband is again with me. I can bear anything Darling when you are with me, and as long as I have your love. But when separated from you, and I know that you are surrounded by so many dangers, and hardships, as you have been on your last expedition I become a weak, nervous Child. Have I not lived a great deal Love, in the last two weeks? When

I look back now at the time, it seems two years, but in each scene I have passed through there has always been one dear face ever before me, and can you doubt whose fact that was? If you do, I don't intend to enlighten you, at least until you come. So there is another inducement." She closed: "Good night *my Hero*. My dreams are all of you." The next month she was with him at his headquarters in McMinnville, Tennessee, when she told sister Mary: "They say we are a love sick couple. At any rate I know my liege Lord is devoted to me. Each day I am forced to love him more. His disposition is *perfect*." John added a postscript: "It would be folly for me to tell you how happy I am, knowing Mattie as you do."[23]

Another aspect of the emerging American marriage, according to Degler, was that the husband conceded that the wife was the moral superior. Such was clearly the case with John. He had never professed religion, but, after the wedding, he regularly rounded up his officers and took them to Sunday worship services with Mattie. He began reading the prayer book she gave him, and he developed the habit of reading Scripture every night. After the Milford skirmish, he wrote: "The dear prayer book that you gave me 'my dear precious One' is before me & I shall read Evening Prayer, 21st day. So my Angel you see what a good influence you exert upon me and I am so much happier." John proudly informed his mother that due to Mattie's example and advice he had become a "much better man." On the last Kentucky raid he told Mattie: "Last night read two Chapters in the Bible & shall do so when I get one: but I can always pray my Idol, & rest assured shall do so, shall try & be better & hope to be enabled at no distant period to accompany you to Communion. We must be alike in all things Except Love, it is utterly impossible for you to equal me in that." When John was killed his youngest brother Key wrote to their mother that he hoped John had gone to a better world. "He was improved so much since he married. He use [sic] to read his bible every night. And say his prayers on his bended knees and go to church every sunday."[24]

After the wedding, John continued to be Mattie's hero, entertaining her with stories of the feats of his men. On the Christmas raid, at Lebanon, Kentucky, Basil Duke took shrapnel from a shell and fell unconscious from his horse. John reported: "When I get back to you my *Darling* shall take great delight in giving you an account of the gallant manner in which his boys brought him across the river while shells were exploding and dashing water over them." After listing the accomplishments of that raid, he asserted: "The greatest pleasure my expedition has afforded is the knowledge that our great success will gratify and delight you." And, before his last raid into Kentucky, John wrote: "Feel confident of success & hope 'My Precious One' to be enabled to send you news soon that will gladden your 'dear heart.' "[25]

With middle Tennessee under enemy occupation, it was considered advisable that Mattie remain within Confederate lines; moreover, the couple wanted to be together. It was not unusual for an officer in the Civil War to have his wife and children nearby. Both of John's sisters came south to be near their husbands — Kitty with General A.P. Hill and Tommie with Basil Duke. But Mattie followed John unusually close.[26]

They absolutely hated to be separated. On the Christmas raid he wrote: "I shall try & get back to you as fast as possible & then my pretty one, nothing shall induce me to again leave you this winter." And nothing did — after that raid they were not apart for more than three days at a time for the next six months. On 17 January 1863, he wrote: "Am determined to have you near me. Cannot bear the thought of your being away from home & my not being with you. . . . If you think it will be pleasant shall bring you up when I go to Winchester, which will be within a few days." Reunited, she wrote: "My life is all a joyous dream now, from which I fear to awaken, and awake I must when my Hero is called to leave me again. My husband wants me to remain with him, and of course I much prefer it."[27]

From John's respected Uncle Samuel Morgan, Mattie received a word of caution: "Now, you must not get angry with me, for saying to you, that I fear you are sticking *too close* to your husband. Not that I am in favor of wives seeking their ease and comfort away from their husbands, whilst they are enduring privations & hardships." That would be selfish, he continued, but when the wife follows too closely, she "might possibly encumber her husband too much with care and anxiety, so much so as to prove injurious to him, especially to one who has necessarily on his mind such a load of care and responsibility."[28]

Wherever they were, John made arrangements for Mattie's escape in case of attack. He provided an ambulance and wagon and kept her informed on the most feasible escape route. She kept her bags packed for "instantaneous movement." They were together at his headquarters in McMinnville on 19 April 1863, when Colonel Robert Minty's Michigan cavalry burst through the picket lines and dashed through the streets eight abreast. Two of Morgan's officers were seriously wounded, creating diversions to give him time to put Mattie in the ambulance and send her racing out of town. John and his headquarters escort escaped on horseback across the fields. Mattie was captured but immediately released.[29]

In June 1863, in preparation for the raid into Indiana and Ohio in July, John applied for leave of absence to take Mattie to Augusta, Georgia, a safe distance from the fighting. There was a special reason for caution now: Mattie was pregnant. General Bragg determined that he could not spare Morgan, so, after seeing Mattie off, John sent telegrams to her in care of telegraph operators along the railroad line to Augusta. On 12 June he sent her a letter: "Today you reached Knoxville and I hope you were not much fatigued. It was a long ride for you My Darling. How much I regretted not being able to accompany you — I should have anticipated all your wants . . . . Enclosed find a sprig of geranium which I send emblematically."[30]

On 20 June, John wrote from Carthage, Tennessee, relating how he had captured the mail from Gallatin along with an ambulance, a large sutler's wagon, and twenty men. "I am so very anxious to see you my 'pretty one.' The time drags heavier each day & although passing through exciting times, still my thoughts are of you My Dearest Wife. The candle is so low that I can scarcely *see,* but could not resist the pleasure of writing. Sent you some late papers captured. Love to Sister Alice. How is our little recruit? God bless you my own Darling Wife." Mattie stayed in Augusta for a few weeks and then traveled to Knoxville to welcome John back from the Indiana-Ohio raid. He was captured and placed in the penitentiary in

Columbus, Ohio; when General Ambrose Burnside pushed into east Tennessee, she had to flee southward. Finally she settled in Danville, Virginia.[31]

Mattie pleaded with officials in Richmond to arrange for the exchange of John, but the weeks passed with no progress. It was painful to Morgan not to be near Mattie during the pregnancy. He made arrangements for her financial support and suggested that she consider moving to Augusta before winter weather. When he received a box of clothing and a letter from his mother, he reported that much of the letter related glowing accounts of Mattie "& above all, that you are a *Christian*." He had written to his wife "the little prayer book, that you presented me with upon our marriage, had been my constant companion, ever since, & that a night has not passed, but that I have read it, & I can say to you that, in so doing I always think of you my Darling. Your daguerreotype I open often during the day and pray that the time may soon come when I may again see you."[32]

In frequent letters he continued pouring out his love for Mattie and the unborn child: "Attend to my little namesake. See its mother, see 'My precious Mattie' that they want for nothing." Basil Duke, also a prisoner of war, had been boasting about his infant son, and John teased that Duke's bragging of his boy's superiority would be shortlived once Mattie's baby arrived. "My precious Wife," he continued, "you must not fail to see to (or about) my little namesake. When you see the Mother, say to her that she is frequently in my thoughts, & that I am exceedingly anxious to see her & her *little* one, that she must be of good heart, that her husband, is well & says he is very proud of *them*." Earlier in the same letter he complained: "But for the uncertainty of your condition, I could bear this incarceration, with a much greater degree of Stoicism." When her letters failed to get through, the suspense became almost unbearable. "If I can hear from you each week & that you are still blessed with health, then I can be as seeming happy as any, but if a week elapses, without a letter, then the little clouds begin to appear & I imagine ten thousand things."[33]

Union officials showed very little interest in exchanging the "horse thief" and "bandit" now that they had him behind bars, so John and six officers escaped on 27 November 1863. One very personal reason for his determination to break out was the need to be with Mattie. He probably did not know it until his return to the Confederacy, but the child was born dead in mid-November in Danville. Hiding by day and traveling by night, he made his way through Union territory and was with Mattie for Christmas.[34]

They were together for a hero's welcome in Richmond in January 1864, after which he reorganized his command and took charge of guarding the lead mines and saltworks in southwest Virginia. Now they were more determined than ever to be together. From headquarters in Abingdon, Virginia, Mattie told John's mother: "I feel perfectly lost when separated from him, and my most earnest prayer is, that I may never have to endure his absence again for as great a length of time as when he was in prison." And even when they were united, they displayed an extreme dependence upon each other. In February 1864 while on leave in Atlanta, they visited John's sister Tommie and others. One of his Hunt relatives, George W. Hunt, reported to John's mother: "Johnnie though looking some years older, than when I saw him three years since in Lexington, is in good health. His wife whom I saw, for the first time a few days since, is a very fine looking and agreeable lady. They are exceedingly devoted to each other. It is amusing to see them separated from each other in the Hotel. *'Tommie, where is the Gen. — Tommie where is Mattie'* is the exclamation of each while seeking the other."[35]

On 11 May 1864, John wrote from Wytheville, Virginia: "Telegrammed to you last night from battlefield, 'My precious wife' & received yours of today. Am perfectly lost without you 'My Sweet One' & if I only knew how long we will remain here would send for you, but my movements are so very uncertain, that I shall be compelled to stand it a little longer. . . . The office is so full that I will have to close. Sending ten thousand kisses. 'My Own Precious One' shall be with you as soon as I can get off but you well know that."[36]

Mattie had been warmly accepted into the Morgan family, and she enjoyed corresponding with John's mother in Lexington. Mattie described the children of John's sisters, Tommie and Kitty, and reported on Key, who as a teenager had dropped out of school to be with his brother in the Confederacy. On 25 February 1864, Mattie declared: "You have great cause dear Mother, to feel proud of your Sons, which I know you do. Key is with us, and in perfect health. I have never seen a youth grow so rapidly." Henrietta Morgan sent Mattie a dress, and Mattie expressed appreciation: "You must certainly dear Mother possess the faculty of knowing not only the desires, but also necessities of those absent from you. I am sure that I must thank you for anticipating mine, in the handsome black silk dress. The handkerchief is a beauty, and each time it touches my lips there will be a kiss in my thoughts for Mother. Tell Florida [a house servant] the work is exquisite, and I thank her for manifesting so much interest in it. . . . I am very desirious of knowing you dear Mother, and until then, believe me with much love to be *your* affectionate daughter."[37]

After John escaped from prison, his brothers Richard and Charlton remained incarcerated for several months. Charlton's sweetheart had rejected him while he was a prisoner, and he found solace writing to Mattie. In one of her warm letters she consoled: "You have my deepest sympathy in *your bereavement*. But I believe the *heart breaker's* heart is more broken and that ere long the same loving accounts will fall upon some other listening ear and past disappointments be forgotten in present enjoyments."[38]

Meanwhile, fearing that one of them might be captured again, John and Mattie made a covenant to be more vigilant than ever. On 1 June 1864, en route to Kentucky on the last Kentucky raid, John warned Mattie to be on the alert for enemy soldiers. "I could not exist if anything should happen to you. I shall faithfully carry out all your desires in regard to myself. How very anxious I am to see you & to hold you in my arms. Do not think I shall permit myself to be separated from you again." And on 27 June from Kentucky, he reaffirmed: "I shall faithfully carry out all your desires in regard to myself." On 4 September 1864, while Mattie was at headquarters in Abingdon, John was in Greeneville, Tennessee, attempting to block a Federal advance. Union troops surprised his pickets, surrounded the house where he had spent the night, and killed him as he tried to escape. Did the fear of being imprisoned and separated from Mattie contribute to his attempt to flee rather than to surrender? It seems possible, yet he was reacting as he always had in similar situations. In previous skirmishes such as this he had always escaped.[39]

Seven months after John was killed, Mattie gave birth to a daughter, whom she named Johnnie Hunt Morgan. The child was a great comfort to Mattie in her grief. When Johnnie was four months old, Mattie observed to John's mother: "She has indeed proved a blessing to me direct from God, and the only happiness I look forward to in the future, is that of rearing her. She is said to be a perfect little Morgan in appearance, and already I imagine she begins to exhibit evidence of having inherited her Father's lovely disposition." The years passed and Mattie married Judge James Williamson, and they reared Johnnie in Green Hill, Tennessee. Mattie died a few days before Johnnie married Joseph W. Caldwell, a Presbyterian minister from Selma, Alabama. Not long after the wedding, Caldwell left for England to attend a church conference, and while he was away, Johnnie died of typhoid fever, leaving John Hunt Morgan with no direct descendants.[40]

In a sense, John Hunt Morgan fought his own personal war, verified by his persistence in conducting independent raids. Certainly he enjoyed the honors, the cheers of the crowd; he especially felt the need to fulfill the expectations of his loved ones and fellow soldiers. As a leader of the Kentucky bloc in Richmond, he dreamed of liberating his home state. When his status declined he attempted to regain it by violating orders and launching the reckless raid into Indiana and Ohio and by striking out in desperation on the last Kentucky raid. In practical terms, to keep his command functional, he needed the horses on Kentucky farms and the abundant shoes and rifles in Union supply depots behind the lines. Always the Morgan legend haunted him — his fans demanded new and greater miracles. In May 1863, Miss Emma Holmes of Charleston celebrated recent successes: "Morgan is himself again. For months past we have heard nothing of him . . . . Morgan is one of my favorite heroes, & I am always delighted to hear of some new & brilliant exploit." His cohorts were equally as demanding. In February 1864, St. Leger Grenfell encouraged Morgan to maintain an independent command and praised him as the Confederacy's foremost cavalry officer, noting that "if public opinion could be expressed and acted upon, you would be placed at once in that independent situation which your gallant conduct has won for you, and your future deed would continue to deserve." To these pressures was added Morgan's wartime marriage and the need, for brief periods, to tear himself from his wife's side and prove to himself, to Mattie, and to the world that he still deserved adolation as the "Thunderbolt of the Confederacy."

## Footnotes

[1] Cecil F. Holland, *Morgan and His Raiders: A Biography of the Confederate General* (New York, 1942), 207; Kenneth P. Williams, *Lincoln Finds a General* (4 vols., New York, 1949-59), IV, 245-47; James A. Ramage, "The Hunts and Morgans: A Study of a Prominent Kentucky Family" (Ph.D. dissertation, University of Kentucky, 1972), 249-50.

[2] *The War of the Rebellion: A Compilation of the Official Records of the Union and Confederate Armies* (128 vols., Washington, 1880-1901), Ser. I, Vol. XX, Pt. 1, 62-71 (hereinafter *O.R.*); Holland, *Morgan*, 166-70, 207; Basil W. Duke, *History of Morgan's Cavalry* (Cincinnati, 1867), 311.

[3] Duke, *History*, 321-22.

[4] Isabella D. Martin and Myrta L. Avary, eds., Mary B. Chesnut, *A Diary from Dixie* (New York, 1929), 242; Holland, *Morgan*, 60-62.

[5] Alice Ready Journal, 3 March 1862, Southern Historical Collection (University of North Carolina Library, Chapel Hill); Holland, *Morgan*, 62-63, 68.

[6] John David Smith and William Cooper, Jr., eds., *Window on the War: Frances Dallam Peter's Lexington Civil War Diary* (Lexington, 1976), 47; Duke, *History*, 20.

[7] Cincinnati *Gazette*, 16 December 1861; Louisville *Journal*, 29 March 1862; Cincinnati *Commercial*, 15 February 1862; Edinburgh *Scotsman*, 21 April 1862; unidentified clippings, 11 December 1861, 14, 18 March, 8 April 1862, Hunt-Morgan Papers (University of Kentucky Library, Lexington) (hereinafter HMP-UK); Ramage, "Hunts and Morgans," 217-23; E. Merton Coulter, *The Confederate States of America, 1861-1865* (Baton Rouge, 1950), 341.

[8] Ready Journal, 3, 8 March 1862. Francis Marion conducted operations against British lines of communication in the American Revolution.

[9] Belle McDowell to Calvin Morgan, 12 October 1862, HMP-UK. On Morgan's family background, see the author's *John Wesley Hunt: Pioneer Merchant, Manufacturer and Financier* (Lexington, 1974).

[10] Ready Journal, 11, 15 March 1862.

[11] Ready Journal, 8 March 1862. Buckner had surrendered at Fort Donelson and was in a northern prison camp.

[12] Ready Journal, 9 March 1862; *O.R.*, Ser. I, Vol. X, Pt. 1, 6-7. Lt. Col. Robert C. Wood, Jr., of the First Mississippi Cavalry, accompanied Morgan. The grandson of Zachary Taylor, Wood outranked Morgan but chose to serve under him nevertheless.

[13] Ready Journal, 9 March 1862.

[14] *Ibid.*, 15, 19 March 1862; Holland, *Morgan*, 79-83.

[15] Ready Journal, 30 April 1862; Holland, *Morgan*, 80, 174.

[16] James B. McCreary Journal, 10 December 1862, carbon of typed copy (William R. Perkins Library, Duke University) (hereinafter McCreary Journal); Edison H. Thomas, *John Hunt Morgan and His Raiders* (Lexington, 1975), 60-62.

[17] Thomas, *Morgan*, 62-63; C.B. Hilliard to Martha Morgan (hereinafter MM), 18 December 1862, John Hunt Morgan Papers, Southern Historical Collection (University of North Carolina Library, Chapel Hill) (hereinafter JHMP-SHC). Basil Duke wrote that Davis attended the wedding. See Duke, *History*, 322. However, biographers of Morgan have been unable to locate corroborating testimony. See Thomas, *Morgan*, 61-62.

[18] McCreary Journal, 21 December 1862.

[19] Mary Cahal to MM, 16 December 1862, JHMP-SHC; Stephen Z. Starr, *Colonel Grenfell's Wars: The Life of a Soldier of Fortune* (Baton Rouge, 1971), 86.

[20] MM to John Hunt Morgan (hereinafter JHM), 6 January 1863, JHMP-SHC; Nashville *Daily Union*, 14 April 1863; James Lee McDonough, *Stones River: Bloody Winter in Tennessee* (Knoxville, 1980), 49, 65-66.

[21] JHM to MM, 23 December 1862, 21 March 1863, JHMP-SHC; Carl N. Degler, *At Odds: Women and the Family in America from the Revolution to the Present* (New York, 1980), 8-19.

[22] JHM to MM, 21 March 1863, JHMP-SHC; Duke, *History*, 376-80.

[23] MM to JHM, 6 January 1863, MM to Mary Cheatham, February [no day] 1863, JHMP-SHC.

[24] JHM to MM, 21 March, 10 August 1863, 1 June 1864, *ibid.*; Francis Key Morgan to Henrietta Morgan (hereinafter HM), 20 September 1864, HMP-UK; Degler, *At Odds*, 8, 26ff.

[25] JHM to MM, 2 January 1863, 31 May 1864, JHMP-SHC.

[26] Francis Key Morgan to HM, 26 November 1863, HMP-UK.

[27] JHM to MM, 23 December 1862, JHM to HM, 12 August 1863, MM to Mary Cheatham, February [no day] 1863, JHMP-SHC; JHM to MM, 17 January 1863, quoted in Holland, *Morgan*, 203.

[28] Samuel D. Morgan to MM, 17 April 1863, JHMP-SHC.

[29] *Ibid.*; JHM to MM, 4 April 1863, 31 May 1864, JHMP-SHC; Holland, *Morgan*, 212-13.

[30] JHM to MM, 12 June 1863, quoted in Holland, *Morgan,* 222. For accounts of the Indiana-Ohio raid, see Thomas, *Morgan,* Lowell H. Harrison, *The Civil War in Kentucky* (Lexington, 1975), and Ramage, " 'Let Him Come!' Indiana's Response to John Hunt Morgan's Raid," *Journal of The Jackson Purchase Historical Society,* 8 (1980), 1-9.

[31] JHM to MM, 20 June 1863, JHMP-SHC; Holland, *Morgan,* 221-22, 263-64.

[32] William Preston Johnston to MM, 30 September 1863, Robert Ould to MM, 30 October 1863, JHM to MM, 12 October, 10, 18 November 1863, JHMP-SHC.

[33] JHM to MM, 30 August, 13 September 1863, *ibid.*

[34] Calvin C. Morgan to HM, 30 December 1863, Morgan and Duke Families Papers (The Filson Club, Louisville); Thomas, *Morgan,* 90.

[35] MM to HM, 29 March 1864, George W. Hunt to HM, 24 February 1864, HMP-UK; Ramage, "Hunts and Morgans," 277-78.

[36] JHM to MM, 11 May 1864, JHMP-SHC.

[37] MM to HM, 25 February, 29 March 1864, HMP-UK.

[38] MM to Charlton Morgan, 1 June 1864, *ibid.;* Charlton Morgan to MM, 11 November, 7 December 1863, 30 March 1864, JHMP-SHC.

[39] JHM to MM, 1, 27 June 1864, JHMP-SHC; Ramage, "Hunts and Morgans," 282-91.

[40] MM to HM, 24 July 1865, HMP-UK; Thomas, *Morgan,* 90-91; Holland, *Morgan,* vii.

[41] St. Leger Grenfell to JHM, 15 February 1864, JHMP-SHC; Thomas L. Connelly and Archer Jones, *The Politics of Command: Factions and Ideas in Confederate Strategy* (Baton Rouge, 1973), 72-81; John F. Marszalek, ed., *The Diary of Miss Emma Holmes, 1861-1866* (Baton Rouge, 1979), 261-62.

# Bibliographical Essay

The John Hunt Morgan Papers and the Alice Ready Journal in the Southern Historical Collection at the University of North Carolina in Chapel Hill have the most valuable information on Morgan's marriage. The Hunt-Morgan Papers at the University of Kentucky have useful letters from Morgan's wife and other family members. Family correspondence is also contained in the Morgan and Duke Families Papers at the Filson Club in Louisville. Basil Duke's *History of Morgan's Cavalry* (Cincinnati, 1867) is a respected account by a participant in the events of Morgan's career.

Lowell Harrison's *The Civil War in Kentucky* (Lexington, 1975) provides an excellent brief overview of Morgan's career, relating it to strategy in Kentucky and the West. In addition to presenting an insightful analysis of the effect of Morgan's repeated attacks on the Louisville and Nashville Railroad, Edison H. Thomas in *John Hunt Morgan and His Raiders* (Lexington, 1975) includes considerable information on Morgan's family life. The most detailed biography is Cecil F. Holland, *Morgan and His Raiders* (New York, 1942). Along with a balanced and restrained account of Morgan's career, Holland wrote a great deal about Martha Ready and her family. The author's Ph.D. dissertation, "The Hunts and Morgans: A Study of a Prominent Kentucky Family" (University of Kentucky, 1972) considers Morgan's career, and the author's *John Wesley Hunt: Pioneer Merchant, Manufacturer and Financier* (Lexington, 1974) discusses Morgan's family background.

**Sophonisba P. Breckinridge**
Courtesy of Special Collections, University of Kentucky Library

# Family Influences on a Progressive
# The Early Years of Sophonisba P. Breckinridge

*by James C. Klotter*

The new baby was born a Breckinridge. In its birthplace of Kentucky, that was both significant and consequential. And, more importantly, the child knew that very early.

Being a Breckinridge meant membership in the state's most prominent political family, with celebrated ancestors and a proud tradition. The very name offered a birthright of advantages — recognition, a kinship network, and deferential treatment. In a more abstract sense the family heritage presented new members with an established philosophy, a sense of the past, and an awareness of future needs. But even at this, even if the Breckinridge heritage gave children models for future emulation, these family exemplars proved less adaptable for the new Breckinridge. After all, the role models were primarily male; Sophonisba Preston Breckinridge was female.

While Sophonisba recognized the genuine accomplishments of some Breckinridge women, she — like all of the children — heard most often of the achievements of the family's men. She knew of the successes of great-grandfather John Breckinridge — lawyer, farmer, slaveholder, introducer of the Kentucky Resolutions of 1798, Jeffersonian United States senator, and U.S. attorney general at his death in 1806. She was aware of the talents of her brilliant and vitriolic grandfather Robert Jefferson Breckinridge, who died in 1871, only five years after her birth. He was Kentucky state representative, Presbyterian minister and moderator of his church's General Assembly, pioneering state superintendent of public instruction, seminary founder, anti-Catholic orator, author of numerous books, editor of several journals, supporter of the Union, and temporary chairman of the 1864 convention that renominated his friend Abraham Lincoln. She learned, too, of the famous leaders of the Preston family whose name she also bore.

But, most of all, Sophonisba Breckinridge's attention was

focused on her father, William Campbell Preston Breckinridge. Born in 1837, "Willie" (as he was called) had been trained in the law, then had fought for the southern cause opposed by his father in wartime. Later W.C.P. Breckinridge would gain national fame for his oratorical powers and would serve five terms as Democratic representative in the United States House. In and out of Congress he took stands on public issues in such a way that the best label for him is simply "progressive Bourbon." Ending his career with seven years of work as editorial writer for his son's paper, he died in 1904 as a respected member of the Lexington community.[1]

In the half-century after his death, historians accorded W.C.P. Breckinridge a major place in state and national history. But over time, historians' perspectives and evaluations changed. By the second half of the twentieth century, his daughter began to receive deserved recognition as an equally important force in America's recent past. Increasing attention to women's role in society soon contributed to Sophonisba Preston Breckinridge's replacement of her illustrious father in new historical dictionaries and encyclopedias. Shortly thereafter, she eclipsed his fame.

All of this was supremely ironic, for Willie Breckinridge's example spurred his daughter's ambition and she desired to follow, not supplant, him. On the other hand, had the father lived to witness her major accomplishments, it seems likely that he would have not only been proud of his offspring, but would have approved her success. For in her, his spirit lived on.

I

Sophonisba Breckinridge — or "Nisba" as family and friends called her — lived a life that amply justified history's favorable evaluations. Thirty-eight years old at her father's death, she already had exhibited that her way departed from traditional patterns of Breckinridge women. A decade earlier, Nisba had been the first woman admitted to the Kentucky bar; in 1901 she received a Ph.D. from the University of Chicago, the first woman to receive that degree in her field; three years later, Dr. Breckinridge earned a J.D. degree from the same university's law school. After that, her career was kaleidoscopic, and even a brief outline of it indicates just how varied were her interests and actions.

As an educator, for example, Nisba became an instructor in the University of Chicago's department of household administration, and, for a time concurrently, also taught at the Chicago School of Civics and Philanthropy. Succeeding Graham Taylor to the deanship of the latter school, she led its transformation into the Graduate School of Social Service Administration at the university. As teacher and administrator, Dr. Breckinridge remained active even after retirement.

Outside the classroom the Kentuckian spent numerous summer vacations as a social worker at Jane Addams' Hull House in Chicago. She also served for a time as that city's health inspector, as first secretary of Chicago's Immigrants Protection League, and as member of the executive committee of the Illinois Consumer's League. Aiding a garment workers' strike and campaigning for a federal child labor law were but two other such activities. Long an advocate of civil rights, Nisba was elected vice-president of the National American Women Suffrage Association (N.A.W.S.A.) in 1911 and held membership very early in both the National Association for the Advancement of Colored People (N.A.A.C.P.) and the Urban League. During the First World War, she aided in the formation and was the first treasurer of the Woman's Peace Party; during peacetime, she represented her country in 1933 as the first woman to serve as official delegate to the Pan-American Congress. No danger of academic isolation existed for her.

Somehow, amidst these myriad activities, the activist scholar found time to combine service with research. Dr. Breckinridge's many books covered such varied topics as a history of legal tender, child delinquency and truancy, state poor laws, woman's rights, and a biography of her reform-minded sister-in-law. Articles appeared in periodicals such as the *Journal of Political Economy,* the *Journal of Home Economics, Survey,* and the *American Journal of Sociology.* For some two decades, she also served as managing editor and contributed to the *Social Science Review.*[2]

Judged as teacher, as interested citizen, or as scholar,

then, Sophonisba Breckinridge receives high marks for concern, achievement, and quality. But if her accomplishments are clear, the reasons for them are less so. What forces shaped the young, southern lady into a strong, mature leader of the Progressive Era? Were her family influences positive or negative? And why, simply, did she follow the path she did? Answers to those questions lie in her pre-Chicago years, for the most part, and, like so many answers to complex questions, are not simple. To understand Sophonisba Preston Breckinridge's motivation and behavior requires an evaluation of her formative years, her Kentucky environment, and, most of all, her family life.

II

Nisba, born on 1 April 1866, eleven months after her father returned from the Civil War, was the second surviving child and the first that Willie could be with from birth. She received much love from a father who had, by his account, built up a surplus of that emotion during wartime. Sister Ella, already four when Nisba arrived, seems to have been her mother's favorite, having received Issa Desha Breckinridge's full attention while the husband and father was away. Sibling rivalry and perhaps some jealousy may have resulted, judging from a reflective Sophonisba's autobiography, written just before her death. She recalled then how Ella, who "was not entirely frank," was also "much cleverer, really cleverer, but she had many distractions. She had great charm and very early became attractive so that boys and young men flock about her." Decidedly unattractive, the thin and sad-looking Nisba reacted in a diametrically opposite way from Ella. When their father, for example, told the two that they could have either one dollar or a "little party" if they got perfect marks, Nisba took the money, Ella the party. Indicative of her later philanthropic pursuits, Nisba saved her dollars until a missionary from the Orient told of Chinese poverty. Then, "I gave her my savings. My mother never forgave me for taking my little savings. . . ." Ella, though a sister, was not a close companion.[3]

Three other children completed the Breckinridge household. Desha, only fifteen months younger than his "Nim," remained a kind friend and in later life defended her as she did him. As young adults, the two argued and disagreed over women's rights, but still expressed sentiments indicating real affection for each other. Brother Robert, on the other hand, was a loner whom the family could never quite control or understand. Sister Curry, some nine years younger, was Nisba's closest female companion in the family, but her sufferings and outlook created a gulf neither could fully bridge, albeit both tried. Although handicapped by dyslexia, Curry had an active mind, a talent for making friends, and, like Nisba, a concern for helping others. Yet the way her older sister remembered Curry reveals much. Recalled Sophonisba: "She was a strange person, much more interesting than I and much more fundamentally honest. One day she looked at me quite seriously and said, 'Of course, Nisba, you do mean all right, but you never had any common sense.' Especially I regret my treatment of her when we were abroad in the Early Nineties. That was when I was horribly[,] wickedly pious, concerned for my own soul, and I made Sunday a dreadful day, even in Paris."

Guilt and jealousy, friendship and affection — these characterize Sophonisba Breckinridge's relationship with her brothers and sisters. While she felt a "very real weakness" in dealing with them, and while she even stated that none had any real affection for her, that emotion and that assertion both seem overstated. And while her sibling interactions contain many elements important in shaping the mature person, they are in themselves not the key.[4]

### III

Parental influences were. Her guide, her motivator, her example, her idol was clearly W.C.P. Breckinridge. For if she loved her mother, she adored and virtually worshipped her father. To the end of her life, in the last days, she still judged others — and herself — by his image and memory. She did so, not in a thoughtless, wistful way, but as an intelligent person who recognized what she was doing.

Sophonisba filled her manuscript autobiography with revelations of Willie's influence on her. Her writing began: "I have wanted to write an account of my father, but I seem unable to make a beginning of a biography of him, while I cannot speak of myself without speaking at length of him." Later, when describing (as she did often) her "dullness," she said that one of the two things that "saved" her was her love for her father and her desire to please him. In assessing her childhood as a good one generally, Nisba recalled, "I was anxious to please my father. He was wonderfully patient and kind." Still later, she noted that at college she sought high marks, "because it pleased my Father to have me make good grades."[5]

Quite evidently, Willie Breckinridge's counsel to his wife when the daughter was but five months old — "Don't let Nisba forget me" — had been taken to heart. The mother tried to teach all the children, she said, to be just like their father. Willie, for his part, took a particular interest in this young daughter who so reminded him of his first child, his "little boy in heaven." Learning her letters from her father's law books, Nisba apparently comprehended quickly, for by the age of seven she already was getting perfect scores. Moreover, she learned from him the unconventional idea that women did not have to be bound to traditional patterns of behavior.[6]

It was a strange lesson from a surprising source at an unexpected time. Women, after all, were still expected to conform to an ideal, an image. The southern lady on her pedestal should, the stereotype often said, be educated in "womanly" pursuits, be refined, be modest, and be virtuous. Compassionate, emotional (rather than logical), and submissive, she should, as one author suggested, "love, honor, obey, and occasionally amuse her husband, . . . bring up his children and manage his household." Seldom did she feel sexual stirrings or passion. In Margaret Ripley Wolfe's words, "If the literature were taken seriously, readers might logically conclude that the South had been populated by a massive outbreak of virgin births."[7]

Most Kentuckians honored this image of southern womanhood. A reporter in 1879 cried out that woman's sphere was that of mother and wife, and nothing further. The next year a state senator made his feelings clear and his options few when he exclaimed, "Give me a wife that can love, honor and look up to me as her lord and master, or give me separation and death." Aging slavery emancipationist Cassius Marcellus Clay praised the "poetry of creation" that existed in his time and condemned any changes that would lead to "communism of the sexes." Modification in the existing mores, said a Louisville minister, would be an assault "upon, not only our common Christianity, but our social order."[8] Legal restrictions supported the established pattern. As late as 1890, the state had no property law for married women, no law permitting women to make wills without their husband's consent, no law giving women full rights to their own earnings, no law granting women guardianship over their own children, and, of course, no law allowing them full voting privileges. As Paul Fuller notes, "Kentucky laws in the rights of women were among the most backward in the country."[9]

Yet, despite all these attempts to shape a society to honor an ideal, the image still conflicted harshly with the reality. Kentucky women on the frontier, from the state's beginning, had fought and died; had — like one of Nisba's relatives — managed large estates; had not only survived but had often prospered when men were absent; had spoken out on issues; and had overcome the emotional and physical destruction of war. By the time Sophonisba Breckinridge reached her teens, this conflict between image and reality was erupting in full force.

A more favorable environment now existed. By 1867, Kentucky had its first suffrage organization; in 1879 suffragist Susan B. Anthony spoke in the state; in 1881, when Nisba was fifteen, the American Woman Suffrage Association (AWSA) met in Louisville, the first such gathering in the South; that same year leaders founded a Kentucky branch, also the first in the region; in 1883, Mary B. Clay (Cassius Clay's own daughter) was elected national president of the AWSA; by 1884 two more of Clay's daughters were writing columns on women's activities in Kentucky newspapers; and in 1888, still another Clay offspring, Laura, became president of the new Kentucky Equal Rights Association. The large, commanding, strong Laura Clay, who — like her sisters — had been influenced in her activities by the divorce of their parents, soon led the equal rights movement in the state and the South. Her Lexington home and aristocratic prominence made her a near and appealing model for young Nisba.[10]

An even closer physical and emotional model, however, was her father. When a youngster at Centre College in the 1850s, Willie had seen women compete with men. Three of his cousins (daughters of the college president) took their work there, but, because of their sex, could not receive degrees. W.C.P. Breckinridge had witnessed the control over her own life exerted by his grandmother, John Breckinridge's widow of a half-century. He recognized the abilities of other women in a talented family. Sophonisba concisely summarized her father's outlook as a result of these experiences: "My father was never a suffragist, but as he had favored the development of facilities for the education of women and negroes he was always for fair play."[11]

Actually, Willie Breckinridge may have been more supportive than his daughter remembered four decades later. He favored coeducational colleges and praised women who voted in local school elections. In an 1898 editorial he admitted that he saw no reason why women should not vote in all elections, although he hedged on that stand at times.[12] His own thought process and reasons for supporting and encouraging his Nisba in her course were revealed in a frank 1902 editorial worth quoting at length. Under the title, "The Problem of the Daughter," Willie wrote:

> It is only when the rare girl, who in spite of all her hereditary instinct to submission and to filling her allotted place in that "sphere" of life (which someone else has assigned her to), finds the virtue of her college life working in her; when she begins to think a little of what she is doing; and after a season of irresolute and uncomfortable protest, comes to the conclusion that artificial activities are not as interesting as real ones. It is only when this unnatural daughter begins to murmur against the usual order of things, . . . that the father is forced to pause and examine. And if he be open-minded, as many such fathers are, moreover, who has maintained a comradeship with

his daughter since her childhood, he begins after a little to agree with her. . . . Later on he begins to wonder why this daughter, for whose intellect and character he, after some years of acquaintance, has a distinct respect, should, in case she does not marry, have no apparent place in life to fly: why, when so many jobs are lacking the doing because of the inadequate supply of intelligent and capable doers, the custom should close the door of activity in the face of a person young, vigorous, intelligent, and with a perfect passion of interest in all the realities of life . . . . He begins to feel with her the troublings of the new "social conscience. . . ."

As a result of all these reflections and awakenings, the father at length begins to question the system which in his circle of society prepares a daughter exclusively for marriage and to be a costly and pleasing plaything in her father's or her husband's home . . . . He wonders if perhaps the system which differentiates so sharply between the activities of a man and a woman is not a perverted one . . . . He begins to comprehend that some of the strange new demands made by women are but the outcome of an unrepressed individuality, are but a part of the development of the new social conscience in which women, as well as men . . . have become the heirs . . . . He becomes rather more sympathetic than disapproving.[13]

In Willie Breckinridge, Nisba had more than a father; she had a helpmate.

During their early years together, the father continually influenced the daughter. But after four years as one of its first women students at Lexington's State College, Sophonisba Breckinridge departed for the unknown of a northern school. In 1884, she entered Wellesley College in Massachusetts as a first-year student. The school's motto, *Incipit vita Nuova* (the new life begins), accurately reflected her future. This eighteen-year-old daughter of an ex-Confederate, who would soon preach the South's cause in the halls of Congress, now found herself in a woman's school in the center of Yankeedom. The opportunity for loneliness, despair, and alienation was obvious. And, like many entering freshmen then and later, she experienced some of these emotions. Yet, above all, she overcame them — and matured both emotionally and intellectually.

Her parents supported Nisba throughout. Writing separately, and frequently, they kept her informed of current Kentucky gossip, of Washington happenings, and of their own lives. Issa Desha Breckinridge's letters frequently focused on the trivial and traditional interests of women of her generation and class, but occasionally on more personal matters as well. Telling Nisba, "You know . . . that you are *your father's idol*," Issa also suggested that Willie loved her, his second-born, more than any of the other children. Turning to her own concerns, the mother told Nisba that if strong and healthy, she could do *"all that God ever wanted women to do!"* She had birth and breeding already; only maturity was required. Privately, Issa Breckinridge wrote a friend that her freshman daughter differed little from her classmates, and was subject "to like troubles to other girls who are not wise." One particular motherly worry was that all the girls wore their hair drawn back in the "modern" fashion.[14]

A more worrisome concern came when Issa and Willie first took their daughter to the college and encountered black students. This issue troubled Mrs. Breckinridge, who asked soon afterwards if Nisba was "thrown with them in any way." Issa wrote that she could not treat blacks as equals, "but they can do you no harm, and I can trust you to treat them properly." Willie responded to the perceived problem more directly. When a friend asked whether he would allow his daughter to be enrolled with blacks, Willie answered firmly: "She got on all right with the boys; I think that she will get on all right with the colored." Nisba later recalled, admiringly, that Frederick Douglass, who visited the Wellesley campus while she was there, "often said that my father was the white man with whom he could most freely and without consciousness of radical differences discuss problems of public concern." The young Kentuckian, however, needed some time to adjust. Nisba noted that she disliked Douglass' "pitiful" story about the harshness of slavery and recalled that when sitting at a dining table with blacks she could serve them all right, "but my own food I could not swallow." Time and experience would overcome many of her prejudices.[15]

Willie Breckinridge continued to support, encourage, and counsel his daughter in this new environment. Writing to Nisba in September 1884, just after she entered school, he discussed her homesickness and, almost harshly, told her that she had been too sheltered for too long. Now she must conquer the emotions within. She apparently did so, for her father's correspondence turned to quieter matters: Study the Bible, "a wonderful book," he advised; avoid "the needle, the schoolroom & the story" and aim instead for chemistry and the sciences, a more profitable field for women; do your own shopping, Willie suggested, and rely on your own tastes, for self-control and self-mastery come from self-dependence. Since a "feeble" will created much unhappiness, he had wanted his baby, "from the hour of your birth," to be strong. Her happiness had long been his chief desire, even when he criticized. Yet as his loving, dutiful, "pure" daughter, his Nisba had always known of his love and of his belief that all would turn out well.

By May 1885, any concerns had apparently vanished. The congressman was comforted, he wrote, by the awareness that his daughter could make her own living, should he die suddenly. "I have loved *you,*" Willie confessed, "all these years; and I know that it is inevitable that you will drift away from me, and I will make no complaint at it." He would be happy if only she remembered that "Duty is the noblest pursuit & compatible with the highest attainment." He added: "You don't know how glad I am that you are not a genius; but a hard-working, dutiful, trained intellect, capable of doing anything because you are willing to undergo the necessary labor and submit to the request[ed] discipline." A young woman, still uncertain of her life's course, received needed encouragement from her father. The results were edifying.[16]

Sophonisba Preston Breckinridge enjoyed school, performed well, and left her mark. Fellow students three times selected the southerner as class president. Grades matched high expectations. Social life flourished. Life seemed good. The attractive Massachusetts countryside, the nearby lake, the New England autumn colors — all were new and delightful experiences for the young southerner. Her small room had a bureau on the left, a table on the right, red cheesecloth over the door, and the family picture on a washstand. The slender-faced, dark-eyed, dark-haired student would sit in the quiet of her room, look out her window, and work, at peace with herself and her school. Wellesley agreed with Nisba and she with it.[17]

Schoolgirl letters reveal both a young, naive, and impressionable girl and a mature, serious, and studious woman. College days were ones of transformation and, more often than not, the student won out over the socialite. Early in her Wellesley career, after describing in some detail a costume party outfit, Nisba added that such future affairs would be missed, because "things like these take so much time and don't pay." By first semester's end, in a mood apparently experienced by few collegiates, she felt so good after exams that she wanted them to return: "They have been so very lovely and I have enjoyed every one." As a sophomore in 1885, she made her first public speech, entered a reading club, tried her hand on the rowing crew, and described herself as being in a "very blissful state."[18]

A "tired girl" by semester's end, Sophonisba recovered and entered her junior year even more ambitious. Sunday school teaching, a public address at a temperance meeting, a debate on her father's favorite topic, the tariff — these combined with usual study to make a school year full.[19] The young Kentuckian matured more during the winter of 1886-87 and began to think seriously of her world, her life, and her future. Early in the term, she wrote Issa: "I am trying very hard this year to make my life as even as possible, that is, to eliminate all the nervous, hurried element & take things calmly. And I hope I am succeeding." This attempt to control her emotions matched an attempt to revise her wearing attire. Several letters passed between mother and daughter concerning Nisba's desire to wear the looser and freer style clothes of "a working woman." The younger Breckinridge also wanted her sister to stop wearing "those heavy dresses and things tight about her waist" that gave headaches, and turn instead to the freedom of the "new" style. The surface issue symbolized the daughter's deeper change.[20]

By March 1887, restlessness mixed with uncertainty, as

Nisba contemplated the future. "I ache to get out and work," she wrote her mother, then less than three weeks later told her father a similar story: "Nothing extraordinary ever happens here[.] That, I suppose[,] is why the days are so happy. And they are happy. I some times wonder how it will seem to go out and fight when all has been so easy here. And yet I shall be glad to go fight — glad to feel some times the delight that must come from doing something hard." She added later: "Sometimes, I think if the Lord wants to make me perfectly content in Heaven He will give hard problems that I can at least solve. But then I suppose all things are really just that are they not?" As she neared her twenty-first birthday, Nisba said she felt "sadly old"; in reality, she was maturing, not only in years but in intellect.[21]

Despite her personal progress and successes, despite Willie's words to the contrary, Nisba approached graduation still dependent on her parents in many ways. Earlier she asked her father what he wanted her to do after school: "I know it will be decided for me, but if I knew what I thought I was working towards it would make it easier. . . ." Three months later Nisba indicated her own hopes when she asked Willie if he would let her work for him. "I will be a 'good girl,'" she promised. A proud father delivered the Wellesley commencement address while a satisfied and equally proud daughter received her long-sought diploma in late spring 1888. Yet Sophonisba Preston Breckinridge left college still uncertain of her future.[22]

But, more important, she had a future, a promising one. The young graduate may still have questioned her worth, intelligence, and abilities, but others recognized her extraordinary talents. Alice Stone Blackwell, the sensitive editorial writer for the *Woman's Journal,* told a Kentuckian, for example, to recruit young Miss Breckinridge to the Woman's Suffrage Association: "She would be a valuable acquisition, I think, being a bright girl & a college graduate." Noted Blackwell also: "Her father's commencement oration is very highly praised — & he said something friendly about woman suffrage, too."[23] But Nisba's recognized high promise remained yet unfulfilled. Ahead lay a turbulent decade that almost destroyed that promise.

## IV

Sophonisba Breckinridge accurately remembered the years immediately following graduation as muddled ones that formed part of "a confused life." She had "pretended" that she would follow in her father's footsteps and study law, but few schools admitted women. Additionally, her mother continued frail and the family, as usual, lacked money. Given all this, Nisba did just what she and her father did not want — she got a high school teaching job in Washington. From 1888 to 1890 she taught mathematics, with little apparent love for her work. Still very religious, Sophonisba also seriously considered joining an Episcopal sisterhood, but did not.[24]

Teaching had certain benefits, of course. She could remain with the family, give her first earnings to her ailing mother, and help with housework. It was probably during this time, also, that Susan B. Anthony spent the winter as a guest of Congressman Breckinridge's family. The women's rights leader used the opportunity to enlighten Nisba on suffrage matters, "to the amusement and sometimes discomfiture of her modest little victim." It was still a learning time, even after college. But in the spring of 1890 a serious attack of what she called the "grip" ended Breckinridge's schoolteaching career in the capital. Returning to Lexington with the rest of the family in the fall, Nisba recovered sufficently to begin sampling once again the social life she had largely foregone at Wellesley. The Kentuckian enjoyed horseback riding and the races. There were friends' dinner parties that attracted the talented of the city. At one such gathering, women in formal evening gowns joined their male guests in rooms ablaze from pink candles in silver candelabra. In the flickering light, the state's nationally known literary figures, the serious-looking James Lane Allen and the younger John Fox, Jr., read portions of their works, and men and women mingled and talked. Despite the romantic atmosphere of that and other parties, however, the single, twenty-four-year-old Sophonisba developed no firm male attachments. In fact, she later admitted to having been in love twice in her youth, but "neither really loved me though. Each for the moment thought that he did. Both married women who were cleverer than I was and both made happy gracious homes."

Although Nisba mentioned no names, one beau was thought to be her former classmate Thomas Hunt Morgan, the brilliant Lexingtonian who would win a Nobel Prize for his work in genetics. But unification of these two famous families and two fine intellects was not to be. Nisba remained single.[25]

Still plagued by health problems, Sophonisba soon joined sister Curry in a sojourn in Europe. Travel, combined with further study, renewed her determination to become a lawyer. Again she went to her father's office, this time to study his books, not just to learn the alphabet from them. In helping Willie prepare cases, his daughter left little doubt of her abilities. Then, almost by accident, Nisba accompanied her brother to Frankfort one day and while there asked the chief justice of the state's highest court if he would examine her for the bar. A wartime comrade of Colonel Breckinridge, the judge agreed and assembled two other justices. It was a tense, unprecedented occasion, and the examination dragged on for over three hours. The decision was favorable — Sophonisba Breckinridge was qualified to practice and was admitted to the bar, the first of her sex so honored in Kentucky.[26] In 1897, this woman the New York *Times* then described as quiet and unassuming, with a clear voice and some of her father's eloquence, was qualified further to practice before the state's highest judicial body. While one goal had been achieved, happiness did not follow.[27]

Emotional peaks and valleys continued to characterize Nisba's post-Wellesley years. Joy over entering her father's firm was tempered by few clients. Being with her family was dampened by her mother's death in 1892. And the long-felt need to work, to accomplish, was unsatisfied by a lawyer's toil. Young attorney Breckinridge finally decided to return to school, there, perhaps, to find whatever it was that could give satisfaction and meaning to her life. But just as she began to make that move, events occurred that shook Sophonisba's confidence to the foundations and tested her emotions to the utmost.

V

Initial rumors in 1893 of her father's longtime sexual involvement with a mistress named Madeline Pollard were easily dismissed as vicious lies. Then came Pollard's lawsuit claiming that Willie had promised to marry her and had not — thus a request for a breach-of-contract judgment. The trial followed, then Willie's admission of an affair, one that perhaps had produced children. The jury's guilty verdict was anticlimactic. Here stood her idolized father, publicly acknowledging that he had been unfaithful, unfaithful to the mother Nisba loved, unfaithful because of a woman so young that she had passed as Willie's daughter. Here stood the man Nisba had modeled her life after, the man whose praise she sought above all other, the man who had advised development of a strong will and who had stressed the importance of duty and self-control. Here stood, above all, her honored father, in disgrace.[28]

Everything could have combined to produce her total repudiation of him. She could have easily rejected Willie Breckinridge and all he represented, and — like Laura Clay — have devoted her attention to the equal rights struggle with increased ferocity. Nisba could have struck out in utter frustration at him for all the pain and embarrassment he had caused. She could, with justification, have turned her back on her father and walked away with few regrets. Yet she could not — and did not — do any of this. The evidence suggests a continuance of love and an outpouring of understanding. She might not accept or approve his course, but she would not allow that act to destroy the image or, for that matter, the reality she called father.

Sophonisba Breckinridge remembered instead Willie's devotion to the dying Issa, calling his aid "endlessly kind." She wrote of all the love and affection her father had given the family, of his deep interest in her own life, of his frankness with her. Nisba recalled the good of the past, apparently accepted Willie's transgression as a deep but single flaw that did not destroy his shining armor, and continued to function as devoted daughter.[29]

But if on the surface Sophonisba displayed no scars, the whole affair may well have left deeper, hidden emotional marks. It would be too much to claim that the scandal sparked Nisba's reform spirit to action, for she had already long shown an inclination to her later course. The change, if there was change, appears to have been more subtle.

Nisba did not abandon many of her father's deepest faiths — his optimism, his sense of America's promise, his devotion to continuing certain traditions — but after the Pollard trial she did impose modifications. Her father's own imperfections seem to have made her more tolerant of the weaknesses of others. If he was not perfect, then she did not have to be either. A burden lifted. Unlike those charity workers who held to the "Victorian ethos" that blamed the poor's condition on individual shortcomings of the "unfortunates," she began to stress instead environmental causes for poverty. As her earlier, deep religious feelings declined in intensity, Sophonisba turned to social welfare work as her outlet for enacting basic Christian values into reality. Rather than follow a more conservative path, she chose to be an innovator who challenged many nineteenth century beliefs. After the scandal, Sophonisba Breckinridge still remained very much her father's daughter, but it was a transformed woman he now knew.[30]

Further unpleasantness awaited. Throughout the rest of the 1890s Nisba faced difficult situations. When Willie asked her to return from the University of Chicago to take care of his new (and third) wife, the daughter did not refuse. She found a woman suffering from serious hysterical attacks and through "sheer will power" Nisba sometimes could control her. But if not, as she wrote, "the results were quite dreadful for she became very abusive, especially about my father. His patience was incredible and he and I would go through these experiences together." Adversity strengthened already close familial bonds.[31]

Returning after a time to Chicago classes, Sophonisba continued to receive evidence of an aging father's devotion and support. In April 1899, Willie reminded Nisba that on each Easter Sunday morning he thanked God that she was such "an unalloyed blessing and comfort" to her family. Four months later, the father expressed his happiness over his daughter's preparation for "independent life-work."[32] News followed news as letters and reports told of the daughter's advancement — a master's degree in 1897, the Ph.D. four years after that, an instructorship, an assistant deanship, then the law degree (with the highest class average) in 1904. After the last honor, a joyful Willie wrote, "I am growing quite famous as your father; a fame very dear to me." By November the proud patriarch looked forward to Nisba's arrival at Thanksgiving. Then, on 20 November 1904, W.C.P. Breckinridge died. The bond that held Sophonisba so close was now broken.[33]

## VI

With her father's death, Nisba severed most close ties to Kentucky. The past she now sought to leave behind. Still, she could not forget the Commonwealth entirely. Through her brother Desha's investments, she drew some income from state businesses. Appeals for her to speak were not always refused, as she returned to plead with the legislature for full suffrage, or to talk on "Women in Industry," or to dedicate a school, or to promote some other cause.[34] As editor of the *Herald,* Desha Breckinridge sometimes called on Nisba to write editorials or signed stories for the paper. She obliged and he reciprocated by reprinting stories favorable to his sister and keeping citizens of the central Bluegrass informed of her activities. One 1911 account from the *World To-day,* for example, praised the good legal mind and varied interests of Dr. Breckinridge, then concluded: "People say that Miss Breckinridge is like her father in many ways, and that she inherited from him her keen mind, her social insight, her unfailing sympathy, and a rare personal charm. But Miss Breckinridge adds to these qualities a genuine humility, a great eagerness to serve, and a willingness to serve in humble ways."[35] Family and Kentucky remained a part of Nisba, but, by leaving both for Chicago, she became a more independent person, accepted for herself and her accomplishments, and not just for her past. Breckinridge's future would lie not in Kentucky but in the northern city. There she would make her most notable accomplishments.

When Nisba first came to Chicago in the 1890s, the city represented many facets of American life. It contained both reactionaries and radicals, and saw both clash in open warfare. The metropolis included luxurious, sheltered mansions on

Prairie Avenue or Lake Shore Drive for the McCormicks, Fieldses, Armours, Pullmans, and other wealthy families, as well as dirty, ill-constructed frame houses for workers near the infamous "Back-of-the-Yards." Both the elite and the forgotten, though, could smell the stench drifting from the stockyards — the manure, the hides, the slaughter refuse, the street garbage, the pollution of Bubbly Creek. Chicago — Carl Sandburg's "Hog Butcher for the World" — inspired Americans by its ability to rebuild from the fire of 1871, and impressed them as the great White City of the World's Columbia Exposition of 1893, yet it shamed them with its unpaved streets, corruption, and class differences. Breckinridge's Chicago was like nothing she had known.

Still, the city attracted, both for its strengths and weaknesses. The paradox of poverty amidst great progress made Chicago more of a mystery, more of a place that required reform and understanding, more of a testing ground for both ideas and people. When Nisba arrived, she had already seen European cities of similar size, but knew well few large urban areas in America — only the nation's capital and Louisville. The latter's population was less than one-eighth that of the city on the lake, however, and its problems had been fewer and far different. Now in this new environment, Breckinridge resided in a metropolis whose population had increased almost six-fold in three decades, in an urban area where three of every four people were foreign-born or whose parents were, in a center of exploding transportation, supply, and merchandising businesses, and in a city pulsating with human energies.

Tragedy was a part of Chicago life in those early years. At the end of the exposition came the assassination of the gray-bearded, dark-eyed former Kentuckian, Mayor Carter Harrison, then the full effects of the Panic of 1893. The Pullman strike of the next year repeated the earlier bitterness workers voiced and owners resented. And the quieter sadness continued, as children suffered malnourishment, disease, and sometimes death. Hope for the future, however, made up the city's psyche as well. Intellectuals saw in the reborn University of Chicago an example that could save the nation and educate its citizens. From its opening in 1892, the school and its president

William Rainey Harper attracted an excellent staff and became a positive symbol of Chicago. Some first-rate cultural attractions added to the image of the White City.[36] This combination of failures and successes, this alliance of "pork and Plato," this massive example of despair and of hope, was a magnet that attracted a remarkably talented group of reformers who sought to bridge the gap between the privileged and nonprivileged. Making an organized, path-breaking attack on urban poverty, they sought to correct this ugliness lurking beneath the American dream. And, in some ways, they succeeded.[37]

Progressivism was emerging and its currents swept Sophonisba Breckinridge into the mainstream. Like other reformers of the period, she was young, unmarried, college-educated, and from a well-to-do family.[38] Many of her allies and their counterparts across America combined a sense of responsibility with a sense of mission. They infused the movement with a strong, moral, almost evangelistic will, yet one that recognized that old answers would not serve them. The new generation translated this reform impulse, this idealistic faith in the future, into a realism that accepted the government's role as vital. These Progressives placed their faith in social democracy, in institutionalized change, in method and technique. Their idols had traditional roots; their principles suggested an "old-fashioned" concept of humanitarianism and morality; their ethos harkened back to personal responsibility. Yet they went further than any before them in their direct efforts to better the lives of the city's poor and ignored. Wrong at times? Certainly. Motivated by mixed and sometimes selfish motives? Yes. Elitist on occasion? Definitely. The reformers could be found guilty on all these and other counts. Still, and above all else, they tried. They cared.[39]

Among this group of reformers in Chicago were numerous women who would influence Breckinridge, as she would them. Sharing a generally similar philosophy and dedicated to like goals, this first generation of professionals in social work formed a tight-knit core that was not always united, not always right, but was seldom inactive. They gave each other emotional and practical support. Dean of Women and very close friend Marion Talbott, for example, offered Nisba a fellowship to attend the University and was credited by Breckinridge as one who clarified her thinking. At Hull House, where Nisba spent her summers, the magnetic yet sometimes remote Jane Addams had already begun the toils that would win her a Nobel Prize in 1931. Joining Addams' work among the immigrants was Julia C. Lathrop, congressman's daughter, Vassar graduate, and the first woman admitted to the Illinois bar. The plain, mournful-looking Lathrop would eventually teach with Nisba, work on similar projects, and then head the United States Children's Bureau in 1912. Another Hull House occupant, Mary E. McDowell, moved "Back-of-the Yards" and began settlement work there. Joining the group later from Wellesley College was Edith Abbott, the daughter of a Nebraska lieutenant governor and sister of the equally well-known Grace. Both Abbotts would form a long and close association with Breckinridge, as would still others, such as Florence Kelley. Like many of her associates, Nisba had spent recent years drifting — a confused, purposeless, and dissatisfied woman. Prepared by her background, family, college days, and Kentucky experience, Breckinridge at last found in Chicago the niche she had long sought. That city, in David Potter's words, "was the frontier for American Women."

By the first decades of the twentieth century, these reformers had overcome obstacles, attracted support, and achieved so much that they became almost heroines. Breckinridge and the others certainly became role models to new generations of women who would follow their professional paths. Sophonisba, not a radical, did assume more extreme stands than many of her fellow reformers. More supportive of blacks than a Graham Taylor, less fearful of immigration than John R. Commons, or Richard T. Ely, or Edward T. Ross, she went beyond those who sought to improve conditions simply by inculcating the poor with the mores of work, thrift, and abstinence. In time, she went beyond the desire simply to improve institutions and sought instead to redo them. Nisba did not fear the state or the new social order she envisioned.[41]

In practice, Breckinridge's philosophy centered on three concrete areas of concern — blacks, women, and the poor generally. Negroes received less attention in her publications than the other two groups, as a rule, but she still emerged as a leading white advocate of black rights. Her stress on environment allowed a view more conducive to understanding the difficulties of Chicago blacks. And, like other reformers, she perceived that blacks differed from immigrant groups in the problems they confronted. Through books, through efforts on the advisory committee of the N.A.A.C.P., and through work with the Association of Black Women, Professor Breckinridge sought to transform public opinion so that blacks could claim their place in a pluralistic society.[42]

More central to her concerns was the women's rights movement. Aside from her father's interest and the influences of Laura Clay and Susan Anthony, Nisba had a further motivation. Her aunt, Mary Desha, had suffered discrimination, yet had made her way in a male world. One of the founders of the Daughters of the American Revolution (D.A.R.) in 1890, Mary at that time had intended an organization devoted chiefly to benefit womankind. Nisba, supportive of her aunt's aims and the founders' goals, later wrote that if she had been at Washington at the beginning of the D.A.R., she probably would have been one of the founders. As it was, Breckinridge did serve on the first executive committee.[43]

But Nisba's interests turned to other organizations, as the Daughters moved away from suffrage and equal rights issues. Increasingly active in the women's movement, Breckinridge was elected as a vice-president of the N.A.W.S.A. in 1911. Acceptance of the office came, however, only after an exchange of letters between Breckinridge and Laura Clay. Alienated more and more by the association's stress on a national suffrage amendment, Clay had begun to inch closer to the states' rights argument of the South. Breckinridge did not want to anger her friend by acceptance of an office she had not even sought. "I know nothing, absolutely nothing of it!" Nisba protested. The older woman responded with assurances that Breckinridge would aid the movement by her political sagacity and an "ability to seize upon and utilize political situations to help the cause which very few women possess." She should accept the post, counselled Clay. Nisba did, finally, and served the cause well.[44]

Breckinridge aided the women's rights movement not only by action but also by the printed word. An early 1906 article advocated stricter laws regulating women's work, in order to protect "mothers . . . of the coming generation." Eight years later, in 1914, Nisba's article on "Political Equality for Women and Women's Wages" indicated that her views had apparently intensified. She noted that females' wages averaged one-third to two-thirds those of males. Admitting the natural barriers in some jobs, she questioned why exclusion existed in others. She pointed out that, of 824 school superintendents in larger cities, only six were women. Obviously, a change was required and Nisba offered a simple answer — political equality. Self-confidence and "a very real new spiritual power" would result.[45]

After passage of the Nineteenth Amendment, the millennium did not come. In a 1923 article, Breckinridge turned to the existing argument that women could still be paid less because they were not the primary breadwinners. Men's wages were not determined this way, she pointed out. And what of single women (like her)? Women wanted just treatment, nothing more. A decade later, Nisba's important study, *Women in the Twentieth Century,* surveyed the entire array of women's work, concluding that the emancipation of wives had been completed legislatively, but not realistically. Breckinridge still attacked the exclusion of females from certain work and found continuing resistance in government work. Yet her book's overall tone was hopeful and reasonable. Successes had been achieved, but some victories still had to be won. So read her message to American women.[46]

Of her three primary areas of reform, Breckinridge's concern for the plight of the poor overshadowed both black and women's rights. This cause stimulated her to greater effort, harder work, and more lasting accomplishments. Of more than a dozen books Nisba wrote, edited, or coauthored, at least nine dealt with some aspect of that problem, whether it be the delinquent child, welfare work, housing, or juvenile-court legislation. Her edited works, in which she compiled documents and case studies totalling over four thousand pages, have continued to be used, and at least two of them are still in print.

Throughout these works and in her articles, Breckinridge

— like others of this "factual generation" — stressed figures and data. When writing about poor housing, she would stagger with statistics, noting that 1,110 people lived in a one-block area of Chicago. Or, in a study she compiled with Edith Abbott, Nisba examined 13,000 delinquency cases and found that one-third of them came from broken homes.[47]

But despite the mass of dry, scientific information given, the professor stressed that such statistics must be the basis for action. At times she also offered her readers some forceful prose and even some morality amid the figures. Breckinridge and Abbott, in examining Chicago's housing, discussed the evils of the "furnished room" where "people of loose habits" met. They explained part ot the overcrowding in housing as a result of an "un-American standard of living."[48] The two authors, however, offered more angry words than moral judgments. Nisba and Edith repeatedly criticized the poor ventilation, the bad or nonexistent plumbing, the dark halls, and the ever-present fire hazards. They accused a city that enforced few ordinances and substituted "the shadow for the substance" of the law. "We still find," Breckinridge and Abbott wrote in a follow-up study, "the same overcrowded areas, alley tenements, dilapidated houses, oppressive density of population, families in outlawed cellar apartments, in dark and gloomy rooms, and in a condition of overcrowding which violates all standards of decency and health." State appropriations were "little short of ridiculous," and a housing code could be labelled as only "inadequate." Their solution to these evils did not differ greatly from those of their progressive counterparts — thorough studies of the problems, better laws and strict enforcement of them, an adequate staff, more appropriations, and, finally, an altering of industrial conditions by business, so that "decent" living standards could be maintained. These studies and the solutions offered presupposed more than they should. They sometimes "sidetracked" rather than advanced reform; they placed too much faith in legal answers to social conditions; and they all simply did not modify as expected. Nevertheless, a confident and pragmatic Breckinridge labored to improve the existing situation, and she did. She tried new answers and rejected old ones in an attempt to fulfill the dream the immigrant poor sought to pursue in the New World.

That was more than most were doing.[49]

Nisba studied not only immigrants' housing, but almost all conditions of their lives. In a paper to the American Home Economics Association in 1919, she told of the wrongs inflicted by citizens upon first-generation Americans. Not only did we — and she used the term we — push them to poor wages, gang labor, and crowded homes, emphasized Breckinridge, but we assumed that because they were different they were inferior. Such assumptions, she declared, would result in a great loss of the "rich contributions" immigrants could make. Keep the original names, with their "charm and beauty," the social worker counselled, and remember that none of the Americans of 1919 "just growed" here. All at one time had been "self-selected" to come to this New World. All were not invited. All did not come for the same reasons. Yet together, she concluded, they made a new and great country. In such speeches and in her books, especially *New Homes for Old,* Dr. Breckinridge showed a sympathy for and understanding of immigrant life that completely reversed the xenophobia of her grandfather, the Reverend Dr. Robert J. Breckinridge.[50]

Nisba's strongest words, her boldest suggestions, came when she discussed the welfare and future of children. Here Breckinridge criticized those — like her — "habituated to the legal mode of thought," for they hindered real aid. In the boldest departure from her father's philosophy, she advocated strong state intervention in child-rearing. If children in their homes were surrounded by immorality, obscenity, and "low associates," then they should "be lifted out bodily at the earliest possible moment." She made a distinction between the "destitute home," where private aid would suffice, and the "degraded home," where the "strong hand of the state" should interfere. Like other reformers of her era, Nisba pressed this point hard, for in the children lay the future. Change them, remove them from their bad environment (or correct it), expose them to new ideas, and the next generation would have few of the evils of the present one, in Breckinridge's vision. Thus most of her reform activity — in housing, among immigrants, in the court system — focused on the children she never bore, but cared about nonetheless.[51]

## VII

Sophonisba Breckinridge's concern for the young was translated to the classroom, and there she directly influenced many future social workers and reformers. Operating out of the University of Chicago's Green Hall, Professor Breckinridge formed one part of a triumvirate of pioneer social workers completed by the two Abbott sisters. In the quiet surroundings of the college, Edith and Nisba would leisurely walk by themselves, their long skirts sweeping the sidewalk, and would become completely absorbed in some common problem. The sprightly Kentuckian in her floppy Panama hat and sheer dress contrasted with the somber Nebraskan in her black hat and dark dress as they walked. Then the two would part as one went to a class or to an office.[52]

In a teaching situation, Nisba did not entrance students with flowing oratory or overwhelm with a forceful presence. A slight woman, who looked as if a breath of wind might blow her away, the professor possessed a "clear treble" voice that was precise, expressive, and effective, though not memorable. Breckinridge, teaching for the most part by the case study method she introduced at the school, stressed facts, the law, and a social welfare approach to her auditors. According to Edith Abbott, Breckinridge respected and had confidence in the young, "in their courage and their ability to right the old wrongs," and displayed this respect in the classroom. Students labelled her liberalism, activism, and advocacy of the oppressed simply "the Breckinridge point of view."[53]

Outside the halls of learning, friends knew a different Breckinridge than the one revealed to students. Acquaintances recalled Nisba's fine, "southern" manners, noting that she displayed such simplicity and such a "genuinely democratic spirit" that few could guess her aristocratic background. A gracious personality, a gentle presence, a dry wit, a vibrant spirit, a creative mind — this was the private Sophonisba. Beneath the surface, behind the soft, Kentucky voice with its trace of an accent, lay also the potential force of an iron will. Energetic and independent, Breckinridge sought what she considered practical, concrete, and attainable aims. Those whose adult minds were not so creative or disciplined as hers, or those who questioned her aims, received little sympathy if they disagreed.[54]

A very private person, Nisba chose to keep secret many individual acts of kindness. At one time, for example, a Green Hall student mentioned that the upcoming Christmas would be her first away from home. Later, when Breckinridge quietly handed the student an envelope containing a round-trip ticket home, she told the youngster that her sole wish was that no one else should know. Other, similar recollections of her thoughtfulness attest to the difference between the sometimes impersonal spirit of her lectures and writings, and the deeper concern she felt within.[55]

Retirement in 1942 ended some of Nisba's closest associations, those with the young minds she had so long molded. The college had been virtually her life since her father's death, and she continued as a part of its community, even if not on the active staff. Yet as time passed, several colleagues, friends, and relatives died. Loneliness increased. Scholarly output declined. She grew old.

Working now in the family papers and on her autobiography, Breckinridge returned to the years before Chicago, and recalled the great happiness and the equally great sadness of that time. She never completed that work, perhaps because the emotions were still too strong. Labor on the autobiography had ceased by 1948, for, by that spring, following a serious illness, the eighty-two-year-old Sophonisba required two nurses. By June her condition had so worsened that old friend Edith Abbott stayed with her almost daily. Breckinridge rallied for a time, became impatient with her inactivity, then suffered a relapse. Still calm, still alert, she sighed a last time, and on 30 July 1948 her life ended.[56]

In the lifetime of Sophonisba Preston Breckinridge, her America had changed from a generally laissez-faire, individualistic civilization to one that placed more responsibility on state and society. The Kentucky of her youth, the Chicago of her maturity, the nation of her entire life had each changed dramatically. Not all the changes had pleased Breckinridge, nor did she accept them all. Yet to the end she apparently remained convinced that her world with all its imperfections greatly improved the one she had encountered as a young, eager Wellesley graduate. If her analysis was correct, Sophonisba Breckinridge could take pride in the fact that she had been an important force in that improvement. As a relative said later: "She was on the side of all good things."[57]

After the usual honors for one of her stature, burial took place in the family plot in the Lexington Cemetery. As the green coffin was placed in the brown soil of the Bluegrass, Nisba once again was near her father. The reformer had returned to the past one last time.

## Footnotes

[1] On other family members see James C. Klotter, "The Breckinridges of Kentucky: Two Centuries of Leadership" (Ph.D. dissertation, University of Kentucky, 1975). The present study focuses on Sophonisba Breckinridge's Kentucky and family ties, not on her later career.

[2] Steven J. Diner, *A City and Its Universities: Public Policy in Chicago, 1892-1919* (Chapel Hill, 1980), 29. No full published biography of Sophonisba Breckinridge exists. Printed sources giving outlines of her career include Christopher Lasch, "Sophonisba Preston Breckinridge," in Edward T. James, ed., *Notable American Women, 1607-1950* (3 vols., Cambidge, Mass., 1971), I, 233-36; Allen F. Davis, "Sophonisba Preston Breckinridge," in John A. Garraty and Edward T. James, eds., *Dictionary of American Biography: Supplement Four, 1946-1950* (New York, 1974), 106-07; Anthony R. Travis, "Sophonisba Breckinridge, Militant Feminist," *Mid-America*, 58 (1976), 111-18; Helen R. Wright, "Three Against Time: Edith and Grace Abbott and Sophonisba P. Breckinridge," *Social Science Review*, 28 (1954), 41-53; and sketches of her by Edith Abbott, Charles E. Merriam, Elisabeth Christman, Russell W. Ballard, Ellen C. Potter, Joseph L. Moss, Martha Branscombe, Arlien Johnson, and Helen R. Wright in pages 417-50 of the *Social Science Review*, 22 (1948). The Travis article should be used with care.

[3] Sophonisba P. Breckinridge, "Autobiography" (University of Chicago Library).

[4] *Ibid.*, and Breckinridge Family Papers (hereinafter B. MSS) (Manuscript Division, Library of Congress), *passim*.

[5] "Autobiography." Nisba's actions in regard to her father were rather typical of many reformers of her class. See, for example, Allen F. Davis, *American Heroine: The Life and Legend of Jane Addams* (New York, 1973), 3, 160.

[6] W.C.P. Breckinridge (hereinafter WCPB) to Issa Desha Breckinridge (hereinafter Issa), 27 October 1867, vol. 257; Issa to WCPB, 30 March 1870, vol. 272; 28 October 1867, vol. 257, B. MSS; "Autobiography"; "Report of Nisba Breckinridge . . . May 9th, 1873," B. MSS boxes. Willie Breckinridge's first wife and their only child had both died by 1860. He married his second wife, Issa Desha, fifteen months later.

[7]Anne Firor Scott, *The Southern Lady: From Pedestal to Politics, 1830-1930* (Chicago, 1970), 4-21, quotation on 4; John Demos, "The American Family in Past Time," *American Scholar*, 43 (1974), 436; Margaret Ripley Wolfe, "The Southern Lady: Long Suffering Counterpart of the Good Ole' Boy," *Journal of Popular Culture*, 2 (1977), 22.

[8]Hopkinsville *South Kentuckian*, 28 October 1879; Frankfort *Daily Kentucky Yeoman*, 27 April 1880; *Illustrated Kentuckian*, 2 (1893), 174; quoted in Thomas D. Clark, *A History of Kentucky* (rev. ed., Lexington, 1960), 405.

[9]Laura Clay, "Kentucky," in Elizabeth Cady Staunton, Susan B. Anthony, Matilda Joslyn Gage, and Ida H. Harper, eds., *The History of Woman Suffrage* (6 vols., Rochester, 1888-1922), IV, 671; Helen Deiss Irvin, *Women in Kentucky* (Lexington, 1979), 96, 99-100; Paul E. Fuller, *Laura Clay and the Women's Rights Movement* (Lexington, 1975), 39-40.

[10]Fuller, *Laura Clay*, 22-29, 16; Clay, "Kentucky," 665-66; Josephine K. Henry, "The New Woman of the New South," *Arena*, 63 (1895), 353-56.

[11]"Autobiography."

[12]Wooster (Ohio) *Voice*, 11 February 1893, B. MSS boxes; Lexington *Morning Herald*, 24 October 1901, 28 September 1898, 4 October 1901, 21 January 1902 (hereinafter *Herald*).

[13]*Herald*, 3 October 1902.

[14]State of Kentucky Matriculators Book (1869-1889), 106, 122, 136, 156 (microfilm, Kentucky State Archives and Records Center, Frankfort); State College to Richard C. Stoll, 31 March 1900, vol. 506, B.MSS; John P. Rousmaniere, "Cultural Hybrid in the Slums: the College Woman and the Settlement House, 1889-1894," *American Quarterly*, 22 (1970), 51; Issa to Sophonisba P. Breckinridge (hereinafter Nisba), 20 September, 2 December 1884; Issa to Fanny Barns, 17 October 1884, B. MSS boxes.

[15]Issa to Nisba, 19 September 1884, B. MSS boxes; "Autobiography"; Nisba to Issa, 17 May [1885?], B. MSS boxes. For a similar but slightly different version of her father's reaction to black students, see Edith Abbott, "Sophonisba Breckinridge Over the Years," *Social Science Review*, 22 (1948), 418. On family racial views generally see James C. Klotter, "Slavery and Race: A Family Perspective," *Southern Studies*, 17 (1978), 375-97.

[16]WCPB to Nisba, 20 September, 3, 8 October 1884, 30 March, 10 May 1885, B. MSS boxes. Many of these 1884-85 letters appear in Helen L. Horowitz, " 'With more love than I can write': A Nineteenth Century Father to his Daughter," *Wellesley*, 65 (1980), 16-20.

[17]"Autobiography"; Nisba to Issa, 1 April 1885, 15 September 1886, B. MSS boxes; Edith Abbott, "Sophonisba Preston Breckinridge: A Supplementary Statement," *Social Science Review*, 23 (1949), 94.

[18]Nisba to Issa, undated (spring 1885); Nisba to WCPB, 22 January 1885; Nisba to Issa, undated (1885), undated (November 1885?), undated (fall 1885), B. MSS boxes.

[19]Nisba to Issa, 20 May 1886; Nisba to WCPB, 1 November 1886; Nisba to Issa, 2 [January?] 1887; Nisba to WCPB, 13 February 1887, B. MSS boxes.

[20]Nisba to WCPB, 1 November 1886; Nisba to Issa, 12, 28 January, 1 February 1887, B. MSS boxes.

[21]Nisba to Issa, 1 March 1887; Nisba to WCPB, 20, 13 March 1887, B. MSS boxes.

[22]Nisba to WCPB, 9 March, 10 June 1887, B. MSS boxes; "Autobiography."

[23]Alice Stone Blackwell to Mary Barr Clay, 28 June 1888, Cassius Marcellus Clay Papers (The Filson Club, Louisville).

[24]"Autobiography." According to Isabelle M. Pettus, "The Legal Education of Women," *Journal of Social Science,* 38 (1900), 239-40, Boston Law School opened its doors to women in 1872, but few others had by 1890.

[25]"Autobiography"; New York *Times,* 29 November 1892; Abbott, "Breckinridge: Supplementary Statement," 94; Lexington *Kentucky Leader,* 19, 26, 31 October 1890; Eugenia D. Potts, "Woman's Work in Kentucky," *Illustrated Kentuckian,* 2 (1894), 254; "Autobiography." See Kentucky Matriculates Book, 106; "Tom" to Nisba, 15 November 1884 and undated [1880s], B. MSS boxes; John P. Myers, "A Lady Ahead of Her Time: Dr. Sophonisba P. Breckinridge," *Kentucky Alumnus,* 44 (1974), 15; and James A. Ramage, "The Hunts and Morgans: A Study of a Prominent Kentucky Family" (Ph.D. dissertation, University of Kentucky, 1972), 313.

[26]"Autobiography"; Curry Breckinridge to "Jack" [Jacqueline], 1 November 1891, vol. 427; Theodore Pickett to Issa, 15 August 1891, vol. 424, B. MSS; "Autobiography"; Potts, "Woman's Work in Kentucky," 254. A story in the 18 January 1897 *Herald* disputed the suggestion that Nisba was the first female admitted to the Kentucky bar, saying that Flora U.W. Tibbitts was examined earlier in 1892. I have not seen evidence, however, supporting that claim. Pettus, "Legal Education of Women," 239-43, notes that Iowa had a woman attorney as early as 1869, and by 1900 Illinois numbered 87 women lawyers, New York 40, and Kentucky "two or three."

[27]New York *Times,* 29 November 1892, 26 January 1897. Some later sources, beginning with one quoted in Abbott, "Breckinridge: Supplementary Statement," 94, said that Nisba used tears to overcome parental objections to her career in law. None of Breckinridge's own recollections support this assertion, which does not seem compatible with her father's other actions. See, for example, WCPB to Nisba, 6 July 1899, vol. 503, B. MSS.

[28]On the scandal, see James C. Klotter, "Sex, Scandal, and Suffrage in the Gilded Age," *Historian,* 42 (1980), 229-43.

[29]"Autobiography"; WCPB to John T. Shelby, 14 September 1893, vol. 459, B. MSS; Lexington *Kentucky Leader,* 22, 27 March 1894.

[30]Clarke A. Chambers and Andrea Hinding, "Charity Workers, the Settlements, and the Poor," in *Who Spoke for the Poor? 1880-1914* (New York, 1968), 21; Robert H. Bremner, *From the Depths: The Discovery of Poverty in the United States* (New York, 1956), 124; Louise C. Wade, "The Heritage from Chicago's Early Settlement Houses," *Journal of the Illinois State Historical Society,* 60 (1967), 416; John D. Buenker, John C. Burnham, and Robert M. Crunder, *Progressivism* (Cambridge, Mass., 1977), 75; B. MSS, *passim;* "Autobiography."

[31]WCPB to Nisba, 7 March 1894 (copy), 24 January, 6 February 1898, B. MSS boxes; "Autobiography."

[32]WCPB to Nisba, 2 April 1899, vol. 502, 31 August 1899, vol. 504, B. MSS.

[33]"Autobiography"; Lexington *Daily Leader,* 15 October 1900; *Herald,* 15 June 1904; Ray Ginger, *Altgeld's America: The Lincoln Ideal versus Changing Realities*

(New York, 1958), 237; WCPB to Nisba, 17 June 1904, vol. 515, 1 November 1904, B. MSS boxes.

[34] Desha Breckinridge to Nisba, 24 February 1906, 30 October, 30 November 1907, 24 August 1927, B. MSS boxes; Nisba to John T. Shelby, 15 May 1917, Box 45, Craig Shelby Papers (University of Kentucky Library); *Herald,* 4 January, 20 February 1914, 28 January 1907, 1 December 1912.

[35] Desha Breckinridge to Nisba, 3 February 1905, B. MSS boxes; Desha Breckinridge to Nisba, 5 October 1914, Lyman Chalkley Papers (University of Kentucky Library); *Herald,* 16 April 1911.

[36] The preceding sketch comes in part from Louise C. Wade's excellent *Graham Taylor: Pioneer for Social Justice* (Chicago, 1964), 1, 55-71; Lloyd Lewis and Henry Justin Smith, *Chicago: The History of Its Reputation* (New York, 1929), 189-335; Bessie Louise Pierce, *A History of Chicago,* III, *The Rise of A Modern City, 1871-1893* (New York, 1957), *passim;* Henry F. May, *The End of American Innocence: A Study of the First Years of Our Own Time, 1912-1917* (New York, 1959), 101-03.

[37] Helen Lefkowitz Horowitz, *Culture & the City: Cultural Philanthropy in Chicago from the 1880s to 1917* (Lexington, 1976), ix (quotation); Allen F. Davis, *Spearheads for Reform: The Social Settlements and the Progressive Movement, 1890-1914* (New York, 1967), vii; Richard Hofstadter, *The Age of Reform: From Bryan to F.D.R.* (New York, 1955), 326; Ginger, *Altgeld's America,* 133.

[38] Davis, *Spearheads for Reform,* 33-35. She did not, however, come from the Midwest as most did. In fact, of twenty-seven women reformers surveyed by Diner, *City and Universities,* 197, Nisba was the only one born in the South.

[39] Davis, *Spearheads for Reform,* 27, 36, 245; Arthur A. Ekrich, Jr., *Progressivism in America: A Study of the Era from Theodore Roosevelt to Woodrow Wilson* (New York, 1974), ix, 13; Robert H. Wiebe, *The Search for Order, 1877-1920* (New York, 1967), 198; Carl N. Degler, *Out of Our Past: The Forces That Shaped Modern America* (New York and Evanston, 1959), 370; Hofstadter, *Age of Reform,* 205. See also Don S. Kirschner, "The Ambiguous Legacy: Social Justice and Social Control in the Progressive Era," *Historical Reflections,* 2 (1975), 69-88, and Diner, *City and Universities,* 67.

[40] "Autobiography"; Jill Conway, "Women Reformers and American Culture," *Journal of Social History,* 5 (1971-72), 167-68, 174; Davis, *American Heroine,* 90-91; Ginger, *Altgeld's America,* 123, 117, 136; Lynn Gordon, "Women and the Anti-Child Labor Movement in Illinois, 1890-1920," *Social Service Review,* 51 (1977), 233, 246; David Potter, "American Women and the American Character," in John A. Hague, ed., *American Character and Culture* (Deland, Fla., 1964), 69. Good sketches of most of these women appear in James, ed., *Notable American Women.*

[41] Dorothy G. Becker, "Social Welfare Leaders as Spokesmen for the Poor," in *Who Spoke for the Poor?,* 11; Gordon, "Anti-child Labor Movement," 246; Wade, *Graham Taylor.*

[42] Sophonisba P. Breckinridge, "The Unshackled Spirit," *Survey* (27 November 1915), 222; *The Crisis,* 9 (1915), 308; Travis, "Militant Feminist," 117. See also Breckinridge, "The Color Line in the Housing Problem," *Survey* (1 February 1913), 575-76; Steven J. Diner, "Chicago Social Workers and Blacks in the Progressive Era," *Social Service Review,* 44 (1970), 408; Charles Flint Kellogg, *NAACP: A History of the National Association for the Advancement of Colored Persons,* I, *1909-1920* (Baltimore, 1967), 124; *The Crisis,* 9 (1915), 308, Diner, *City and Universities,* 131.

[43] James C. and Freda Campbell Klotter, "Mary Desha, Alaskan Schoolteacher of 1888," *Pacific Northwest Quarterly*, 71 (1980), 78, 86; Flora Adams Darling, *Founding and Organization of the Daughters of the American Revolution* (Philadelphia, 1901), 16, 20, 58, 107-09; "Autobiography." Both Nisba and Curry Breckinridge refused to see Mary Desha after 1894, however, since she had been active in opposition to their father in the Pollard affair. "Autobiography."

[44] Nisba to Laura Clay, 29 October 1911; Clay to Nisba, 1 November 1911 (copy), Nisba to Clay, 3 November 1911, Box 6, Laura Clay Papers (University of Kentucky Library). See also Catherine W. McCulloch to Clay, 30 October 1911, Clay Papers; Fuller, *Laura Clay*, 124-27; and a comment in *Diplomats and Demagogues: The Memoirs of Spruille Braden* (New Rochelle, N.Y., 1971), 121.

[45] Sophonisba P. Breckinridge, "Legislative Control of Women's Work," *Journal of Political Economy*, 14 (1906), 107-09, quotation on 109; idem, "Political Equality for Women and Women's Wages," in James P. Lichtenberger, ed., *Women in Public Life* (Philadelphia, 1914), 122-33, quotation on 132. See also Edith Abbott and Sophonisba P. Breckinridge, "Employment of Women in Industries — Twelfth Census Statistics," *Journal of Political Economy*, 14 (1906), 14-40.

[46] Sophonisba P. Breckinridge, "The Home Responsibilities of Women Workers and the 'Equal Wage,'" *Journal of Political Economy*, 31 (1923), 521, 543; idem, *Women in the Twentieth Century; A Study of Their Political, Social and Economic Activities* (New York, 1933), 103-05, 344. See also idem, "Widows and Orphan's Pensions in Great Britain," *Social Service Review*, 1 (1927), 249-57; idem, "Separate Domicil for Married Women," *ibid.*, 4 (1930), 37-52; and idem, "The Activities of Women Outside the Home," in *Recent Social Trends in The United States: Report of the President's Research Committee on Social Trends* (New York, 1933), 709-50.

[47] Bremner, *From the Depths*, 140; Sophonisba P. Breckinridge and Edith Abbott, "Housing Conditions in Chicago, III: Back of the Yards," *American Journal of Sociology*, 16 (1911), 457; Ginger, *Altgeld's America*, 228.

[48] Wade, "Chicago's Settlement Houses," 420; Sophonisba P. Breckinridge and Edith Abbott, "Chicago's Housing Problem: Families in Furnished Rooms," *American Journal of Sociology*, 16 (1910), 293-94, 296-98; idem, "Back of the Yards," 450, 468.

[49] Breckinridge and Abbott, "Chicago Housing Conditions, IV: The West Side Revisited," *American Journal of Sociology*, 17 (1911), 33; idem, "Chicago's Housing Conditions, V: South Chicago at the Gates of the Steel Mills," *ibid.*, 176; Bremner, *From the Depths*, 161, 201-03.

[50] Sophonisba P. Breckinridge, "Education for the Americanization of the Foreign Family," *Journal of Home Economics*, 11 (1919), 188-89; idem, *New Homes for Old* (New York, 1921), 3-5. A New York *Times* reviewer of the latter work wrote in the 20 November 1921 issue: "One gets the very strong impression from Miss Breckinridge's book that study of the needs of the immigrant families convicts Americans of having been culpably heedless of the obligations of humanity . . . ."

[51] Sophonisba P. Breckinridge, "The Community and the Child," *Survey* (4 February 1911), 785-86; Gordon, "Anti-Child Labor Movement," 235. See also Breckinridge and Edith Abbott, *The Delinquent Child and the Home* (New York, 1912), 175-77; Breckinridge, "Family Budgets," in *Standards of Child Welfare: A Report of The Children's Bureau Conferences* . . . (Washington, D.C., 1919), 34-43; idem, "Summary of the Present State Systems for the Organization and Administration of Public

Welfare," *Annals of the American Academy of Political and Social Science,* 105 (1923), 93-103; idem, *The Family and the State* (Chicago, 1934); and idem, "Government's Role in Child Welfare," *Annals of the American Academy of Political and Social Science,* 212 (1940), 42-50.

[52]Eleanor K. Taylor, "The Edith Abbott I Knew," *Journal of the Illinois State Historical Society,* 70 (1977), 178-79. Abbott, in an interesting admission, told John C. Baker in a 26 November 1948 letter that she enjoyed Nisba not only for her gifted and quick mind, but also because "she was so lovely to look at." Copy, Papers of Edith and Grace Abbott (University of Chicago Library).

[53]Wright, "Three Against Time," 41-42; Abbott, "Breckinridge: Supplementary Statement," 93; idem, "The Debt of the School of Social Service Administration," *Social Service Review,* 22 (1948), 448; Taylor, "Abbott I Knew," 182-83; Abbott, "Breckinridge Over the Years" 420, 422. On her ideas on the social welfare profession, see Sophonisba P. Breckinridge, "Frontiers of Control in Public Welfare Administration," *Social Service Review,* 1 (1927), 84; idem, "Public Welfare Organizations with Reference to Child Welfare Activities," *ibid.,* 4 (1930), 376-419; and idem, "The New Horizons of Professional Education for Social Work," *ibid.,* 10 (1936), 437-49.

[54]Taylor, "Abbott I Knew," 182; Abbott, "Breckinridge Over the Years," 417; Charles E. Merriam, "A Member of the University Community," *Social Science Review,* 22 (1948), 424; Katherine F. Lenroot, "Friend of Children and of the Children's Bureau," *ibid.,* 427, 429; Wade, *Graham Taylor.*

[55]Abbott, "Breckinridge Over the Years," 421.

[56]W.C.P. Breckinridge had given the family papers to Sophonisba; she turned them over to the Library of Congress. See Fayette County Will Book 9, p. 593 (microfilm, University of Kentucky Library) and Worthington C. Ford to Nisba, 23 March 1905, B. MSS boxes. [Marguerite Woolley?] to Robert W. Woolley, 2 August 1948, Robert W. Woolley Papers (Manuscript Division, Library of Congress); Edith Abbott to W.H. Courtney, 6 April, 10 July 1948, Abbott Papers. Breckinridge's estate totalled $10,418. *Ibid.*

[57]James C. Klotter interview with Scott D. Breckinridge, Lexington, 22 May 1980.

# Bibliographical Essay

The most revealing source of Sophonisba P. Breckinridge's motivations, outlook, and early career is her unpublished autobiography in the University of Chicago Library. This frank, unorganized document of over one hundred, generally unnumbered, and often repetitive pages has been seldom consulted by previous scholars. It deserves more attention. Sophonisba Breckinridge's own sizeable collection of papers in the Library of Congress should be supplemented by the even more massive Breckinridge Family Papers at the same institution. The Papers of Edith and Grace Abbott, at the University of Chicago Library, are also revealing. Other collections add to the picture presented in these chief sources.

Printed secondary sources on Sophonisba Breckinridge are few. Sketches of her life appear in *Notable American Women, 1607-1950* (3 vols., Cambridge, Mass., 1971); in the *Dictionary of American Biography: Supplement Four, 1946-1950* (New York, 1974); in numerous articles in volumes 22, 23 and 28 of the *Social Science Review* (1948, 1949, and 1954); and in Anthony R. Travis, "Sophonisba Breckinridge, Militant Feminist," *Mid-America,* 58 (1976), 111-18. A good compilation of Sophonisba's college correspondence with her father is Helen L. Horowitz, " 'With more love than I can write': A Nineteenth Century Father to His Daughter," *Wellesley,* 65 (1980), 16-20. The same author's *Culture and the City: Cultural Philanthropy in Chicago from the 1880s to 1917* (Lexington, 1976) is also helpful.

Many writers owe a great debt to the sound scholarship available on the Chicago reformers. Sources of particular aid include Allen F. Davis, *Spearheads for Reform: The Social Settlements and the Progressive Movement, 1890-1914* (New York, 1967); his excellent *American Heroine: The Life and Legend of Jane Addams* (New York, 1973); Louise C. Wade's fine *Graham Taylor: Pioneer for Social Justice* (Chicago, 1964); her "The Heritage from Chicago's Early Settlement Houses," *Journal of the Illinois State Historical Society,* 60 (1967); and Steven J. Diner, *A City and Its Universities: Public Policy in Chicago, 1892-1919* (Chapel Hill, 1980). Numerous other useful studies exist.

For Sophonisba's family background and Kentucky setting, see James C. Klotter, "The Breckinridges of Kentucky: Two Centuries of Leadership" (Ph.D. dissertation, University of Kentucky, 1975); Hambleton Tapp and James C. Klotter, *Kentucky: Decades of Discord, 1865-1900* (Frankfort, 1977); Paul E. Fuller, *Laura Clay and the Women's Rights Movement* (Lexington, 1975); and the Lexington newspapers.

Breckinridge's own writings often reveal more about her method than they do her personality. As a rule, they are not easy reading. Her numerous books and articles remain, however, important contributions in the field.

# Augustus Owsley Stanley
# Early Twentieth Century Democrat

*by Thomas W. Ramage*

The Kentucky and American public came to know him as "A.O."; to relatives and friends he was "Owsley." But he was officially named Nudicut Owsley Stanley soon after his birth on 21 May 1867, in Shelbyville, Kentucky. Later, at about age ten, he persuaded his parents to change his first name to Augustus, after his grandmother Augusta Owsley, so that no one would call him "No" Stanley.[1] The boy's father, William Stanley, had been a Confederate soldier who attained captaincy in the famed Orphan Brigade. Later, William served briefly as the associate editor of the Shelby *Sentinel* and then as a Christian or "Campbellite" minister. A.O.'s mother, Amanda Owsley, was a niece of a former Kentucky governor.[2]

In fall 1886, the nineteen-year-old Stanley entered the Kentucky Agricultural and Mechanical College at Lexington, where he displayed a marked talent for oratory. After graduating from Danville's Centre College in June 1889, he taught school for four years in several Kentucky towns. During that time he also read law, and in 1894 he was admitted to the bar. Opening his practice in Flemingsburg, Kentucky, where his father was pastor of a church, Stanley made his first attempt at winning political office. He won the Fleming County Democratic nomination for county attorney, but was defeated in the 1897 election by his Republican opponent.[3]

Stanley's Flemingsburg law practice did not prosper, and in 1898 he moved to the Ohio River town of Henderson, a prosperous little city situated in Kentucky's Pennyroyal district. Arriving there on St. Patrick's Day, 1898, with less than one hundred dollars in his pocket, he quickly made friends with some of the important people in the city, including the mayor, Irvin Thompson, and the circuit court judge, John L. Dorsey, who was later to become his law partner. Within several years Stanley had established a thriving law practice.[4]

**Augustus Owsley Stanley**
Portrait in oil, by Pasquale Farina, in Kentucky Historical Society Collection

Yet, despite his newly-won affluence, the old ambition to win political office persisted. To ingratiate himself with leaders of the Democratic party and to make himself well-known, Stanley campaigned enthusiastically for Democratic candidates in these years. At the state Democratic convention in June 1900, he was designated a presidential elector for William Jennings Bryan. Two years later, after a grueling contest, he was elected, at age thirty-five, congressman from Kentucky's Second District. In the interim before the Fifty-eighth Congress convened, Stanley married Sue Soaper, a Henderson girl whose father was a prominent tobacco agent.[5]

Stanley's political philosophy at this time aligned him with a group which could be called laissez-faire progressives. Closely resembling nineteenth-century liberals in holding strong laissez-faire concepts, favoring a minimum of federal control, they were nonetheless willing to use government to oppose special privilege. The young Second District congressman thought of himself as a devoted disciple of Thomas Jefferson, and his speeches are filled with encomiums for states' rights and the laissez-faire concept of government. Yet he also supported much progressive legislation aimed at restoring competition and denying special privileges to special interests, despite the fact that these measures usually entailed federal intervention and federal expansion.[6]

As a new congressman, Stanley soon discovered what many others before him had: that a few powerful men on both sides of the House ruled the country; the rest were merely followers. He also learned that the average congressman's time was consumed in dealing with such unstatesmanlike matters as the establishment of new mail routes, pension claims, the distribution of garden seed, and government inquiries. Stanley, however, was not content to be an average congressman. Patiently biding his time, he determined that when the right moment arrived he would make himself both known and respected.[7]

Such an opportunity presented itself in 1904, when under the whiplash of economic adversity, the dark tobacco growers of Kentucky and Tennessee began petitioning Congress for relief. Paid low prices for their product, the tobacco farmers blamed the tobacco companies for their economic miseries, alleging that these companies had formed a monopoly and were not competing with one another. Some of the farmers and small tobacco dealers believed that the repeal of the six-cent tax on tobacco in the natural leaf, which had been levied in 1872, would restore competitive buying by permitting the farmer to sell his crop directly to the consumer, thereby breaking the trust's monopoly.[8]

Keenly aware of the farmers' unhappy plight, Stanley took up their cause without a moment's hesitation. Not only did his own district lie in the affected area, but, more importantly, he had a profound sympathy for the underdog farmers. Early in 1904 he introduced two bills to aid the hard-pressed tobacco growers. A little later, at a meeting of two or three hundred tobacco growers at Guthrie, Kentucky, he urged the farmers to organize and withhold their tobacco from the trust until they received a fair price. Taking Stanley's advice, the tobacco farmers in September 1904, organized the Dark District Tobacco Planters' Association to sell their products at higher prices.[9]

Despite the repeated attempts of Stanley and others to repeal the tobacco tax, the bill to accomplish this failed to pass, usually floundering in Senator Nelson W. Aldrich's Finance Committee. Moreover, the companies which purchased the dark tobacco refused to buy any of the Planters' Association tobacco and would deal only with independent farmers, derisively labeled "Hill Billies" by members of the Planters' Association.[10] Frustrated and angry, some of the tobacco farmers, calling themselves "Possum Hunters," organized the "Silent Brigade" and began intimidating the "Hill Billies." Later in 1905 the "Possum Hunters" turned to violence — they began burning and blowing up tobacco warehouses in western Kentucky towns in what were called "nightriding" activities.[11]

While sympathetic to the plight of the farmers, on numerous occasions Stanley deplored the use of violence. He urged the tobacco people to cultivate the twin virtues of patience and obedience to the law. Even so, some critics implied that the Henderson lawmaker encouraged nightriding. During the 1908 congressional election, for example, the Republicans claimed that he had made a speech in which he had said: "If you can't raise tobacco, raise corn; if you can't raise corn, raise oats; if you can't raise oats, raise hell." But Stanley denied that he had advised farmers to "raise hell," and the evidence does not support the view that he encouraged nightriding.[12]

The fight to repeal the six-cent tobacco tax reached a successful conclusion in 1909 when the newly elected president, William Howard Taft, called a special session of Congress to revise the tariff. Stanley and his associates were able to gain enough Republican support to include an amendment to repeal the tax in the Payne-Aldrich tariff. Although elimination of the tax was hailed as a victory for the tobacco farmers, it did not afford the relief they sought because it did not allow them to stem and twist their tobacco, and there was very little demand for tobacco in its natural condition.[13]

Nonetheless, Stanley was widely acclaimed for his part in winning repeal of the six-cent tax. When newspapers and farmers mentioned the tax repeal amendment, they usually called it the "Stanley bill" despite its having been drafted by the commissioner of revenue and introduced by a Republican. As a result of his leadership in this fight, Stanley's popularity soared, and he became practically unbeatable in his congressional district.[14] In the 1904 and 1908 Democratic congressional primaries, for example, Stanley was unopposed, and in the 1906 primary his one opponent dropped out before election day. The only time Stanley experienced any difficulty in winning the regular election was in 1908, when the Republicans accused him of having incited the nightriders. Even then, he was reelected by a plurality of over four thousand votes.[15]

One of Stanley's principal claims to fame while serving as a United States representative was his role in sponsoring and conducting an investigation of the gigantic United States Steel Corporation. This billion-dollar concern, put together by J.P. Morgan during the movement toward combination in the late 1890s, was an inviting target for those who opposed giant corporations. Producing 60 percent of the nation's iron and steel and owning over 1,000 miles of railroad, 112 ore ships, and immense reserves of iron ore, coal, and limestone, the size of U.S. Steel alone was enough to convince many that it was a monopoly. Moreover, its pricing policies, its purchase of the Tennessee Coal, Iron, and Railroad Company during the Panic of 1907, and its labor policies also aroused the suspicion of its critics.[16]

Thus, at a time when the public was becoming increasingly concerned about the "malefactors of great wealth," the growing public demand for the prosecution of the Steel Corporation was not surprising. To forestall federal prosecution, the company adopted a policy of cooperating with government officials and of seeking their approval before initiating practices which might be labeled monopolistic. Even so, mounting criticism forced the House in 1905 to pass a resolution calling for an investigation of the corporation, and shortly thereafter President Roosevelt's Commissioner of Corporations, James R. Garfield, also began an investigation which dragged on into the Taft administration. Early in 1909, the Senate authorized its Judiciary Committee to make an inquiry into U.S. Steel's acquisition of the Tennessee Coal, Iron, and Railroad Company.[17]

This was the state of affairs in 1910 when Congressman Stanley focused his attention upon the U.S. Steel Corporation; his reasons are not difficult to discern. With the tobacco tax successfully repealed and with a federal antitrust suit against the American Tobacco Company then in progress, there was little more that he could do in that direction. Motivated as he was by a deep-seated antipathy to large combinations which stifled competition and created artifically high prices, as well as by his ambition to further his and his party's political fortunes, that he should continue his "trust-busting" efforts was perhaps natural. He later stated that his attention had been drawn to the Steel Corporation because of a statement by its board chairman Elbert H. Gary, to the effect that the dissolution of U.S. Steel would be impossible because of the financial havoc such an action would entail. "To me," commented Stanley, "this seemed equivalent to the remark of Louis XIV, 'I am the State' and I determined to see if the trust was immune."[18]

On 9 June 1910, Stanley sponsored a resolution requesting President Taft to furnish the House with all information possessed by the executive dealing with possible violations of the

Sherman Antitrust law by U.S. Steel. When the Taft administration refused to comply with the resolution, the Kentucky congressman introduced another resolution on 20 June calling for an investigation of the steel giant. Two days later he delivered an eloquent speech before the House in support of his resolution. "The greatest crime of the steel trust," Stanley asserted, "is not the plundering of the consumer. . . . When its complete history is written, its blackest pages will record its treatment of the toiler, its crucifixion of labor, its degradation, its cold and inhuman pilfering of its own employees." Furthermore, he charged that U.S. Steel had been "defiantly defended by an ex-President," that it had been given "a clean bill of health by the Attorney-General," and that it had "paid hush money" and was "a secret partner of the Republican party." Despite this oratorical support for his resolution, the Republican-dominated House refused to authorize an investigation of U.S. Steel.[19]

When the Sixty-second Congress assembled early in April 1911, Representative Stanley again introduced his resolution for a steel inquiry. With the Democrats in control of the House for the first time since 1892, the Rules Committee approved the resolution on 3 May, and almost two weeks later it was approved by the House. The House also created a nine-man investigating committee, consisting of five Democrats and four Republicans, with Stanley as its chairman.[20]

The Stanley Committee hearings began on 27 May 1911 and ended on 13 April 1912. During that time there was a parade of important witnesses before the committee, including Elbert H. Gary, board chairman of the United States Steel Corporation, Commissioner of Corporations Herbert Knox Smith, former President Theodore Roosevelt, Attorney General George W. Wickersham, Andrew Carnegie, and Louis D. Brandeis.

After listening to its last witness, the Stanley Committee settled down to the difficult task of formulating its reports which, by the end of July were completed and ready for formal presentation to the House. The majority report, presented to Congress on 2 August, clearly reflected the views of Chairman Stanley. It charged that U.S. Steel stock had been heavily watered and that the company had maintained prices at an artifically high level, restricted production, divided territory, stifled competition, and restrained trade through price-fixing schemes. Also, according to the report, the run on the Trust Company of America during the Panic of 1907 was attributable to a statement by George W. Perkins (the report hinted that Perkins' motive in making the statement was to force that company to sell its Tennessee Coal and Iron Company stock). The report further declared that Theodore Roosevelt had exercised bad judgment in 1907 in approving the Tennessee Coal and Iron Company deal. It denounced U.S. Steel as an enemy of labor and as a corporation which exerted an injurious influence upon U.S. business.

Stanley and his fellow Democratic committeemen, in their majority report, also included proposals for curbing the trusts. First, they suggested a bill to define corporate practices which under the Sherman Act constituted restraint of trade. The report called for the enactment of a second measure — largely the brain child of Louis D. Brandeis — giving any injured party the legal right to institute dissolution proceedings against a corporation and placing the burden of proof upon the defendant. A third bill, which was largely the work of Stanley and which was directed against interlocking directorates, forbade directorship in two corporations engaged in interstate commerce. A fourth measure prohibited persons or corporations who owned stock in a manufacturing industry from owning stock in a railroad. Finally, the report suggested a bill excluding corporations guilty of illegal practices from interstate commerce.[21]

After consulting with congressional Democratic leaders, and with their approval, Stanley introduced three antitrust bills during August. All three were modeled on remedies suggested by the majority report. When the House did not pass his measures, Stanley again introduced his antitrust program when the Sixty-third Congress met in May 1913.[22] In the meantime the Kentuckian had been working with President Woodrow Wilson to win his support for his antitrust program. Shortly after becoming president, Wilson invited Stanley to his office; for two hours, the Kentucky congressman briefed the president on the U.S. Steel Corporation and on the committee's proposed legislation. Despite his keen interest in the trust question, Wilson did not address the issue until the fall of 1913. At Wilson's request, Congressman Stanley sent a long letter to the president on 9 December, summarizing his views on the subject.[23]

Since he was then campaigning for the Democratic senatorial nomination, Stanley was eager to get one of his bills passed. Yet he knew his chances of accomplishing this were very slim, for several reasons. One obstacle was that a considerable number of other representatives had introduced antitrust legislation and were just as anxious as he to see their bills passed. More importantly, Henry D. Clayton of Alabama was chairman of the House Judiciary Committee, which was charged with the responsibility of drafting the legislation, and any legislation coming out of that committee was likely to bear his name. Although the prospect of Chairman Clayton's stealing some of his thunder did not please Stanley, he acknowledged the privilege of seniority and worked to put his stamp upon the committee version of the antitrust measures. Toward this end he made repeated visits to see Attorney General James C. McReynolds, Commissioner of Corporations Luther Conant, Jr., and the president himself, and he also appeared before the Judiciary Committee.[24]

The final version of the the Clayton Act bore a striking resemblance to parts of earlier Stanley bills and recommendations. Its sections on interlocking directorates and on giving damage benefits to persons injured were "almost verbatim reproductions" of Stanley bills. Indeed, the similarities were so obvious that one partisan observer said that Clayton had merely "erased Stanley's name" from his bills and substituted his own. Moreover, the same commentator concluded that the Stanley investigation and report "were a mine of information and of incalculable assistance to the framers of both the Clayton and the Federal Trade Commission acts. A survey of progressive legislation enacted by Congress in the last quarter century would disclose that the essentials of that committee's findings and proposals are now embodied in statutory law."[25]

Not everyone, however, was equally enthusiastic. Some critics belittled the Stanley investigation as a cheap political move, calculated to win votes for the Democratic party. Obviously, the hearings were partly motivated by partisan politics, and undoubtedly they contributed to some extent in placing the Republican party in an unfavorable light.

Yet, even though the investigation may have been used by the Democrats to gain political advantage, its wider effects remain to be considered. By focusing public attention on the U.S. Steel Corporation, the Stanley Committee hearings forced a hesitant Taft to initiate dissolution proceedings against that corporation. Moreover, the Justice Department's case rested largely upon U.S. Steel's questionable acquisition of the Tennessee Coal, Iron, and Railroad Company in 1907. This was the part of the suit which angered Theodore Roosevelt because he had tacitly approved the deal and because this part of the suit made it appear that he was either a knave or a fool. Although Taft had not read the suit before it was filed, this did not exculpate him in the eyes of an angry Roosevelt. After this, all possibility of healing the breach between the two men had disappeared. The Taft administration's initiation of the suit against U.S. Steel was, in the words of one historian, a bombshell whose "explosion changed the course of American politics," and that suit was filed primarily because of the Stanley hearings.[26]

Again, the Stanley investigation helped to bring about a climate of opinion favorable to the passage of the Underwood Metal Tariff Bill. The Stanley hearings revealed that prior to the formation of the U.S. Steel Corporation in 1901 the price of steel manufactured in the United States was less than its European equivalent; after 1901, however, the situation had been reversed. This and other information stimulated House Democrats and twenty insurgent Republicans to pass the Underwood Metal Tariff Bill in January 1912. Although the bill also passed the Senate, Taft vetoed it, and Congress could not muster the necessary votes to override his veto. The tariff question, however, did become an important issue in the presidential election of 1912.[27]

While the steel investigation was taking place in 1912, Stanley was also busily involved in state and national politics, especially since 1912 was a presidential election year. As early as September 1911, he had indicated a marked preference for Speaker of the House Champ Clark for the Democratic presidential nomination. On the whole, Kentuckians leaned toward Clark for the presidential nomination, despite some strong support for New Jersey Governor Woodrow Wilson.

The real struggle in Kentucky, however, was not between Clark and Wilson, but between two opposing Democratic party factions, which were fighting for control of the party within the state. On the one hand was the combine of former Governor J.C.W. Beckham, which espoused the "dry" cause, supported Wilson, and were allied with the coterie of Governor James B. McCreary. Arrayed against them were the "wets" who had gathered around their chieftains — Senator-elect Ollie M. James, Louisville *Courier-Journal* editor Henry Watterson, and Representatives Stanley and J. Campbell Cantrill. The "wet" forces had suffered a stinging defeat at the state convention in 1911 and were determined in 1912 to wrest control of the party machinery from their adversaries. But this was not to be. At the May convention the Beckham-McCreary forces were victorious, although the delegates to the Democratic national convention were instructed for Clark.[28]

Stanley attended the Democratic National Convention in Baltimore and continued to work for Clark. Despite Clark's waning popularity as the vote proceeded, Stanley and the Kentucky delegation remained loyal to the Missourian for forty-five ballots, until Wilson became the choice of his party for the nomination. After the convention, Stanley returned to Kentucky to do battle with the Republicans. Running virtually unopposed in his own election, he concentrated on helping the national ticket and, throughout the campaign, hammered away on two issues: the tariff and the trust problem. The Democrats made good use of the Stanley Committee's finding, devoting one chapter in their national campaign book to its work. Reelected to serve a fifth term in the House, Stanley was also greatly pleased with Wilson's victory.[29]

After his successful reelection to the House in 1912, the Kentucky Representative set his sights on a United States Senate seat. Circumstances in 1913 seemed to Stanley auspicious for achieving that goal. The current senator was a Republican. With no Democratic incumbent to challenge, Stanley's chief opponents in the race for the senatorial nomination were young

Beckham and aging Governor McCreary. Beckham had defeated his erstwhile ally McCreary for the senatorial nomination in 1906, only to lose the election in the Kentucky General Assembly two years later when several Democrats switched their votes to the Republican candidate. Beckham's supporters claimed that he had been betrayed and that the Democrats ought therefore to vindicate this wrong by nominating him in 1913. McCreary for his part hoped to use his gubernatorial office as a springboard into the Senate.

Originally scheduled for August 1913, the primary election was postponed until August 1914, because of the ratification of the Seventeenth Amendment. Stanley was thus forced into the undesirable position of having to choose between running for the House or the Senate; he could not run for both. After giving the matter serious consideration, he decided to seek the Senate post.

The campaign, which evolved principally into a contest between Stanley and Beckham, was a no-holds-barred affair with Beckham emphasizing Stanley's proliquor position and Stanley claiming that Beckham was the tool of the Louisville and Nashville Railroad Company. Beckham won the 1 August primary with 72,677 votes to 65,871 for Stanley and 20,257 for McCreary. Although the Louisville *Evening Post* observed that the primary was "unusually orderly and fair," later events challenged that report. During a trial concerning alleged voting irregularities in eastern Kentucky, one man testified that he had "bought votes for Beckham . . . at the rate of $3 a head."[30]

Temporarily blocked in his effort to win election to the Senate, Stanley pondered his next political move. He could not run for Congress again — at least not for two years — and, besides, that course did not promise to put him any nearer his long-standing senatorial goal. Neither could he remain politically inactive, for to do so would be to court political oblivion. After careful consideration, he decided to take the advice of friends and try to capture the Democratic gubernatorial nomination. In the Democratic primary Stanley faced five other candidates — some of whom counted on the same backers as he. His chief opponent, however, was former Secretary of State Harry V. McChesney, an avowed state prohibitionist who was supported by the Beckham organization. As in earlier contests, Stanley was portrayed as the tool of the liquor interests; he, on the other hand, accused McChesney of being a "professional lobbyist" for the corporations. In the August 1915 primary, Stanley defeated McChesney by a substantial plurality.[31]

The Democratic platform, written by a convention late in August, called for better roads, a constitutional amendment permitting the use of convict labor on public roads, better schools, and an antitrust act. Other planks provided for a workmen's compensation law, a corrupt practices act, an antipass law, aid to farmers' organizations, an increase in the powers of the State Railroad Commission, an antilobby law, and the revision of the state's tax laws. Finally, the platform squarely favored the county unit law (local option). Interpreting his primary victory as a decision in favor of the county unit law, Stanley pledged, if elected, to exert "all the power vested in me to prevent . . . further agitation" on the liquor question.[32]

After a "dry"-"wet" battle at their Lexington convention, the Republicans nominated Edwin P. Morrow, an excellent stump speaker and nephew of Kentucky's first Republican governor. The G.O.P. platform rejected national and statewide prohibition; it favored the county unit law, submission of the question of women's suffrage to the electorate, and a tax revision downward. Actually, there was so little difference between the Democratic and Republican platforms that both parties were forced to look elsewhere for issues.[33]

The campaign was one of the most colorful in Kentucky's history. Although warm personal friends, Stanley and Morrow, who "fought each other . . . when personal abuse and tradition was the fashion," verbally hammered each other unmercifully. But, after mutual denunciations, they were often seen together eating and drinking in the friendliest manner. Focusing his attack upon the McCreary administration, Morrow announced that his theme during the campaign would be the "broken promises" of the McCreary administration. He also claimed that the Republicans had taken a stronger stand in favor of the county unit law than had the Democrats. In contrast Stanley attempted to focus on national issues and to identify himself with the Wilson administration. He also emphasized the evil of "invisible government."[34]

On one occasion, Morrow and Stanley shared the same platform. Speaking first, Morrow thrilled the crowd with his brilliant oratory. Stanley, who had drunk too much bourbon prior to the engagement, managed to sit quietly during Morrow's address, but when he rose to make his own speech "his head swam and his knees buckled." Nauseated, he staggered to the back of the platform where he vomited. Then, embarrassed but not at a loss for words, he returned to the speaker's stand where he said: "Gentlemen, I beg you to excuse me. Every time I hear Ed Morrow speak, it makes me sick at my stomach."[35]

The outcome of the 2 November election was very close. On the day following the election, both sides claimed victory, and both accused the other of election fraud. Finally, on 10 November, with all counties reported, Stanley's unofficial plurality was set at 366. The next day, Morrow reluctantly conceded defeat and promised to accept the verdict regardless of how it was achieved. Stanley's official margin of victory was later put at a slim 471 votes.[36]

In his inaugural address, Governor Stanley indicated that his would be a progressive administration. He solemnly pledged to reduce the expenses of government, to appoint only those people who were needed and who would faithfully carry out their duties, and to see that the platform pledges of his party were enacted into law. The 1916 General Assembly, like many other previous sessions, was marked by an intense partisanship on the part of administration and antiadministration forces. It was controlled by a so-called "bipartisan combine" of Republicans and Democrats.[37] Despite the bickerings and fightings of this session, the Stanley administration was able to push its priority legislation though the legislature. This included an antipass law, a corrupt practices act, an antilobby act, an antitrust measure, a workmen's compensation bill, and a convict labor bill. Commenting on the work of the legislature, Stanley stated that the Assembly's achievements constituted a "compend of progressive legislation of which all lovers of clean and good government may be justly proud."[38]

Governor Stanley also called a special session of the legislature to meet in mid-February 1917, to revise Kentucky's tax structure. For several years businessmen and other interested parties had been demanding a revision of the tax laws as a means of raising enough revenue to meet the state's financial obligations and also to rectify what they considered an inequitable system. During its sixty-day session, the legislature passed several bills which modified Kentucky's tax system. The new laws, embodying the principle of classifying property for tax purposes, lowered the tax rate, placed new taxes upon certain items, and established a Tax Commission of three to supervise the administration of the tax laws and to make assessments on certain kinds of property. Not all Kentuckians were pleased with the new tax system. One group of landowners, organized into the Kentucky Taxpayers' League, demanded repeal of the new laws which they claimed placed a light tax burden on corporations and a heavier one on farmers.[39]

In fall 1917 Governor Stanley was deeply concerned with the primary and regular elections for state legislative offices. Those forces favoring prohibition throughout Kentucky were diligently working for candidates who would support statewide prohibition in the 1918 General Assembly. Then, too, he would be opposed by the pro-Beckham forces. Stanley realized that his continued political success depended in part on a satisfactory disposition of the prohibition question. He could not ignore the fact that the forces calling for state and national prohibition were almost daily gaining strength. By summer 1917 Stanley was convinced that the wisest policy was to eliminate the issue by letting the voters decide it, and in an open letter, he expressed "an earnest desire" to have the issue thus resolved in an honest election "without joker, equivocation or delay."[40]

As a result of the fall elections the Stanley forces succeeded in retaining control of the General Assembly. Meeting early in 1918, legislators quickly ratified the Eighteenth Amendment and passed a statewide prohibition amendment — to be voted on in November 1919. The legislature also passed a tax levy bill, a measure strengthening the workmen's compensation law, the first legislative redistricting bill in twenty-five years, and a bill creating a state budget system. Moreover, increased funds were appropriated for the state's charitable, penal, and educational institutions. Amid the intense anti-German hysteria of World War I, the legislature also enacted a controversial bill to prohibit the teaching of the German language in Kentucky's elementary and secondary schools. Declaring that the bill would "defeat the very laudable purpose for which it was enacted," Stanley vetoed the measure. The governor's action was condemned by some groups as "un-American and unpatriotic," and one Protestant minister went so far as to brand Stanley a "traitor and coward."[41]

In August 1918 the opportunity for which Stanley had been waiting since his defeat for the U.S. Senate in 1914 came with the death of Senator Ollie M. James. With the support of the State Central and Executive Committee, the Kentucky governor secured the nomination of his party. The Republicans nominated a Louisville physician, Dr. Ben L. Bruner, as their candidate for the Senate seat. During the campaign, Bruner charged that Stanley as governor had "failed to keep faith with the people," alleging the creation of offices, the increase of state expenses, and the misuse of his pardoning power as examples of his failures. Moreover, the Republican nominee also accused Stanley of being unpatriotic in his veto of the anti-German language bill and of having been nominated in an undemocratic way. Countering Bruner's attacks, Stanley contended that his defeat would be interpreted by America's allies and enemies alike as a vote against Wilsonian and Democratic war policies. After a spirited contest, Stanley defeated Bruner by the narrow but safe margin of 5,590 votes.[42]

The change from the governor's office in Frankfort to Capitol Hill in Washington was much to Stanley's liking. Although he was admittedly only too happy to lay aside the "multitudinous and harrassing cares of this pestiferous job" as governor, Stanley could justly take pride in the achievements of his administration. Under his leadership the Kentucky General Assembly enacted Kentucky's first workman's compensation law; strengthened the corrupt practices act; passed antipass, antilobby, and antitrust laws; and increased appropriations for the improvement of the state's charitable, penal, and educational institutions. But of all the achievements of his gubernatorial administration, Stanley remembered the revision of the tax laws which put the state on a pay-as-you-go basis and the adoption of the state's first budget system as the "most epochal thing I did."[43]

After resigning as governor of Kentucky on 19 May 1919, Stanley was sworn in as the junior senator from Kentucky. He was assigned to the important Committee on Interstate Commerce and to the less important Committee on Patents. During his first session in the Senate, in keeping with a time-honored custom, he said very little on the floor. But he did live up to his preelection pledge to stand behind President Wilson; thus he supported the women's suffrage amendment and the League of Nations.[44]

In fall 1919, Senator Stanley devoted much of his time trying to defend his adminstration in the Kentucky gubernatorial election. After a hotly-contested primary, Governor James D. Black had won the Democratic nomination and the support of Stanley in the election. The Republican gubernatorial nominee, Edwin P. Morrow, and the opposition press unmercifully attacked the Stanley-Black administration, accusing it of "extravagance and broken promises." Traveling to Kentucky mostly on weekends, Stanley eloquently defended his administration while he was also campaigning for Black. Despite these efforts, however, Governor Black was buried by the electorate.[45]

Much of Stanley's Senate career was devoted to a fight for personal liberty. When the Senate was considering the Cummins Railroad Bill in 1919, Stanley opposed the antistrike section of the bill on the ground that it violated the employee's natural, inalienable right to quit his job whenever he desired. "There are certain rights," Stanley pointed out, "that came from God, that no government ever created, that no government should ever destroy." Despite forceful arguments, the Cummins Bill passed with its antistrike provisions.[46]

The Kentuckian began another losing campaign several months later when he opposed passage of the Willis-Campbell bill, which was designed to restrict a doctor's freedom to prescribe wine and liquor. The Senate "wets," led by Stanley, knew that they could not muster enough votes to defeat the bill, but they hoped to win enough support to place effective restrictions upon what they considered illegal searches and seizures. Early in August 1920, Stanley offered an amendment to the bill, making it a misdemeanor subject to a maximum punishment of one year's imprisonment and a one thousand dollar fine for any federal official or agent to search the "property or premises" of any person without a warrant. The Stanley amendment passed in the Senate, but was quickly emasculated by a determined majority in the House under the watchful eye of the Anti-Saloon League lobby.[47] When the bill again came before the Senate, Stanley led the fight against it, even though he recognized that his fight might lead to his untimely retirement. But he reminded his Senate associates that he had sworn to uphold and defend the Constitution and would "rather go down to the vile dust from which . . . [I] sprang, unwept, unhonored, and unsung — aye, better the oblivion of the humblest citizen true to his country, than to wear the toga of a Senator, the heart of a coward and the purpose of a traitor." The Senate adopted the Willis-Campbell bill by an overwhelming majority, and later President Warren G. Harding signed it into law.[48]

Early in 1922, Stanley began making a series of speeches which clearly reflected his new emphasis on personal freedom. Addressing a Chicago businessmen's club in mid-January on "The Perils of Paternalism," he denounced all despotic and sumptiary laws as infringements upon personal rights. For the passage of these laws he blamed the progressives, and the remedy for this condition, he declared, was a return to "the time-tried conservatism and wisdom of the continentals." As a result of his conservative crusade, several newspapers began mentioning him as a possible candidate for the 1924 Democratic presidential nomination.[49]

Meanwhile, in the Senate, the Kentucky lawmaker continued to foster the image of a conservative who was also a loyal Democrat. On the important Four Power Treaty, which pledged the United States, Great Britain, France, and Japan to respect one another's possessions in the Pacific, Stanley along with twenty-three other Democrats and four Republicans voted against it. Like many other Democrats, Stanley also unsuccessfully opposed passage of the Fordney-McCumber Tariff in 1922.[50] At the beginning of the Sixty-eighth Congress which met early in December 1923, Stanley was appointed to the important Democratic steering committee which shaped party legislative policies and strategies. During the first session, Stanley's attendance record, like those of many of his colleagues facing reelection, was spotty. Before the session ended, however, he supported the Soldiers' Bonus Bill, proposed a constitutional amendment giving Congress the power to prohibit or regulate child labor, and introduced a measure making it possible for cooperative farm associations to sell or exchange their surplus products abroad for finished goods.[51]

But Stanley spent most of 1924 in his home state in preparation for his senatorial election. After easily defeating his little-known Democratic opponent, John J. Howe, in the August primary, Stanley then turned his attention to the general election. Sensing a possible victory, the Republicans nominated a wealthy Louisville businessman, Frederic M. Sackett. Never previously elected to public office, Sackett promised, if elected, to support fully Republican policies and the strict enforcement of prohibition.[52] Having made some powerful enemies over the years, such as the Anti-Saloon League and the Ku Klux Klan, Stanley found himself in deep political trouble. Primarily empasizing national issues, he attacked the Harding-Coolidge administration and defended his own record. His determined efforts were not enough, however, to prevent Sackett from defeating him by more than 24,000 votes.[53] Commenting upon his defeat, Stanley said:

> The day must come in the life of every honest public servant when he must choose between being right and being popular. My friends and foes alike must admit I was true to my convictions; that like Paul I "bore witness to the light" as God gave me to see the light. He who lives by the sword must fall by the sword.[54]

After the election, Stanley returned to Washington to attend the last session of the Sixty-eighth Congress. During the debate on a Washington, D.C. traffic bill, imposing stiff penalties on hit-and-run drivers, Stanley, who opposed the bill, delivered what might be considered his farewell address;

> In leaving this body I can say nothing of more importance . . . than to repeat what I have so often reiterated on the floor of the Federal Senate, what we must have . . . is the respect for the law.
>
> Duty itself is obedience to the law out of respect for the law. The law was once obeyed because it was respected, and it was respected because it was respectable. Today the thing that menaces us more than all threatened internecine strife, is the universal disregard and the universal contempt for law. . . . You must approach the enactment of the law with care, with prudence, with sane and serious consideration, if you expect that law, when enacted, to receive the reverent obedience of the people of the United States.[55]

After leaving the Senate in 1925, Stanley resumed the practice of law, this time in Washington and Louisville. During the next few years, the ex-senator engaged in a lucrative practice which gave him a measure of financial security, but he still had his eye on the Senate. To keep his name before the people and to maintain contact with his political friends in Kentucky, he continued to make speeches and to participate actively in Kentucky politics. He seriously considered running in the Democratic senatorial primaries of 1930 and 1936, but in both instances abandoned the idea because of the opposition he would face.[56]

Stanley had been appointed early in 1930 to the International Joint Commission by President Herbert C. Hoover. The IJC, which was created under the terms of the Treaty of 1909 between the United States and Canada, performed judicial, investigative, administrative, and arbitral functions when called upon by the two governments. Stanley served on the commission from 1930 until early 1954, when the Eisenhower administration pressured him into resigning. During his twenty-four years' tenure on the IJC, most of the "references" involved disputes concerning the division of boundary waters. One of the most important matters to be considered by the IJC was the St. Lawrence Seaway and Power project which the Commission supported.[57]

Through his more than two decades on the IJC, Stanley worked diligently and patiently to persuade the United States government to make more extensive use of the Commission. Stanley believed that the IJC afforded a fine example of how nations could resolve their differences through reasoned discourse instead of through armed conflict. He never ceased to think that one of the Commission's greatest achievements was "the part it played in drawing closer and closer together two powerful and friendly nations alike in fundamental institutions, social conditions, and spiritual aspirations." Moreover, after the beginning of the Cold War, he was deeply convinced that the United States and Canada were "the last best hope for the maintenance of . . . Freedom" against an "undisciplined, barbarous and ferocious adversary."[58]

In mid-January 1954, the Eisenhower administration pressured Stanley into resigning his IJC position. His period of retirement was shortlived. Early in 1958, declining health and old age forced him to bed, and on Tuesday night, 12 August, he passed away at age ninety-one. After a Washington funeral service, Stanley's body was taken to the Capitol Rotunda in Frankfort where his flag-draped casket lay in state. He was buried in the historic Frankfort Cemetery near the graves of other Kentucky governors.[59]

Stanley's years of public service were marked by important and substantial achievements. As a representative, he labored long and diligently to prevent tobacco companies from exploiting the tobacco farmer. With comparable fervor and determination, he tried to prohibit the United States Steel Corporation and other trusts from perpetrating what he considered to be violations of the Sherman Antitrust Act. Although the 1914 bill to correct these abuses bore the name of Henry D. Clayton of Alabama, many of its sections were strikingly similar to earlier bills which Stanley had introduced.

During Stanley's gubernatorial years, his administration redeemed every pledge of the 1915 Democratic platform. More significant perhaps was the revision of the state's tax system, which brought about what some considered a more equitable sharing of the tax burden as well as increased revenues. As a United States senator, Stanley's main effort was directed at preventing what he regarded as the federal government's unconstitutional and unjustifiable interference with the inalienable personal liberty of the individual.

Stanley's years on the International Joint Commission were marked by no spectacular achievements. Yet he served for more than twenty years steadfastly devoted to the improving of relations between the United States and Canada. Shortly after Stanley's death, Republican Senator Thruston B. Morton declared that the Democrat's life was an "inspiring example of dedicated public service." Stanley himself was well satisfied with his life. Six years before his death, he wrote; "Approaching the sunset of life, I am at peace with my soul and with Paul I can truly say — 'I have fought the good fight, I have kept the faith.' "[60]

## Footnotes

[1] *Biographical Directory of the American Congress, 1774-1949* (Washington, 1950), 1853; G. Glenn Clift, *Governors of Kentucky* (Cynthiana, Ky., 1942), 117-18; *The National Cyclopaedia of American Biography* (51 vols., New York, 1893-1960), XLIII, 422-23; Henderson (Ky.) *Twice-A-Week Gleaner*, 22 June 1906; author's interview with A.O. Stanley, Jr., 15 September 1966.

[2] Ed Porter Thompson, *History of the Orphan Brigade* (Louisville, 1898), 785; Louisville *Times*, 8 April 1921; Lexington (Ky.) *Herald*, 9 February 1900.

[3] *The Kentucky Alumnus*, 7 (1916), 16-18; *Annual Register of the State College of Kentucky* (Lexington, 1885-86); Lexington *Herald*, 26 December 1915; Henderson *Twice-A-Week Gleaner*, 22 June 1906.

[4] Henderson *Twice-A-Week Gleaner*, 22 June 1906; Louisville *Courier-Journal*, 25 October 1953; author's interview with A.O. Stanley, Jr., 1 December 1960.

[5] Louisville *Courier-Journal*, 5 August, 5 November 1902; Henderson *Daily Gleaner*, 30 April 1903.

[6] Arthur S. Link, *Wilson: The New Freedom* (Princeton, N.J., 1956), 241. See also Link, "The Progressive Movement in the South, 1870-1914," *North Carolina Historical Review*, 23 (1946), 172-95.

[7] Augustus Owsley Stanley (hereinafter AOS) to William Stanley, 12 December 1903, Stanley Papers (University of Kentucky Library, Lexington) (hereinafter cited as SP).

[8] Joseph C. Robert, *The Story of Tobacco in America* (New York, 1949), 149-50; Horace C. Filley, *Cooperation in Agriculture* (New York, 1929), 247; Anna

Youngman, "The Tobacco Pools of Kentucky and Tennessee," *Journal of Political Economy,* 18 (1910), 37-39; James O. Nall, *The Tobacco Night Riders of Kentucky and Tennessee, 1905-1909* (Louisville, 1939), 5-8.

[9]Henderson, *Twice-A-Week Gleaner,* 2 February 1904; Nall, *Night Riders,* 9-11, 19-24.

[10]Harry H. Kroll, *Riders in the Night* (Philadelphia, 1965), 57; Nall, *Night Riders,* 19-29.

[11]Nall, *Night Riders,* 43-50.

[12]Henderson *Daily Gleaner,* 7 August 1907, 20 September 1908.

[13]Louisville *Courier-Journal,* 10 April, 6 August 1909; Nall, *Night Riders,* 186-88.

[14]Charles H. Fort to AOS, 13 May 1909, SP.

[15]Louisville *Courier-Journal,* 4 November 1908.

[16]*Report of the Commissioner of Corporations on the Steel Industry* (Washington, 1911), 12, 63; Robert H. Wiebe, *Businessmen and Reform* (Cambridge, Mass., 1962), 43-44.

[17]Wiebe, *Businessmen and Reform,* 45-46; Ida M. Tarbell, *The Life of Elbert H. Gary* (New York, 1925), 184-85; John H. Garraty, *Right-Hand Man: The Life of George W. Perkins* (New York, 1960), 246-47; *Congressional Record,* 58th Congress, 3rd Session, 1525; Arundel Cotter, *The Authentic History of the United States Steel Corporation* (New York, 1916), 189-90; Robert H. Wiebe, "The House of Morgan and the Executive, 1905-1913," *American Historical Review,* 65 (1959), 57.

[18]Louisville *Courier-Journal,* 20 June 1910; Brooklyn *Daily Eagle,* 18 June 1911, n.c., SP.

[19]*Cong. Record, Appendix,* 61st Cong., 2d Sess., 399-403.

[20]*Cong. Record,* 62d Cong., 1st Sess., 85, 918, 966; Louisville *Courier-Journal,* 4 May 1911.

[21]*House Report No. 1127,* 62d Cong., 2d Sess., 161, 183-87, 190, 213-16.

[22]New York *Times,* 22 January 1913; *Cong. Record,* 63d Cong., 1st Sess., 1832-33.

[23]Louisville *Courier-Journal,* 22 January 1913; Arthur C. Walworth, *Woodrow Wilson* (2 vols., New York, 1958), II, 328, 330; AOS to Woodrow Wilson, 9 December 1913, Woodrow Wilson Papers (Manuscript Division, Library of Congress).

[24]AOS to Mrs. Amanda O. Stanley, 10 December 1913, SP; AOS to William Stanley, 19 January 1914, SP; U.S. House of Representatives, Committee on Judiciary, *Hearings Before the Committee on the Judiciary House of Representatives Sixty-Third Congress Second Session on Trust Legislation* (Washington, 1914).

[25]Robert W. Woolley, "Politics is Hell," unpublished autobiography, Robert W. Woolley Papers (Manuscript Division, Library of Congress), Ch. 15, p. 5.

[26]George E. Mowry, *Theodore Roosevelt and the Progressive Movement* (Madison, Wis., 1946), 189-91; William H. Harbaugh, *Power and Responsibility: The Life and Times of Theodore Roosevelt* (New York, 1961), 314-15; Gabriel Kolko, *The Triumph of Conservatism* (New York, 1963), 170.

[27]*Cong. Record, Appendix,* 61st Cong., 2d Sess, 400.

[28] Louisville *Evening Post*, 29 May 1912; Lexington *Herald*, 30 May 1912; Louisville *Courier-Journal*, 30 May 1912.

[29] Henderson *Daily Gleaner*, 1, 20 September, 11 October 1912; *The Democratic Text-Book, 1912* (New York, 1912), 259-61.

[30] Louisville *Evening Post*, 1, 12 August 1914; Louisville *Times*, 4 February 1915.

[31] Henderson *Daily Journal*, 28 July 1915; Owensboro *Daily Messenger*, 29 July 1915; Louisville *Courier-Journal*, 6, 22 August 1915.

[32] Lexington *Herald*, 6 September 1915; Owensboro *Inquirer*, 10 August 1915.

[33] Cincinnati *Enquirer*, 16 June 1915; Lexington *Herald*, 16 June, 1 September 1915.

[34] AOS to A.B. Guthrie, Jr., 29 December 1949, SP; Louisville *Courier-Journal*, 21 September 1915; Lexington *Herald*, 21 September 1915.

[35] Louisville *Courier-Journal*, 23 October 1960.

[36] AOS to Robert W. Woolley, 17 December 1915, SP; Lexington *Leader*, 3, 12 November 1915; Louisville *Courier-Journal*, 23 November 1915.

[37] Henderson *Daily Journal*, 7 December 1915; Louisville *Courier-Journal*, 3 January 1916; Orval W. Baylor, *J. Dan Talbott* (Louisville, 1941), 83.

[38] Cincinnati *Enquirer*, 19 March 1916.

[39] Louisville *Courier-Journal*, 26 April 1917.

[40] Cincinnati *Enquirer*, 19 November 1916, 15 July 1917; Henderson *Daily Gleaner*, 17 November 1916; *Kentucky Post*, 13 July 1917.

[41] Henderson *Daily Gleaner*, 22 March 1918; Cincinnati *Enquirer*, 24 March, 7 April 1918.

[42] Cincinnati *Enquirer*, 22 September 1918; Louisville *Courier-Journal*, 22 September, 6 November 1918.

[43] AOS to Robert W. Woolley, 23 January 1918, Woolley Papers; Louisville *Courier-Journal*, 25 June 1950.

[44] Lexington Herald, *20 May 1919; Congressional Directory*, 67th Cong., 2d Sess., 183-84; Henderson *Daily Gleaner*, 27 May, 12 June, 26 October 1919; *Cong. Record*, 66th Cong., 1st Sess., 633-35, 8786-88, 8802-03.

[45] Louisville *Courier-Journal*, 9 September, 26 November 1919.

[46] *Cong. Record*, 66th Cong., 2d Sess., 358, 509, 664-74, 795, 811, 896, 989, 952.

[47] New York *Times*, 9 August 1921; *Cong. Record*, 67th Cong., 1st Sess., 4723-24, 4726.

[48] *Cong. Record*, 67th Cong., 1st Sess., 7849-56; Henderson *Morning Gleaner*, 18, 19, 23 November 1921.

[49] Printed copy of speech delivered by A.O. Stanley at Chicago, Ill., 12 January 1922, SP; Henderson *Morning Gleaner*, 14, 26, 27 January, 23 February 1922.

[50] New York *Times*, 11 December 1921; Henderson *Morning Gleaner*, 11 May 1922; *Cong. Record*, 67th Cong., 2d Sess., 6573.

[51]Henderson *Morning Gleaner*, 6 December 1923; *Cong. Record*, 67th Cong., 2d Sess., 12033, 12999-13000, 68th Cong., 1st Sess., 10142; Louisville *Courier-Journal*, 29 May 1924.

[52]Louisville *Courier-Journal*, 7 September 1924.

[53]Henderson *Gleaner and Journal*, 9 November 1924; Louisville *Courier-Journal*, 6, 7 November 1924.

[54]Henderson *Morning Gleaner*, 20 March 1925.

[55]*Cong. Record*, 68th Cong., 2d Sess., 3790-93.

[56]Henderson *Morning Gleaner*, 11 February 1925; author's interview with Mrs. Amanda W. Rose, 14 Febrary 1961.

[57]Louisville *Courier-Journal*, 10 May 1930; Lawrence J. Burpee, *Good Neighbors* (Toronto, 1940), 3-10.

[58]*Cong. Record, Appendix*, 81st Cong., 2d Sess., 4026; AOS to Louis S. St. Laurent (copy), 30 June 1950, SP; AOS to George Spence (copy), 9 November 1928, SP.

[59]Louisville *Courier-Journal*, 28 January 1954, 13, 14, 16, 17 August 1958.

[60]*Cong. Record*, 85th Cong., 2d Sess., 17226; AOS to Ewing Galloway (copy), 18 August 1952, SP.

# Bibliographical Essay

For the study of the life of Augustus O. Stanley, the A.O. Stanley Papers at the University of Kentucky are indispensable. The Theodore Roosevelt, William H. Taft, Woodrow Wilson, and Robert W. Woolley Papers in the Library of Congress are also helpful. Also useful were newspapers: the Louisville *Courier-Journal,* which was generally pro-Stanley, and the *Evening Post* which was generally anti-Stanley; the Henderson, Ky., newspapers; the Lexington *Herald;* and the New York *Times.*

For national politics during Stanley's active political career the following books were helpful: Blair Bolles, *Tyrant from Illinois: Uncle Joe Cannon's Experiment with Personal Power* (New York, 1951); David Chalmers, *Hooded Americanism* (1965); Paolo E. Coletta, *William Jennings Bryan* (Lincoln, Neb., 1964); William H. Harbaugh, *Power and Responsibility: The Life and Times of Theodore Roosevelt* (New York, 1961);

Gabriel Kolko, *The Triumph of Conservatism* (New York, 1963); Arthur S. Link, *Wilson* (5 vols., Princeton, N.J., 1947-65); Henry F. Pringle, *The Life and Times of William Howard Taft* (2 vols., New York, 1939) and his *Theodore Roosevelt* (New York, 1931); Arnold S. Rice, *The Ku Klux Klan in American Politics* (New York, 1962); Andrew Sinclair, *The Available Man: The Life Behind the Masks of Warren Gamaliel Harding* (New York, 1965); Andrew Sinclair, *Prohibition* (Boston, 1962); James H. Timberlake, *Prohibition and the Progressive Movement, 1900-1920* (Cambridge, Mass., 1963); Arthur C. Walworth, *Woodrow Wilson* (2 vols., New York, 1958). On Kentucky politics and problems see: John H. Fenton, *Politics in the Border States* (New Orleans, 1957); Harry H. Kroll, *Riders in the Night* (Philadelphia, 1965), and James O. Nall, *The Tobacco Night Riders of Kentucky and Tennessee, 1905-1909* (Louisville, 1939).

# Holman Hamilton
# A Bibliography

*by Sherrill Redmon McConnell*

Holman Hamilton left a legacy of biographies and histories that attest to his careful scholarship, discipline, and regard for fluent, unpretentious prose. There are historians with longer lists of publications to their credit, but Professor Hamilton was remarkably prolific, especially for a latecomer to the profession. His record is all the more impressive to people who remember how much time he put into his classroom lectures and the long hours he spent advising students, guiding theses and dissertations, and enthusiastically shouldering the many other responsibilities of academic and community life.

This bibliography lists Holman Hamilton's published historical writings — his books, scholarly articles, and other essays. No effort has been made to include newspaper articles and editorials he penned as a journalist in the 1930s and 40s; nor have I listed the solicited contributions on historical topics that appeared in Lexington dailies in the 1970s. With characteristic energy, Hamilton regularly reviewed books for *The Journal of American History, The Journal of Southern History, Mid-America, The Register of the Kentucky Historical Society, The Indiana Magazine of History,* and other journals. The reviews listed here, representing only about one-fourth of the total number he wrote, are included to suggest the breadth of his reading.

Few texts survive of the dozens of formal lectures and addresses Hamilton delivered before professional meetings, college gatherings, and civic groups as diverse as the Central Kentucky Council of Teachers of Social Studies and the Garden Club of America. Because Hamilton was accustomed to taking such engagements seriously — invariably speaking from a prepared text — it seems appropriate to include some of the lectures which found their way into print and even a few which did not.

## Books

*Zachary Taylor: Soldier of the Republic.* Indianapolis and New York: Bobbs-Merrill, 1941.

*Zachary Taylor: Soldier in the White House.* Indianapolis and New York: Bobbs-Merrill, 1951. Reissued together as *Zachary Taylor.* Hamden, Connecticut: Archon Books, 1966.

*White House Images and Realities.* History of American Civilization Lectures. Gainesville: University of Florida Press, 1958.

*Prologue to Conflict: The Crisis and Compromise of 1850.* Lexington: University of Kentucky Press, 1964. Paperback edition, New York: W.W. Norton and Company, 1966. Based upon his dissertation, "The Compromise of 1850," University of Kentucky, 1954.

*The Three Kentucky Presidents: Lincoln, Taylor, Davis.* The Kentucky Bicentennial Bookshelf. Lexington: University Press of Kentucky, 1978.

## Articles

"Zachary Taylor in Illinois." *Journal of the Illinois State Historical Society,* 34 (March 1941): 84-91.

"Zachary Taylor and The Black Hawk War." *Wisconsin Magazine of History,* 24 (March 1941): 305-15.

"The Vincennes Days of Zachary Taylor." *Indiana Magazine of History,* 37 (March 1941): 65-71.

"Zachary Taylor in Mississippi: Notes and Documents." *Journal of Mississippi History,* 3 (April 1941): 130-39.

"Zachary Taylor and Minnesota." *Minnesota History,* 30 (June 1949): 97-110.

"An Indiana College Boy in 1836: The Diary of Richard Henry Holman." *Indiana Magazine of History,* 49 (September 1953): 281-306.

"'A Youth of Good Morals': Zachary Taylor Sends His Only Son to School." *Filson Club History Quarterly,* 27 (October 1953): 303-07.

"Democratic Senate Leadership and the Compromise of 1850." *Mississippi Valley Historical Review*, 41 (December 1954): 403-18. Pelzer Prize.

"Texas Bonds and Northern Profits: A Study in Compromise, Investment, and Lobby Influence." *Mississippi Valley Historical Review*, 43 (March 1957): 579-94.

" 'The Cave of the Winds' and the Compromise of 1850." *Journal of Southern History*, 23 (August 1957): 331-53.

"Claude Bowers' High School Diaries." *Indiana Teacher*, 109 (November-December 1964): 97.

"The Sixty-First Annual Meeting of the Organization of American Historians." *Journal of American History*, 55 (September 1965): 349-68.

"Versatility and Variety: Hoosier Literary, Political, and Diplomatic Prominence, 1871-1901." *Indiana Magazine of History*, 65 (June 1969): 103-14.

"The Kentucky Civil War Round Table." *Civil War Times Illustrated*, 11 (August 1972): 44-47.

"Lincoln Memorial University and the Lincoln Collection: The Tone, The Spell, The Scholarship, The Challenge." *Lincoln Herald*, 75 (Summer 1973): 53-54.

"Before 'The Tragic Era': Claude Bowers' Earlier Attitudes Toward Reconstruction." *Mid-America*, 55 (October 1973): 235-44.

Coauthor with James L. Crouthamel, "A Man for Both Parties: Francis J. Grund as Political Chameleon." *Pennsylvania Magazine of History and Biography*, 97 (October 1973): 465-84.

"Lincoln and His Fellow Kentucky Presidents." *Lincoln Herald*, 80 (Summer 1978): 53.

" 'This Most Unnecessary and Senseless War': Zachary Taylor writes from Mexico." *Kentucky Review*, 1 (Spring 1980): 64-73.

# Edited Works and Introductions

"Lincoln and Herndon: Religion and Romance." Introduction to facsimiles of William H. Herndon, "Abraham Lincoln, Miss Ann Rutledge, New Salem. . . .," and "Lincoln's Religion." Lexington: University of Kentucky Library Associates, 1959.

Coeditor with Gayle Thornbrough, *Indianapolis in the "Gay Nineties": The High School Diaries of Claude G. Bowers*. Indianapolis: Indiana Historical Society, 1964.

"The Sage of Salt River." Introduction to *Hundred Proof: Salt River Sketches and Memories of the Bluegrass*, by William H. Townsend. Lexington: University of Kentucky Press, 1964.

Introduction to *Hail Kentucky! A Pictorial History of the University of Kentucky*, by Helen Deiss Irvin. Lexington: University of Kentucky Press, 1965.

Editor and introduction to *Three American Frontiers: Writings of Thomas D. Clark*. Lexington: University of Kentucky Press, 1968.

"The Genial Squire." Introduction to *The Collected Writings of J. Winston Coleman*. Lexington: Winburn Press, 1969. Also appears in *Meet Squire Coleman*, by Holman Hamilton and Edward T. Houlihan. Lexington: privately printed, 1973.

Introduction to *The Circuit Rider: A Tale of the Heroic Age*, by Edward Eggleston. 1874. The Novel as American Social History. Lexington: University Press of Kentucky, 1970.

Foreword to *High Peaks*, by C.V. Whitney. Lexington: University Press of Kentucky, 1977.

Introduction to *Lewis Cass*, by Andrew C. McLaughlin. 1899. American Statesmen. New York: Chelsea House, 1980.

## Contributions to Cooperative Works

"The Battle of Okeechobee," "The Battle of Palo Alto," "The Battle of Resaca de la Palma," and "The Campaign of 1848." *Dictionary of American History*. Edited by James Truslow Adams. New York: Charles Scribner's Sons, 1940.

"Slavery and Expansion: The Crisis and Compromise of 1850." *Major Crises in American History: Documentary Problems*. Edited by Leonard Levy and Merrill D. Peterson. New York: Harcourt, Brace & World, 1962.

"Democracy and Manifest Destiny." *The Democratic Experience*. Coauthored by Carl N. Degler, Arthur S. Link, Louis B. Wright, David M. Potter, and others. Chicago: Scott, Foresman and Co., 1963. Revisions, 1968, 1973, and 1979.

"Zachary Taylor." *American People's Encyclopedia*, 18. New York: Grolier, 1969.

"Zachary Taylor." *Encyclopedia Americana,* 26. New York: Americana Corporation, 1969.

"Margaret Mackall Smith Taylor." *Notable American Women: A Biographical Dictionary, 1607-1950.* Edited by Edwin T. James. Cambridge: Harvard University Press, Belknap Press, 1971.

"The Election of 1848." *The History of American Presidential Elections.* Edited by Arthur M. Schlesinger. New York: Chelsea Press, 1971.

## Addresses and Lectures

"Ashland Then and Now." Annual reception sponsored by the University of Kentucky and the Henry Clay Memorial Foundation, Lexington, July 23, 1956.

"Highlights and Sidelights of Colorful Kentucky." Delivered before Garden Club of America, Southern Zone, Lexington, May 2, 1957.

"Some Highlights and Sidelights of American History." Annual dinner meeting of the Allen County-Fort Wayne Historical Society, Fort Wayne, Indiana, March 1, 1958. Reprinted in *Old Fort News,* 21 (October-December 1958): 7-14.

"Old Rough and Ready — Kentucky's Hero President." WBLG Radio, presented by the Daughters of the American Revolution, Lexington, February 2, 1964.

"The American Presidency and the Civil War." Civil War Round Table, Louisville, February 9, 1964 and Filson Club, Louisville, April 6, 1964.

"The Dramatic Days of 1850." Tau Chapter, Phi Alpha Theta, University of Kentucky, Lexington, October 14, 1964.

"The Role of Biography in the Study of American History." Inaugural address, Hyland-Price Lecture Series, Washington College, Chesterton, Maryland, October 17, 1967.

"Claude Bowers and Popular History in the 1920s." Distinguished Professor Lecture, University of Kentucky, Lexington, December 6, 1972. Holman Hamilton Papers, Margaret I. King Library, University of Kentucky.

"The Kentucky Heritage." Boone Day Address, Frankfort, Kentucky, June 7, 1972. Reprinted in *The Register of the Kentucky Historical Society,* 70 (July 1972), 225-30.

"The American Presidency: Men, Myths and the Institution." American College of Physicians, Kentucky-Tennessee Regional Meeting, Lexington, Ky., October 11, 1974.

"Commencement Then and Now." Commencement address, University of Kentucky, Lexington, May 10, 1975.

"Two Prominent Hoosier Author-Politicians: The Albert Beveridge-Claude Bowers Friendship." Annual dinner meeting, Allen County-Fort Wayne Historical Society, Fort Wayne, Indiana, February 2, 1977.

"Presidential Leaders and Leadership." Featured address at 30th National Convention of Omicron Delta Kappa, Williamsburg, Virginia, March 4, 1978. Excerpts appear in *The Circle: The News Magazine of Omicron Delta Kappa*, 57 (Spring 1978): 5-6.

"Claude Bowers: Historian as Activist — Activist as Historian." Visiting Distinguished Professor Lecture, University of Houston, Houston, Texas, March 7, 1979.

"Jefferson Davis." Distinguished Transylvanians Lecture Series, Transylvania University, Lexington, October 4, 1979.

"Clio with Style." Presidential Address, Southern Historical Association, Atlanta, Georgia, November 15, 1979. Reprinted in *Journal of Southern History*, 46 (February 1980), 3-16. Excerpts appear in the *Organization of American Historians Newsletter*, 8 (July 1980), 9-12.

# Book Reviews

Robert S. Henry, *The Story of the Mexican War*, in *Journal of Southern History*, 16 (August 1950), 371-72.

James C.N. Paul, *Rift in the Democracy*, in *Journal of Southern History*, 18 (August 1952), 374-76.

Edward S. Wallace, *General William Jenkins Worth: Monterey's Forgotten Hero*, in *Mississippi Valley Historical Review*, 41 (June 1954), 131-32.

T. Harry Williams, editor, *With Beauregard in Mexico: The Mexican War Reminiscences of P.G.T. Beauregard*, in *Mississippi Valley Historical Review*, 43 (September 1956), 317.

John A. Garraty, *The Nature of Biography*, in *Journal of Southern History*, 24 (May 1958), 232-33.

George Dallas Masgrove, *Kentucky Cavaliers in Dixie*, in *Civil War History*, 4 (September 1958), 343-44.

Howard P. Nash, Jr., *Third Parties in American Politics*, in *Mississippi Valley Historical Review*, 46 (September 1959), 311-12.

James P. Shenton, *Robert John Walker, A Politician from Jackson to Lincoln*, in *Mid-America*, 44 (January 1962), 59-60.

Norma L. Peterson, *Freedom and Franchise: The Political Career of B. Gratz Brown*, in *The Register of the Kentucky Historical Society*, 64 (April 1966), 161-62.

William Y. Thompson, *Robert Toombs of Georgia*, in *Journal of Southern History*, 33 (August 1967), 403-04.

Richard Allen Heckman, *Lincoln vs. Douglas: The Great Debates Campaign*, in *Journal of American History*, 54 (December 1967), 666-67.

William Barrow Floyd, *Jouett-Bush-Frazer: Early Kentucky Artists*, in Lexington *Herald-Leader*, June 30, 1968.

Glenn W. Price, *Origins of the War with Mexico: The Polk-Stockton Intrigue*, in *Hispanic American Historical Review*, 48 (November 1968), 706-07.

George W. Smith and Charles Judah, editors, *Chronicles of the Gringos: The U.S. Army in the Mexican War, 1846-1848*, in *Journal of Southern History*, 35 (May 1969), 264-65.

James P. Baughman, *Charles Morgan and The Development of Southern Transportation*, in *Florida Historical Quarterly*, 48 (July 1969), 99-100.

Clifton J. Phillips, *The History of Indiana, 1880-1920*, in *Indiana Magazine of History*, 45 (September 1969), 229.

Francis Paul Prucha, *The Sword of the Republic: The United States Army on the Frontier, 1783-1846*, in *Journal of American History*, 56 (September 1969), 375-76.

Edgar B. Nixon, editor, *Franklin D. Roosevelt and Foreign Affairs*, in *The Register of the Kentucky Historical Society*, 68 (January 1970), 88-89.

Paolo E. Coletta, *William Jennings Bryan*, in *The Register of the Kentucky Historical Society*, 68 (July 1970), 273-74.

Jerome L. Clark, *1844*, in *Journal of American History*, 57 (September 1970), 425-26.

T. Harry Williams, *Huey Long*, in *The Register of the Kentucky Historical Society*, 68 (October 1970), 376.

Stanley G. Payne, *The Spanish Revolution*, in *Hispanic American Historical Review*, 50 (November 1970), 765.

Frances Lea McCurdy, *Stump, Bar, and Pulpit: Speechmaking on the Missouri Frontier*, and Waldo W. Braden, editor, *Oratory of the Old South, 1828-1860*, in *American Historical Review*, 76 (October 1971), 1221-22.

Henry Cohen, *Business and Politics in America from the Age of Jackson to the Civil War: The Career Biography of W.W. Corcoran*, in *Mid-America*, 53 (October 1971), 268-69.

Patricia Watlington, *The Partisan Spirit: Kentucky Politics, 1779-1792*, in *Georgia Historical Quarterly*, 56 (Winter 1972), 594.

Frederick Merk, *Slavery and The Annexation of Texas*, in *Journal of Southern History*, 39 (May 1973), 295-96.

Fletcher M. Green, *The Role of the Yankee in the Old South*, in *The Register of the Kentucky Historical Society*, 71 (July 1973), 322-23.

Jean H. Baker, *The Politics of Continuity: Maryland Political Parties from 1858-1870*, in *Journal of American History*, 60 (March 1974), 1128-29.

William Barney, *The Road to Secession: A New Perspective on The Old South*, in *American Historical Review*, 79 (April 1974), 583-84.

Dumas Malone, *Jefferson The President: Second Term, 1805-1809*, in *History: Reviews of New Books*, 2 (July 1974), 191.

Frank Freidel, editor, *Harvard Guide to American History*, in *The Register of the Kentucky Historical Society*, 73 (January 1975), 88-90.

Fawn M. Brodie, *Thomas Jefferson: An Intimate History*, in *Journal of Southern History*, 41 (February 1975), 107-09.

Jesse L. Holman, *The Prisoners of Niagara or Errors of Education: A New Novel Founded on Fact* (1810, republished, 1973), in *The Register of the Kentucky Historical Society*, 74 (January 1976), 58-59.

Kenneth Franklin Neighbors, *Robert Simpson Neighbors and the Texas Frontier*, in *The Register of the Kentucky Historical Society*, 76 (January 1978), 69-70.

John Chester Miller, *The Wolf by The Ears: Thomas Jefferson and Slavery,* in *American Historical Review,* 83 (June 1978), 803.

Irving H. Bartlett, *Daniel Webster,* in *Journal of American History,* 65 (March 1979), 1113-14.

*Scholarly Communication: The Report of the National Enquiry,* in *Journal of Southern History,* 45 (November 1979), 588-89.

Thomas D. Clark, *Historic Maps of Kentucky,* in *The Register of the Kentucky Historical Society,* 78 (Spring 1980), 157-58.

## Articles about Holman Hamilton

Betty Tevis, "Dr. Holman Hamilton." Official football program, University of Kentucky vs. University of Georgia (October 26, 1974), 50-51.

James A. Ramage, "Holman Hamilton: A Biographical Sketch." Published to honor the subject at his retirement dinner, Lexington, Kentucky, April 29, 1975.

Lexington *Herald,* June 9, 1980.

Lexington *Leader,* June 9, 1980.

Lexington *Kentucky Kernel,* June 12, 1980.

" 'Clio with Style.' " *Organization of American Historians Newsletter,* 8 (July 1980), 9.

"Holman Hamilton," St. Paul's School, Concord, N.H., *Alumni Horae,* 60 (Summer 1980), 95-96.

"In Memoriam," *Civil War Round Table Newsletter,* 24 (September 1980), the entire issue devoted to Holman Hamilton, including Richard R. Roberts, "History and Circuses."

Charles P. Roland, "Holman Hamilton." *Journal of Southern History,* 46 (November 1980), 643.

_____, "Lexington Newsletter," January 1981, 16.

[James C. Klotter], "In Memoriam: Holman Hamilton," *The Register of the Kentucky Historical Society*, 79 (Winter 1981), 63-64.

"Tribute to Dr. Hamilton," *Kentucky Alumnus*, 51 (Summer 1981), 22-23.

Vincent DeSantis, "Holman Hamilton," *The Register of the Kentucky Historical Society*, 80 (Spring 1982), 134-39.

# Contributors

**Charles J. Bussey** is associate professor of history at Western Kentucky University, Bowling Green.

**Thomas D. Clark,** emeritus professor of history at the University of Kentucky and Indiana University, lives in Lexington.

**James C. Klotter** is general editor at the Kentucky Historical Society, Frankfort.

**Sherrill Redmon McConnell** is director of the Kentuckiana Historical Collections, University of Louisville Archives, and archivist, Kornhauser Health Sciences Library.

**James A. Ramage,** professor of history, teaches at Northern Kentucky University, Highland Heights.

**Thomas W. Ramage** is associate professor of history in the Department of History, Political Science, and Philosophy at Augusta College, Augusta, Georgia.

**Peter J. Sehlinger** teaches in the School of Liberal Arts of Indiana University at Indianapolis, where he is professor of history.

**Thomas E. Templin,** who lives in Lexington, wrote his dissertation on Henry "Light Horse Harry" Lee.

## INDEX

— A —

Abbott, Edith, 141, 144, 146-47, 153n
Abbott, Grace, 141, 146
Abingdon (Va.), 113-14
Abolition. *See* slavery
Adair, John, 59
Adams, John, 45-46
Addams, Jane, 123, 141
agrarian philosophy, 41
*Alabama Review*, 28
Aldrich, Nelson W., 158
Alexandria (Va.), 47
Alicante (Spain), 85
Allen, James Lane, 134
Amato, James G., 29
American Home Economics Association, 145
*American Journal of Sociology*, 123
American Party. *See* Know-Nothing Party
American Tobacco Company, 160
American Women Suffrage Association (AWSA), 127
*Amistad* affair, 84-87, 92
Anthony, Susan B., 127, 134, 142
Antifederalists, 40
Anti-Saloon League, 172-73. *See also* Prohibition
antislavery. *See* slavery
antitrust legislation, 162-64
Armour family, 139
Articles of Confederation, 38-40
Atlanta (Ga.), 113
*At Odds: Women and the Family in America from the Revolution to the Present*, 108
Augusta (Ga.), 111

— B —

Baltimore, 47-48; riots of 1812, 47-48
Baltimore *Federal Republican*, 47-48
Bank of Kentucky, 59
Bank of the United States, 53n
banks: state, 64-65; Corcoran and Riggs, 64; Rothschild, 81
Barbados, British West Indies, 49
Barcelona (Spain), 92
Bardstown (Ky.), 57
Baring Brothers (England), 81
Bartolomé de las Casas, Father, 89
battles. *See* individual names; Revolution, American; Civil War
Bayard, James A., 55
Beckham, John Crepps Wickliffe, 165-66
Beckwith, George, 49
Belmont, August, 78
Benjamin, Judah P., 78
Benton, Eliza McDowell, 76
Benton, Thomas Hart, 76
Berea College (Ky.), 23
Beveridge, Albert J., 9, 16
Black, James D., 171
blacks: 130, 141-42. *See also* equal rights movement; Negroes; slavery
Blackwell, Alice Stone, 133
Blair, Francis P., 69n
blind, Louisville school for, 59
"Bloody Monday," 77-78
"Book Thieves," 4
Boutwell, George, 66
Bowerfind, Henry and Clara, 18
Bowerfind, Suzanne. *See* Suzanne B. Hamilton
Bowers, Claude G., 8-9, 15-16, 18-21, 28
Brackenridge, Hugh Henry, 34, 44
Bragg, Braxton, 103, 106-07, 111
Brandeis, Louis D., 161-62
Brandywine, Battle of, 35
Breckinridge, Curry, 125, 135, 152n
Breckinridge, Desha, 125, 135
Breckinridge, Ella, 124
Breckinridge family, 125; papers of 147, 153n
Breckinridge, Issa Desha, 124-25, 130, 135-36, 148n
Breckinridge, John, 121
Breckinridge, John C., 76, 79, 106

Breckinridge, Robert, 125
Breckinridge, Robert Jefferson, 121, 144
Breckinridge, Sophonisba: **120**; bibliography on, 153-54; daughter, 121-38, 152n; educator, 123, 134, 146-47; lawyer, 122-23, 129-33, 135, 138, 150n; social reformer, 123, 137-45, 152n; student, 122, 137-38, 141; writer, 123, 125, 138, 143-45, 147
Breckinridge, William Campbell Preston, 122, 124-28, 131, 133-38
Britain: Cornwallis' army, 36; impressment of Americans, 47; in Four Power Treaty, 172
Bruce, Rebecca Gratz. See Rebecca Bruce Morgan
Bruner, Ben L., 170
Bryan, William Jennings, 157
Buchanan, James, 65, 78-80, 85, 92, 97
Buckner, Simon Bolivar, 76, 104
Buena Vista, Battle of, 19
Burnside, Ambrose, 112
Burr, Aaron, 34, 46

— C —

cabinet officers, U.S. See individual names
Calderón. See Saturino Calderón Collantes
Caldwell, Johnnie Morgan. See Johnnie Hunt Morgan
Caldwell, Joseph W., 115
Calhoun, John C., 16, 80
California, 19, 61
Camp Cooke (Cal.), 19
"Campbellite" (Christian), 155
Canada, in Treaty of 1909, 174. See also International Joint Commission
Cantrill, J. Campbell, 165
Cantrill, Stanley, 165
Caribbean, 49-50. See also Cuba

Carnegie, Andrew, 161
Carter, Ann Hill. See Ann Carter Lee
Carthage (Tenn.), 111
Cass, Lewis, 82, 84, 86
Castalian Springs (Tenn.), 101
Castile (Spain), 90
Catholic: anti-Catholicism, 121; culture in Spain, 89-90; University of Chile, 24
cemetery: Church of England (Madrid), 87; Kentucky State (Frankfort), 175
Centre College (Ky.), 128, 155
Chambers, John Sharp, 4
Charleston (S.C.), 115
Chase, Salmon P., 66
Cheatham, Benjamin, 106
Cherokees, 42
Chicago: city of contrasts in 1890s, 138-39; Hull House in, 141; reformers in, 144-45; School of Civics and Philanthropy, 123; University of, 137-40, 146; "White City" of Columbia Exposition, 139
child labor and welfare, 123, 141, 143-45, 173
Children's Bureau, U.S., 141
Chile: 8, 24, 26, 28; Catholic University of, 24, 26
Christmas raid of Kentucky, Morgan's, 107
Christy, Susan Preston, 90, 93n
civil rights, 123. See also blacks; equal rights
Civil War: 20, 49, 67-68, 76; Bragg invasion (1863), 103; Morgan in, 99-116; prewar studies, 97
Clark, Champ, 164-65
Clark, George Rogers, 76
Clark, Thomas D., 18, 21
Clark, William, 76
Clay, Cassius M., 127-28; daughters of, 127
Clay, Henry, 16, 57, 59, 61, 80

## INDEX

Clay, Laura, 127-28, 136, 142
Clay, Mary B., 127
Clayton, Henry D., 163; Act, 163-64, 175
"Clio with Style," 11-13
Cold War, 175
Coleman, John Winston, Jr., 4, 17
Collantes, Saturino Calderón, 84, 86
Columbia Exposition (1893), World's, 139
Columbus (Ohio), Union penitentiary at, 111-12
"Committee of 21," 66
Commons, John R., 141
compromise. *See* John J. Crittenden; Compromise of 1850
Compromise of 1850: 6, 21-22; political reactions to, 61-62
Conant, Luther, Jr., 163
Concord (N.H.), 14
Cone, Carl B., 24
*Confederacy,* Atlanta, 103
Confederate States of America: 75, 93, 155; agents in Madrid, 88; executive mansion (Montgomery, Ala.), 28; Morgan in the army of, 99-116; Mexico and, 73, 93; Preston as envoy to, 73, 93; "Thunderbolt of the Confederacy," 116
Constitutional convention (1849), Kentucky, 57, 60, 76
constitutions. *See* Constitutional convention; U.S. Constitution
Continental Congress, 35
Corcoran (W.W.) and Riggs banking firm, 64
corporations. *See* monopoly; U.S. Steel Corporation; antitrust legislation
Cortes, the, 84
Cortés, Hernán, 89
Coulter, E. Merton, 103
Creeks (Indians), 42
Crittenden, John J., and compromise proposal, 66-67
Cuba, acquisition of, 73, 79-80, 82- 83, 85-87, 92, 97
Cumberland Island (Ga.), 50
Cumberland River, 99
Cummins Railroad Bill, 171
Cushing, Caleb, 62-63

—D—

*Daily Courier,* Louisville, 82
*Daily Union,* Nashville, 107
Danville (Va.), 112-13
Daughters of the American Revolution (D.A.R.), 142
Davis, Jefferson: 3-4, 27-28; as secretary of war, 62-63
De Havilland, John, 88
Degler, Carl M., 22, 108-09
*Democratic Experience,* 22
Democratic party: candidates, 77, 79, 159, 163-64, 166; in Congress, 162, 164, 166; in 20th century, 155-76; national conventions, (1864) 67, (1880) 93, (1912) 165; state (Kentucky) conventions, (1900) 157, (1912) 165; state Central and Executive Committee, 170
Democratic-Republican Societies, 43
Democrats: 57, 59, 68, 70n, 76, 78, 80, 155. *See also* Democratic party
Depression, the Great, 1, 15
Desha, Issa. *See* Issa Desha Breckinridge
Desha, Mary, 142, 152n
*Dictionary of American History,* 23
disunion, 22, 33, 41. *See also* unionism
Dixon, Archibald, 60-61
Dobbin, James, 62
Dominican Republic, 88
Dorsey, John L., 155
Douglas, Stephen A., 61
Douglass, Frederick, 130
Draper, Simon, 64.
"Drys." *See* prohibition
Duke, Basil W., 76, 101, 110, 112
Duke, Tommie Morgan, 110, 113

Dunbar Prize (Williams College), 15

— E —

Eaton, W. Clement, 5
Edinburgh *Scotsman,* 103
Eighteenth Amendment, 169
Eisenhower, Dwight D., 20; administration, 174-75
Ely, Richard T., 141
equal rights movement, 123, 141-43. *See also* blacks; women's suffrage
Eutaw Springs, Battle of, 36

— F —

Fallón, Christopher, 80-81
farmers. *See* Tobacco Planters' Association
federal: "advance," 114; prisoners, 99; union, 51. *See also* Union army; unionism
*Federal Republican,* Baltimore, 47
Federal Trade Commission acts, 163
Federalism, 37, 40, 45. *See also* Federalist party; "Baltimore riots"; Henry Lee
Federalist party, 33, 43, 45-48. *See also* Federalism
Fields family, 139
Fifth Armored Division, 19
Fifty-eighth Congress, 157
Fillmore, Millard, 22
Filson Club: collections, 16; *History Quarterly,* 4
First Mississippi Cavalry, 117n
Flatt, Don, 27
Flemingsburg (Ky.), 155
Florida (person), 114
Foote, Henry S., 21
Fordney-McCumber Tariff, 173
Forrest, Nathan Bedford, 107
Fort Donelson, 117n
Fort Henry, 102
Fort Knox, 19
Fort Wayne (Ind.): 13-14, 16; historical society, 5; *Journal-Gazette* 15, 17-18, 20-21; Public Library, 14, 16
Four Power Treaty, 172
Fox, John, Jr., 134
France: in Four Power Treaty, 172; language of, 89; naval war with U.S., 45-46; Revolution in, 43
Franco-American army, 36
Frankfort (Ky.): 17; Cemetery, 175; Constitutional convention, 60
Franklin College (Ind.), 24
Free Soil party: faction in Pierce's cabinet, 62; 1852 presidential ticket, 62
Freneau, Philip, 34, 42
Fugitive Slave Law, 22, 61, 66
Fulbright Professorship, 8, 24
Fuller, Paul, 127
funding and assumption (fiscal measures), 41

— G —

Gallatin, Albert, 55n
Gallatin (Tenn.), 104, 111
Garden Club of America, 181
Garfield, James R., 160
Gary, Elbert H., 160-61
Georgetown College (Ky.), 23
Georgia: Cumberland Island, 50; opposition to whiskey tax, "back country," 43; Revolutionary War in, 35
German immigrants: anti-German hysteria, WWI, 170; language bill, 170; Ohio River settlement, 77-78. *See also* "Bloody Monday"
Germantown, Battle of, 35
Gilpin, Henry D., 85
governor: of Indiana, 25; of Kentucky, 155, 175; of Missouri, 76; of Nebraska (lt.-governor), 141; of Virginia, 31, 75, 76. *See also* individual names
Great Britain. *See* Britain
Green, Fanny, 90
Greene, Nathaniel, 35-36, 50; daugh-

ter of, 50
Greenville (Tenn.), 114
Grenfell, George St. Leger, 106, 107, 116
Guggenheim Fellowship, 19
Guilford Court House, Battle of, 36
Guthrie, Adam, 57
Guthrie, James: **58;** bibliography on, 70-71; business entrepeneur, 58-60, 63, 65, 67; lawyer-politician, Kentucky, 57, 59, 63; Treasury Secretary, 57, 62-63, 68; Senator, 67; Unionist (Democrat), 57, 60, 63, 65-68
Guthrie (Ky.), 158
"Guthrie Report" of Committee of 21, 66

— H —

Hale, John P., 62
Hall of Distinguished Alumni (University of Kentucky), 24
Hallam Professorship, 9
Hamilton, Alexander: 33, 37; fiscal program, 41, 53n; political philosophy, 43, 45; Whiskey Rebellion tribunals, 44
Hamilton, Allen, 13-14
Hamilton, Helen Knight, 13-14
Hamilton, Holman: **2, 12;** bibliography on, 181-90; educator, 3-4, 7, 21-25, 27-30; historian-author, 3-4, 14, 16-18, 20-23, 25-28, 181-89; honoree, 19, 21, 23-24; journalist, 3, 14, 17-18, 20, 25-26; speaker, 3-4, 5, 11, 13, 23-24, 28-29; student, 3, 5-6, 14, 19
Hamilton, Katherine, 14
Hamilton, Susan, 19
Hamilton, Suzanne ("Susie") Bowerfind, 5, 11, 13, 18-19
Hancock, George, 75
Hardee, William J., 102, 106
Harding, Warren G., 172
Harper, William Rainey, 140
Harrison, Carter, 139

Hartsville battlefield, 99
Harvard University, 74
Havana cigars, 90
Haynes Lectures (Marshall University), 23
Hill, A.P., 110
Hill, Kitty Morgan, 110, 114
"Hill Billies," 158
historians: 11, 13, 18, 20. *See also* individual names
History of American Civilization Lectures (University of Fla.), 23
*History of American Presidential Elections,* 23
Hobart College, 23
Hoffman, Mary, 15
Holmes, Emma, 115
Hoover, Herbert C., 174
House of Burgesses, 34
Howard, Oliver O., 16
Howe, John J., 173
Hull House (Chicago), 123, 141
*Hundred Proof,* 23
Hunt, George W., 113
Hunt, John Wesley, 103
hurricane claims of 1844, 86-87

— I —

Illinois Consumer's League, 123
immigrants, 60, 77; conditions of, 140-42, 145, 152n. *See also* Germans; Irish
Immigrants Protection League, (Chicago), 123
Independent Treasury Act, 63
Indiana: "Book of the Year," 20; Historical Society, 28; *Magazine of History,* 181; Morgan's 1863 raid, 115; University, 23-24
*Indianapolis in the "Gay Nineties,"* 22
Indians, northwestern, 42
Inns of Court (London, G.B.), 34
International Joint Commission (IJC), 174-76
interstate commerce, 171

Irish immigrants: Ohio River settlement, 77-78. See also "Bloody Monday"
Irving, Washington, 89
Isabel II, Queen of Spain, 84, 90

— J —

Jackson, Andrew, 59
Jacksonian Democracy, 57, 63
James, Marquis, 20
James, Ollie M., 165, 170
Jay Treaty, 38-40, 53n
*Jefferson and Hamilton: The Struggle for Democracy in America,* 15
Jefferson County (Ky.): courthouse, 16; Preston plantation, 73
Jefferson, Thomas: 46, 73; political philosophy of, 42-43, 46, 80, 121
Johannsen, Robert W., 27
Johnston, Albert Sidney, 74-75, 102-03
Johnston, Josiah Stoddard, 75
Johnston, William Preston, 79
*Journal-Gazette* (Fort Wayne, Ind.), 15, 17-18, 20-21
*Journal of American History,* 27
judiciary, U.S. federal, 45
Julian, George W., 62

— K —

Kansas-Nebraska Bill, 61, 77
Kelley, Florence, 141
Kentuckiana collections, 4
Kentucky: Agricultural and Mechanical College, 155; Bank of, 59; Bicentennial Bookshelf, 27; budget system, 170-71; Constitutional convention (1849), 57, 60, 76; Equal Rights Association, 127; General Assembly enactments, 168-71; Historical Preservation Committee, 28; Historical Society, 17, 28; Indian danger, 42; last Virginia governor, 31, 42-43, 51; Morgan's (Civil War) raids, 107-10, 114-15; National Peace Conference delegation, 65; Resolutions (1798), 121; State Cemetery, 175; statehood, 42, 57; Tax Commission, 169; tax laws, 169, 171; tobacco growers rebellion, 157-58; use of Mississippi River, 38-40; Virginia Convention delegation, 40. See also individual names of officials
Kipling, Rudyard, 14
Know-Nothing party, 60, 77
Knoxville (Tenn.), 111
Ku Klux Klan, 173

— L —

labor. See Cummins Railroad Bill
Laffoon, Ruby, 4
La Granja (Spain), 91
laissez-faire concept of government, 157
Lathrop, Julia C., 141
League of Nations, 171
Lee, Ann Hill Carter, 43, 49-50
Lee, Charles, 34
Lee, Henry, 34, 38, 51n
Lee, Henry "Light Horse Harry": 32; bibliography on, 55-56; congressman, 38-42; Federalist (nationalist), 31, 34, 39-43, 45-47, 49-51, 53n; husband and father, 31, 37, 43, 47-51; militia commander, 31, 43-44, 51; participant in Baltimore riots, 47-48; Revolutionary officer, 31, 34-37, 47 *(Memoirs);* Virginia Assembly member, 38, 45; Virginia governor, 31, 42-43, 51
Lee, Matilda Lee, 37, 42, 46-47, 49
Lee, Robert E., 31, 49, 51, 56
Lee's Legion, 35-36
Leon Lillo et Compagnie (France), 81
Lewis, John L., 25
Lexington (Ky.): Cemetery, 134; - Fayette County Historic Commis-

# INDEX

sion, 28; Friends of the Public Library, 28; Hamilton home, 30; Morgan family, 103, 113; Wickliffe estate, 93
Lexington (Ky.) *Herald,* 122, 138
Liberal Union coalition, 84
"Light Horse Harry" Lee. *See* Lee, Henry "Light Horse Harry"
Lincoln, Abraham, 3, 16, 65, 67, 83, 88
Lincoln Memorial University, 23
Lincoln National Life Foundation, 4, 16
*Lincoln, Taylor, Davis, The Three Kentucky Presidents,* 27
Lingen, James, 48
Link, Arthur S., 22
local option issue (county unit law), 167. *See also* Prohibition
Lopez, Narciso, 80
*Louisiana Progress,* 17
Louisville, 16-17, 59, 77, 174. *See also* "Bloody Monday"; German immigrants; Irish immigrants
Louisville *Courier-Journal,* 165
Louisville *Evening Post,* 167
Louisville and Nashville Railroad, 65, 67-68, 166
Louisville, Maysville and Lexington Railroad, 60
Loyalists, 35-36

— M —

McChesney, Harry V., 166-67
McClellan, George B., 67
McClelland, Robert, 62
McCormick family, 139
McCreary, James B., 165-67
McDowell, James, 76
McDowell, Mary E., 141
McMinnville (Tenn.), 109, 111
McMurtry, R. Gerald, 16
McReynolds, James C., 163
McVey, Frank L., 1, 4, 17-18
Madison, James, 34, 39, 40-41, 43, 47-48, 55n

Madrid (Spain), 90-91
Magoffin, Beriah, 79
*Major Crises in American History,* 23
Mallory, Stephen, 79
Marcy, William, 62
Marion, Francis, 35, 116n
"Marion of the War" (Morgan), 103
Marseilles (France), 83-84
Marshall, Humphrey, 77-78
Marshall University, 23
Mason, James, 80
Maximilian, emperor of Mexico, 93
*Memoirs of General William T. Sherman,* 67
*Memoirs of the War in the Southern Department of the United States,* 47
Memorial Hall (University of Kentucky), 30
Memphis State University, 23
Meriwether, David, 61
Mexican War, 19, 74, 97
Mexico, 73
Milford (Tenn.), 108-09
militia, 43-44
Mississippi River free navigation issue, 38-40
Mississippi Senate chamber, 28
Mississippi Valley Historical Association: Pelzer Prize, 21; *Review,* 21
Missouri, 76; Compromise line, 66
monopoly: tobacco company trust, 158; U.S. Steel combination, 159-60
Monroe, James, 55n
Morehead State University, 23, 27
Morgan, Charlton, 114
Morgan family, 113. *See also* individual names
Morgan, Henrietta, 109, 112-14
Morgan infants: son of Morgan and Rebecca, 102; child of Morgan and Mattie, 111-13
Morgan, Johnnie Hunt, 115
Morgan, John Hunt: **100**; bibliogra-

phy on, 118-19; Confederate hero, 102-13, 116; correspondent, 99, 108-14; husband of Martha, 106-10
Morgan, Key, 109, 114
Morgan, Kitty. *See* Kitty Morgan Hill
Morgan, Martha Ready, **100**; 99-116
Morgan, Rebecca Gratz Bruce, 102
Morgan, Richard, 114
Morgan, Samuel, 110
Morgan, Thomas Hunt, 135
Morgan, Tom, 105
Moroccan-Spanish war, 92
Morrow, Edwin P., 167-68, 171
Morton, Thruston B., 176
Mount Vernon, 34
Murfreesboro (Tenn.), 105, 107-08
Murray State University, 23

— N —

Napoleon III, 83
Nashville (Tenn.): penitentiary, 105; *Daily Union*, 107
National American Women Suffrage Association (N.A.W.S.A.), 123
National Association for the Advancement of Colored People (N.A.A.C.P.), 123, 142
National Bank, 59
*National Gazette* (Philadelphia), 42
National Peace Conference, 57, 65-68
National Recovery Act, 16
national unity. *See* nationalism; Unionists
nationalism: "Jackson-Taylor," 22; Lee philosophy, 37, 39, 41, 49-50. *See also* Unionists
nativist. *See* Know-Nothing party
naval war of 1798 (U.S. and France), 45-46
Nebraska: Abbots of, 141, 146; territory, 77
Negroes, free, 60. *See also* blacks; equal rights; slavery
Nelson County (Ky.), 57

Nevins, Allan, 20
*New Homes for Old*, 145
New Mexico, 61
New Orleans, 17, 59
New York *Times*, 18, 63
*New Yorker*, 18, 20
newspapers, 63, 90, 103, 107. *See also* individual names; Baltimore riots of 1812
Nicholson, A.O.P., 69n
nightriding, 158
Nineteenth Amendment, 143. *See also* women's rights movement
Nobel Prize, 135, 141
Northern Kentucky University, 23
*Notable American Women*, 23

— O —

O'Donnell, Leopoldo, 84
Ohio-Indiana raid, Morgan's, 111
"Old Rough and Ready." *See* Zachary Taylor
One Hundred Fourth Illinois Cavalry, 99-100
Oneida Baptist Institute, 26
Orange County (Va.), 17
Ostend Manifesto, 80
Owsley, Amanda. *See* Amanda Owsley Stanley
Owsley, Augusta, 155

— P —

Pan-American Congress, 123
Panics (national economic): of 1893, 139; of 1907, 160
Paris (France), 83, 90
*Party Battles of the Jackson Period*, 15
Patents, U.S. Senate Committee on, 171
Paul (Saint), 176
Paulus Hook, Battle of, 35
peace mission to Russia, 55n
Pearl Harbor, 19
Pelzer Prize, 21

Pennsylvania, 43-44, 81
Pennyroyal of Kentucky, 155
Perkins, George W., 162
Perry, Horatio J., 88, 90
Perryville, Battle of, 105
Peter, Frances, 102
Philadelphia *National Gazette,* 42
Philippines, 19
Pierce, Franklin, 57, 61-62, 85
Pittsburgh (Pa.), 44
political parties, 43. *See also* individual names
Polk, James Knox, 80, 85
Polk, Leonidas, 106
Pollard, Madeline, 136-37, 152n
"Possum Hunters." *See* nightriding
Potter, David M., 22
Powell, Lazarus, 61, 69n
Prather, Elizabeth. *See* Elizabeth Prather Guthrie
presidents, United States: 25-27, 40, 61. *See also* individual names
Preston, Caroline, 73
Preston family, 121
Preston, Francis, 75-76
Preston, James Patton, 75
Preston, Margaret ("Mag") H. Wickliffe: 74, 83-84, 89, 92; influence on husband, 79, 90-91
Preston, Peg and Carrie, 83, 91
Preston, Susan. *See* Susan Preston Christy
Preston, Wickliffe, 91
Preston, William: **72;** bibliography on, 95-98; congressman, 76-78; conservative (Whig-Democrat), 74-79, 93; diplomat, 73, 78-93; Kentucky lawyer-politician, 73, 76, 93; soldier, 73, 76, 93
Preston, William, Sr., 73
Preston, William Campbell, 76
Prince William County (Va.), 34
Princeton (College of New Jersey), 34
Progressivism: 122, 124, 136-37; legislation, 157, 162, 172; reformers, 140-46, 151n

Prohibition, 165-67, 169, 171-72
*Prologue to Conflict: The Crisis and Compromise of 1850,* 6, 8, 21-22, 26
Pullman family, 139
Pullman strike of 1894, 139

— R —

railroad: 60, 81. *See also* individual names
Ready, Alice, 101, 103-04, 111
Ready, Charles, 101-02, 105
Ready, Mrs. Charles, 105
Ready, Horace, 101, 106
Ready, Martha. *See* Martha Ready Morgan
Ready, Mary, 101, 109
reformers. *See* Progressivism; Chicago
religious liberty in Spain, 90
Report on Manufactures, 53n
republicanism, 31
Republican party: 43, 47-48, 92, 158-59; candidates, 46, 155, 166-68, 170-71, 173; conventions, 121, 167; in Congress, 159, 161, 164, 172
Revolution: American, 31, 34-37, 41, 47, 51n, 73; French, 43
Richmond (Va.), 112-13
Roland, Charles P., 27
Roosevelt, Franklin D., 4, 25
Roosevelt, Theodore, 25, 160-62, 164
Rosemont plantation (Miss.), 28
Ross, Edward T., 141
Rothert, Otto A., 4, 16-17
Rothschild banking interest, 81
Rowan, John, 59

— S —

Sackett, Frederic M., 173
Sacre Coeur convent school (Paris), 83
Sandburg, Carl, 139

*Saturday Review,* 20
Schlesinger, Arthur, Jr., 20
*Scotsman,* Edinburgh, 103
Scott, Winfield, 61-62
secession movement, 65-67
Second (Congressional) District of Kentucky, 157, 159
Second Kentucky Cavalry, 105
sectionalism, 92. *See also* slavery, unionism
Seventeenth Amendment, 166
Seward, William H., 88
Shays' Rebellion, 39
Shelbyville (Ky.), 155
Sherman Antitrust Act, 160-62, 175
Sherman, William T., 67
Shirley plantation (Va.), 43
"Silent Brigade." *See* nightriding
Singletary, Otis A., 23
Sixty-eighth Congress, 173
Sixty-second Congress, 161
Sixty-third Congress, 162
slavery: antislavery, 49, 60, 83-85, 87, 127, 130; proslavery, 60, 73-75, 80, 83. *See also* Compromise of 1850; Fugitive Slave Law
Slidell, John, 78; resolution, 82-84, 92
Smith College, 18
Smith, Herbert Knox, 161
Smyser, Jacob, 71
Soaper, Sue. *See* Sue Soaper Stanley
social work professionals, 140-41
Soldiers' Bonus Bill, 173
Soulé, Pierre, 80
South Carolina, 35, 65, 76
Southern Campaign, Revolutionary War, 35-36
Southern Historical Association, 11
Southern Rights faction, 62
Spain, 28, 38, 73, 78-93. *See also* Amistad affair; Cuba; William Preston
Spanish-Moroccan war, 92-93
St. Lawrence Seaway and Power project, 174

St. Paul's School (N.H.), 14
Stanley, Amanda Owsley, 155
Stanley, Augustus Owsley, **156;** bibliography on, 179-80; congressman, 157-65; Kentucky governor, 167-71, 175; Senator, 166-67, 171-76. *See also* antitrust legislation; Stanley Committee
Stanley Committee, 161-64
Stanley, Sue Soaper, 157
Stanley, William, 155
Staples, Charles R., 4
State College (Ky.), 129
states' rights, 76, 142. *See also* disunion
Stauffer, Betty Taylor, 17
Stones River (Tenn.), Battle of, 107-08
Stratford plantation (Va.), 37-38; 46-47
Stuart, James E.B. ("Jeb"), 103

—T—

Taft, William Howard, 159-61, 164
Talbott, Marion, 140-41
Tapp, Hambleton, 18
tariff: 64, 86-87, 164, 173
Tassara, Gabriel García y, 82
tax: on tobacco, 157-58; on whiskey, 43. *See also* Kentucky tax laws
Taylor, Graham, 123, 141
Taylor, Zachary, 3-5, 16, 19-20, 27, 117
Tennessee: Civil War in, 99-110, 114; Coal, Iron and Railroad Company, 160, 162, 164; regiment, 101; Technological University, 28; "The Belle of," 106
Texas, 61, 74-75
Thirteenth Amendment, 66
*Three American Frontiers: Writings of Thomas D. Clark,* 22-23
*Three Kentucky Presidents: Lincoln, Taylor, Davis,* 8, 27-28
Thompson, Irvin, 155
Thornbrough, Gayle, 22

"Thunderbolt of the Confederacy." See John Hunt Morgan
*Time* magazine, 20
Tobacco Planters' Association, Dark District, 158
Townsend, William R., 4-5, 18, 23, 29
Trapp, Claude, 4
treaties: Four Power, 172; U.S. and Spain, 85 (1795), 86-87 (1860); U.S. and Canada, 174 (1907)
"trust-busting," 160
Trust Company of America, 162
Tudor Hall (Indianapolis), 18
Tyler, John, 65, 85

— U —

Underwood Metal Tariff Bill, 164
Union army, 104-05, 114-15
unionism, 57, 62-63, 65-66, 88, 121
United States Children's Bureau, 141
United States Constitution, 39-41, 66-67, 172, 176
United States government: Congress, 38-39, 45, 61, 65, 68, 75-76, 80, 84-85, 92, 122, 134, 157-61; House of Representatives, 76, 122, 157-60, 161-64; Justice Department, 164; Senate, 57, 59, 76, 166, 170-73; Supreme Court, 85; Treasury Department, 63-65, 68; treaties, 85-87, 172, 174. *See also* individual names of officials
United States Steel Corporation, 159-64, 175
University of Chicago, 123
University of Chile, 24
University of Florida: American Civilization Lectures, 23; Press, 22
University of Houston (Texas), 28-29
University of Kentucky: 1-5, 13, 26-27, 30; Alumni Association, 9, 26; Hallam Professorship, 26; History Department graduate program, 1-3, 5-7, 9, 21, 23; Library, 6, 7; Teacher awards, 24, 26. *See also* University Press of Kentucky
University of Louisville, 60
University of Missouri, 23
University of Notre Dame, 23, 25
University Press of Kentucky, 10, 23, 27
University of Temuco, 24
University of Texas, 26
University of Valparaiso, 24
Urban League, 123
Utah Territory, 61

— V —

Valley Forge, 35
Van Buren, Martin, 85
Vietnam War, compared to Revolution, 35
Virginia: 33, 38, 42, 45, 113; congressmen, 45, 75; Convention of 1788, 39-40; General Assembly (legislature), 38, 42, 45, 53n, 65; governors, 31, 75, 76; Indian danger, 42; militia, 51n; Revolutionary war in, 35-36, 41

— W —

war: *See* Revolution; names of participants; War of 1812; World War
War of Independence. *See* Revolution (American)
War of 1812, 47-48
Warren, Louis, 4, 16
Washington (D.C.), 45, 134, 173-74. *See also* National Peace Conference; United States government
Washington *Constitution,* 82
Washington, George, 31, 34, 38-41, 43, 45, 49, 51
Washington *Union,* 82
Webster, Daniel, 16, 64
Wellesley College, 129-33, 141, 147
Western Kentucky University, 23

West Indies, 55n
Westmoreland County (Va.), 34
West Virginia, 42
"wet"-"dry" factions. *See* Prohibition
Whig party, 57, 59, 63, 68n, 75, 77-78
Whiskey Rebellion of 1794, 31
Wickersham, George W., 161
Wickliffe, Margaret Howard. *See* Margaret Wickliffe Preston
Wickliffe, Robert, 3, 74, 79, 93
Wickliffe, Robert Woolley, 88
Williams College, 5, 14-15
Williams, Kenneth P., 99
Williams, T. Harry, 28
Williamson, James, 115
Willis-Campbell bill, 171-72
Wilson, Samuel M., 4
Wilson, Woodrow, 162-63, 165, 168, 170-71
Winchester (Ky.), 110
Wolfe, Margaret Ripley, 126
Woman's Peace Party, 123
*Women's Journal,* 133
women: assessments of, 126-30, 138, 143; lawyers, 141, 150n; reformers, 140-41, 151n; rights of, 127, 142-43. *See also* women's suffrage
*Women in the Twentieth Century,* 143
Women Suffrage Association, National American (N.A.W.S.A.), 123, 133, 142
women's suffrage, 123, 127, 142, 146, 167, 171
Wood, Robert C., 104, 117n
Wood, Trist, 17
*World-Today,* 138
World War: First (I), 123, 170; Second (II), 1, 18
Wytheville (Va.), 113

— Y —

Yale University, 74
Yorktown (N.Y.), 31, 36
Young (J.P.) Lectures, Memphis State University, 23

— Z —

*Zachary Taylor: Soldier in the White House,* 20-22
*Zachary Taylor: Soldier of the Republic,* 18-19